THE DEATH-DEFYING
DOCTOR MIRAGE

SECOND
LIVES

JEN VAN METER | ROBERTO DE LA TORRE | DAVID BARON

CONTENTS

Collection Cover Art: Jelena Kevic-Djurdjevic

Editors: Alejandro Arbona (#1-4)
and Kyle Andrukiewicz (#3)
Editor-in-Chief: Warren Simons

The Death-Defying Doctor Mirage®: Second Lives. Published by
Valiant Entertainment LLC. Office of Publication: 350 Seventh
Avenue, New York, NY 10001. Compilation copyright ©2016 Valiant
Entertainment, Inc. All rights reserved. Contains materials originally
published in single magazine form as The Death-Defying Doctor
Mirage: Second Lives #1-4. Copyright ©2015 and 2016 Valiant
Entertainment LLC. All rights reserved. All characters, their distinctive
likeness and related indicia featured in this publication are
trademarks of Valiant Entertainment LLC. The stories, characters,
and incidents featured in this publication are entirely fictional. Valiant
Entertainment does not read or accept unsolicited submissions of
ideas, stories, or artwork. Printed in the U.S.A. First Printing.
ISBN: 9781682151297.

THE DEATH-DEFYING DOCTOR MIRAGE®

SECOND LIVES

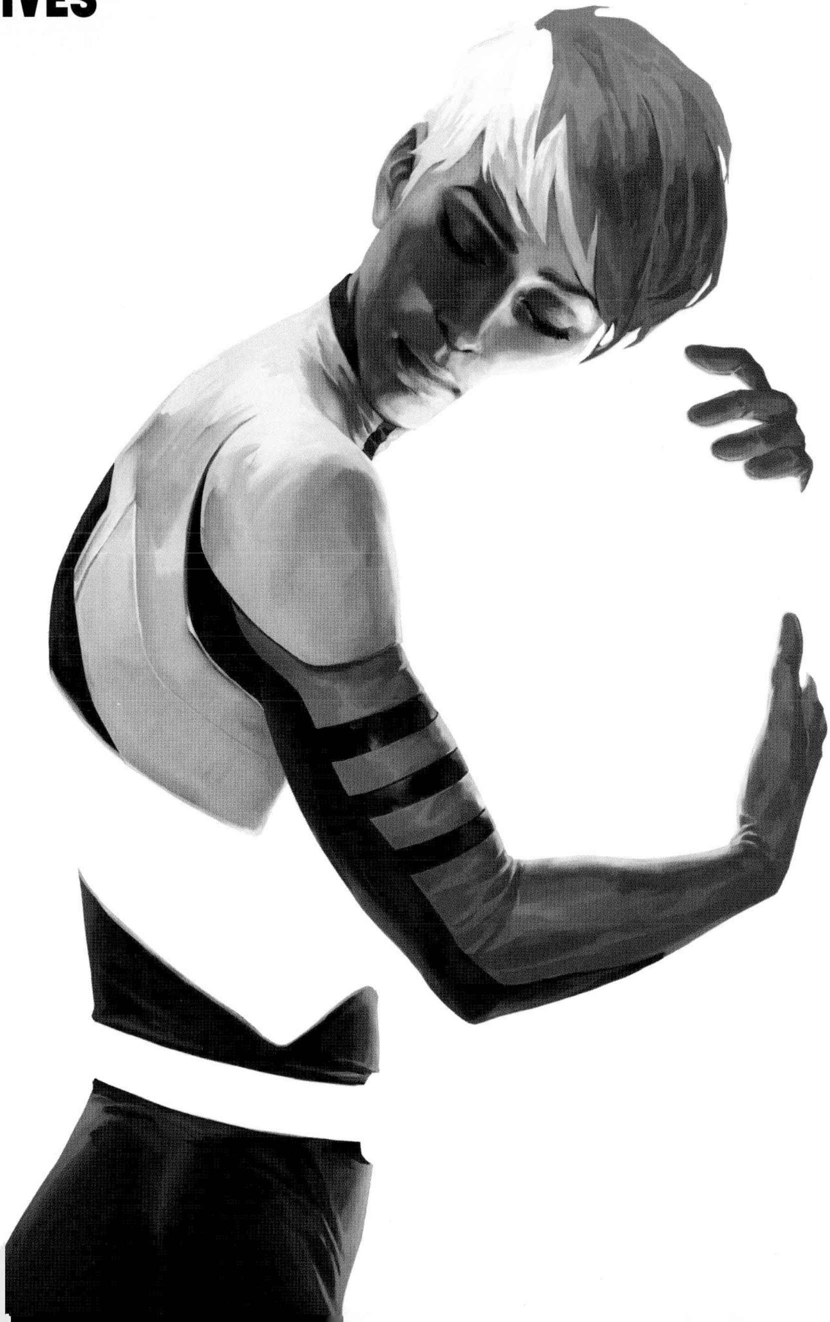

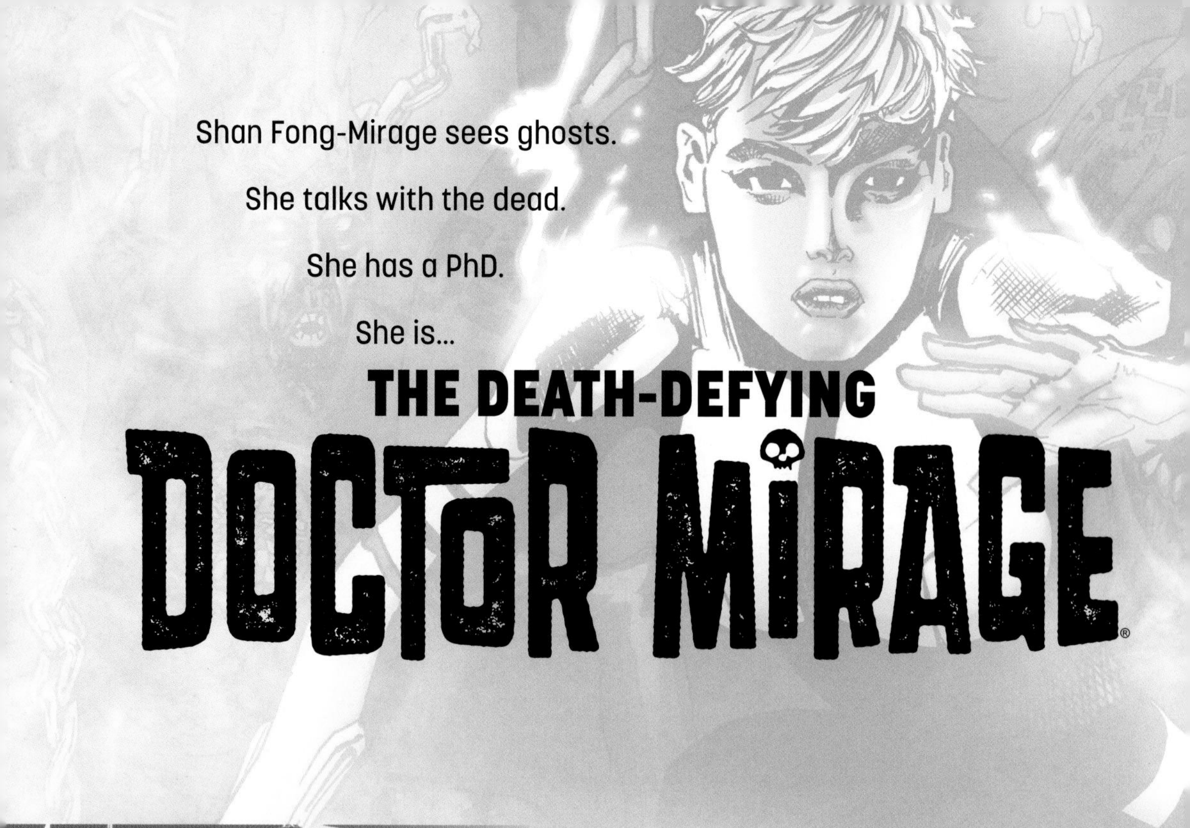

Shan Fong-Mirage sees ghosts.

She talks with the dead.

She has a PhD.

She is...

THE DEATH-DEFYING DOCTOR MIRAGE®

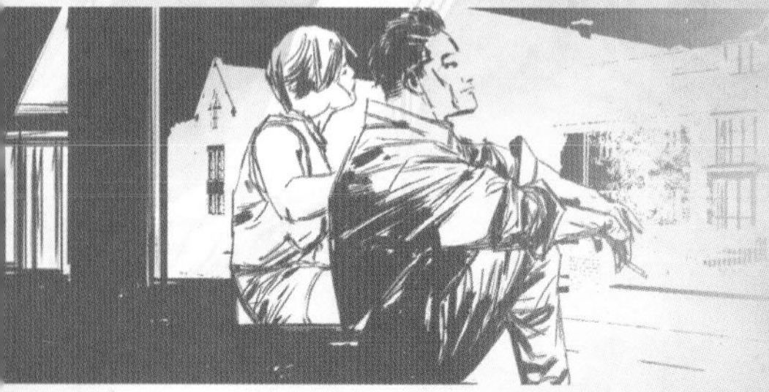

Shan met a man named Hwen. They fell in love got married, and had adventures.

They made a good team. Their agent Leo got them on TV as paranormal investigators.

THEN HWEN DIED.

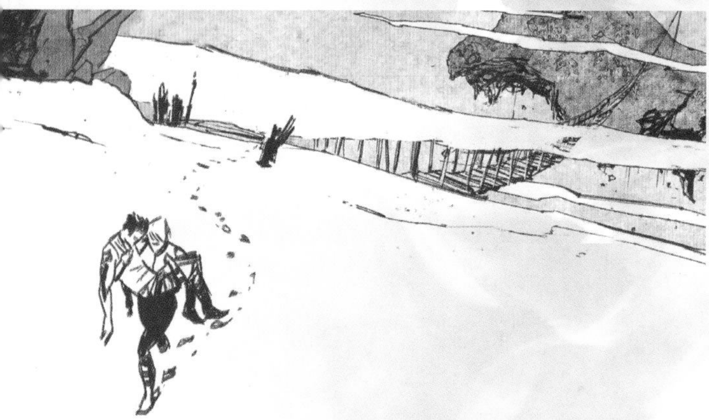

Shan was alone for years, until she ventured beyond the veil of death and brought back Hwen's spirit.

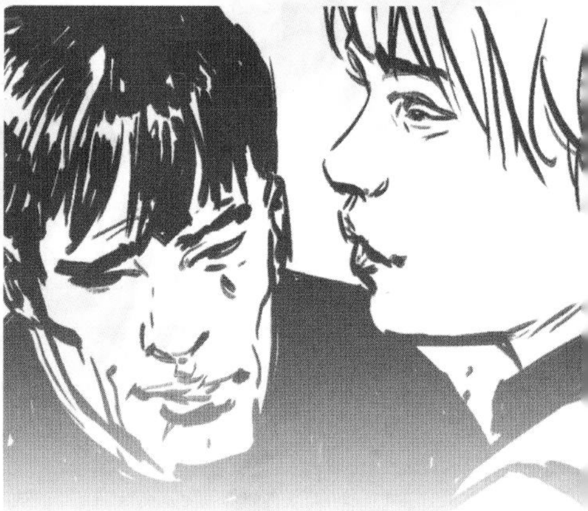

Now Shan has a ghost husband who she can't even touch, and who only she can see...

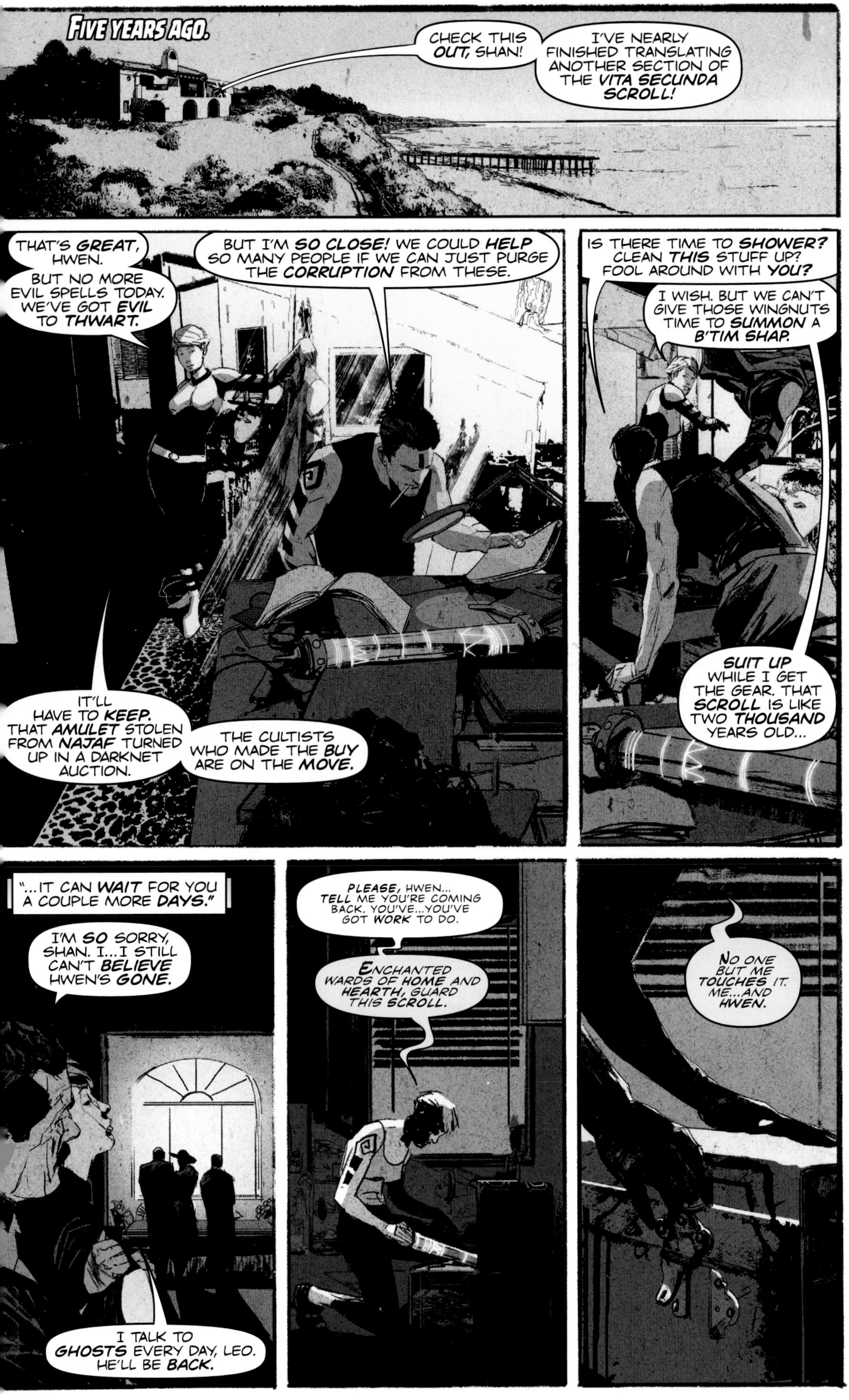
FIVE YEARS AGO.
CHECK THIS OUT, SHAN!
I'VE NEARLY FINISHED TRANSLATING ANOTHER SECTION OF THE VITA SECUNDA SCROLL!
THAT'S GREAT, HWEN.
BUT NO MORE EVIL SPELLS TODAY. WE'VE GOT EVIL TO THWART.
BUT I'M SO CLOSE! WE COULD HELP SO MANY PEOPLE IF WE CAN JUST PURGE THE CORRUPTION FROM THESE.
IT'LL HAVE TO KEEP. THAT AMULET STOLEN FROM NAJAF TURNED UP IN A DARKNET AUCTION.
THE CULTISTS WHO MADE THE BUY ARE ON THE MOVE.
IS THERE TIME TO SHOWER? CLEAN THIS STUFF UP? FOOL AROUND WITH YOU?
I WISH. BUT WE CAN'T GIVE THOSE WINGNUTS TIME TO SUMMON A B'TIM SHAP.
SUIT UP WHILE I GET THE GEAR. THAT SCROLL IS LIKE TWO THOUSAND YEARS OLD...
"...IT CAN WAIT FOR YOU A COUPLE MORE DAYS."
I'M SO SORRY, SHAN. I...I STILL CAN'T BELIEVE HWEN'S GONE.
I TALK TO GHOSTS EVERY DAY, LEO. HE'LL BE BACK.
PLEASE, HWEN... TELL ME YOU'RE COMING BACK. YOU'VE...YOU'VE GOT WORK TO DO.
ENCHANTED WARDS OF HOME AND HEARTH, GUARD THIS SCROLL.
NO ONE BUT ME TOUCHES IT. ME...AND HWEN.

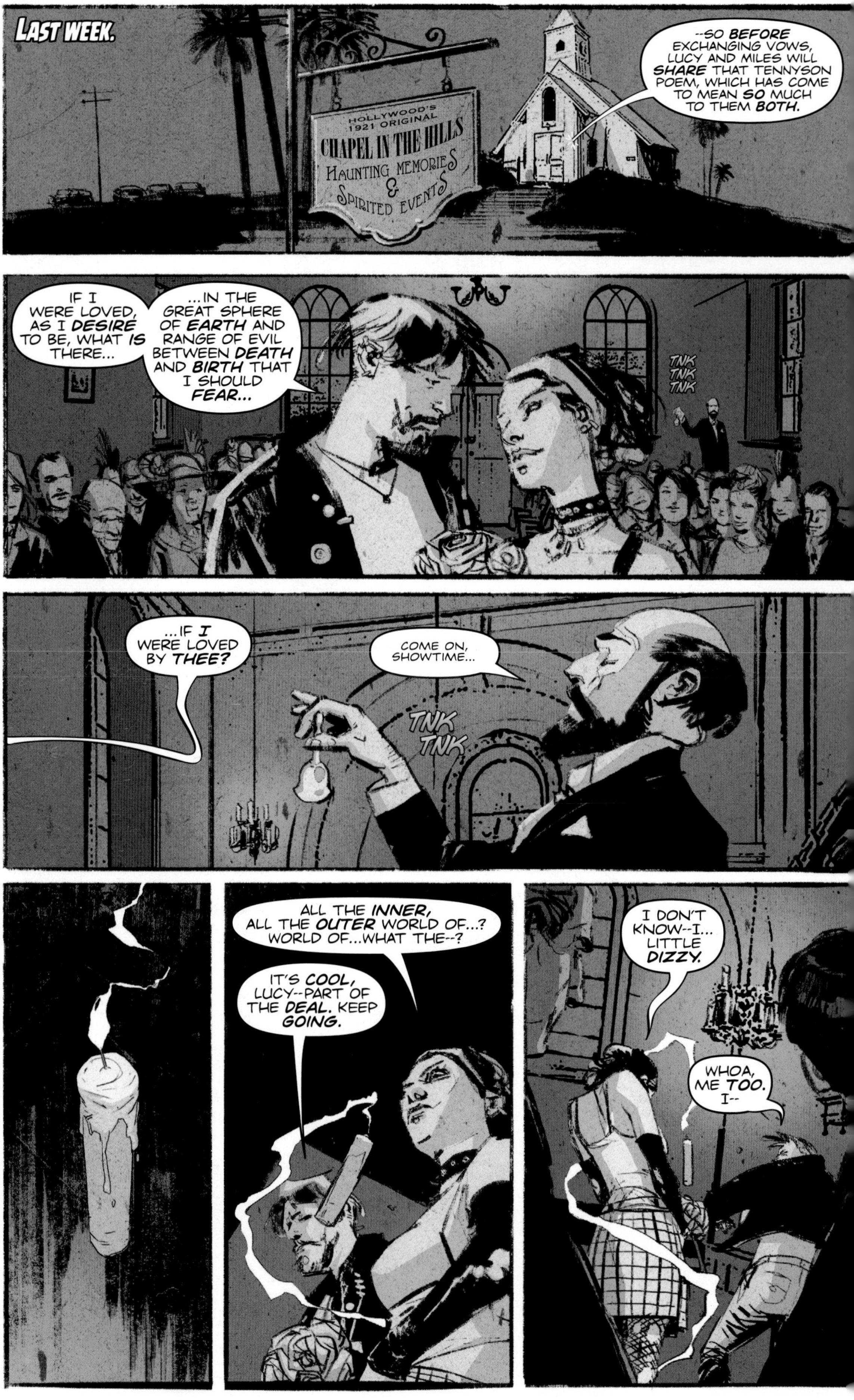
LAST WEEK.
HOLLYWOOD'S 1921 ORIGINAL
CHAPEL IN THE HILLS
HAUNTING MEMORIES & SPIRITED EVENTS
--SO BEFORE EXCHANGING VOWS, LUCY AND MILES WILL SHARE THAT TENNYSON POEM, WHICH HAS COME TO MEAN SO MUCH TO THEM BOTH.
IF I WERE LOVED, AS I DESIRE TO BE, WHAT IS THERE...
...IN THE GREAT SPHERE OF EARTH AND RANGE OF EVIL BETWEEN DEATH AND BIRTH THAT I SHOULD FEAR...
TNK TNK TNK
...IF I WERE LOVED BY THEE?
COME ON, SHOWTIME...
TNK TNK
ALL THE INNER, ALL THE OUTER WORLD OF...? WORLD OF...WHAT THE--?
IT'S COOL, LUCY--PART OF THE DEAL. KEEP GOING.
I DON'T KNOW--I... LITTLE DIZZY.
WHOA, ME TOO. I--

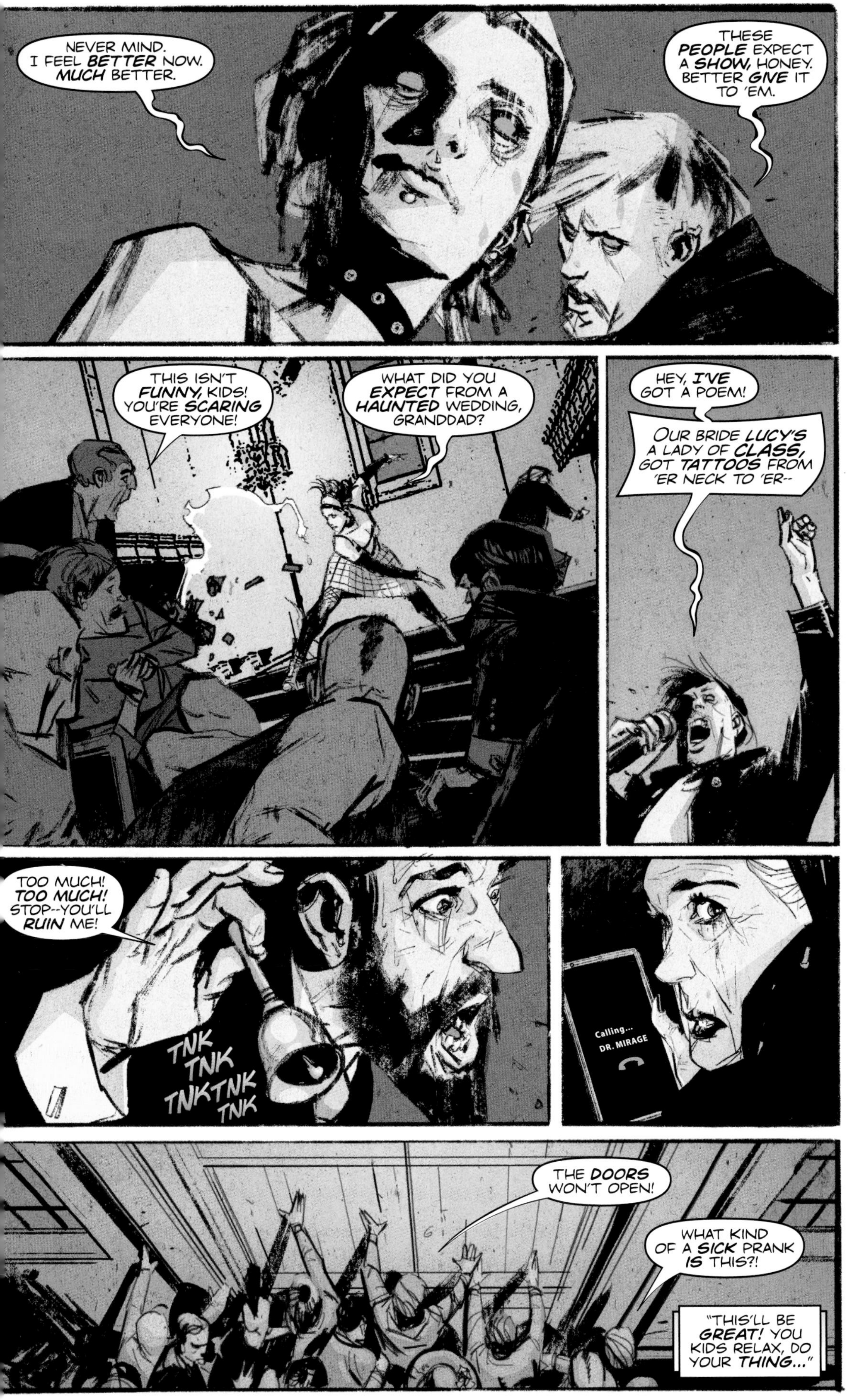
NEVER MIND. I FEEL BETTER NOW. MUCH BETTER.
THESE PEOPLE EXPECT A SHOW, HONEY. BETTER GIVE IT TO 'EM.
THIS ISN'T FUNNY, KIDS! YOU'RE SCARING EVERYONE!
WHAT DID YOU EXPECT FROM A HAUNTED WEDDING, GRANDDAD?
HEY, I'VE GOT A POEM!
OUR BRIDE LUCY'S A LADY OF CLASS, GOT TATTOOS FROM 'ER NECK TO 'ER--
TOO MUCH! TOO MUCH! STOP--YOU'LL RUIN ME!
TNK TNK TNKTNK TNK
Calling...
DR. MIRAGE
THE DOORS WON'T OPEN!
WHAT KIND OF A SICK PRANK IS THIS?!
"THIS'LL BE GREAT! YOU KIDS RELAX, DO YOUR THING..."

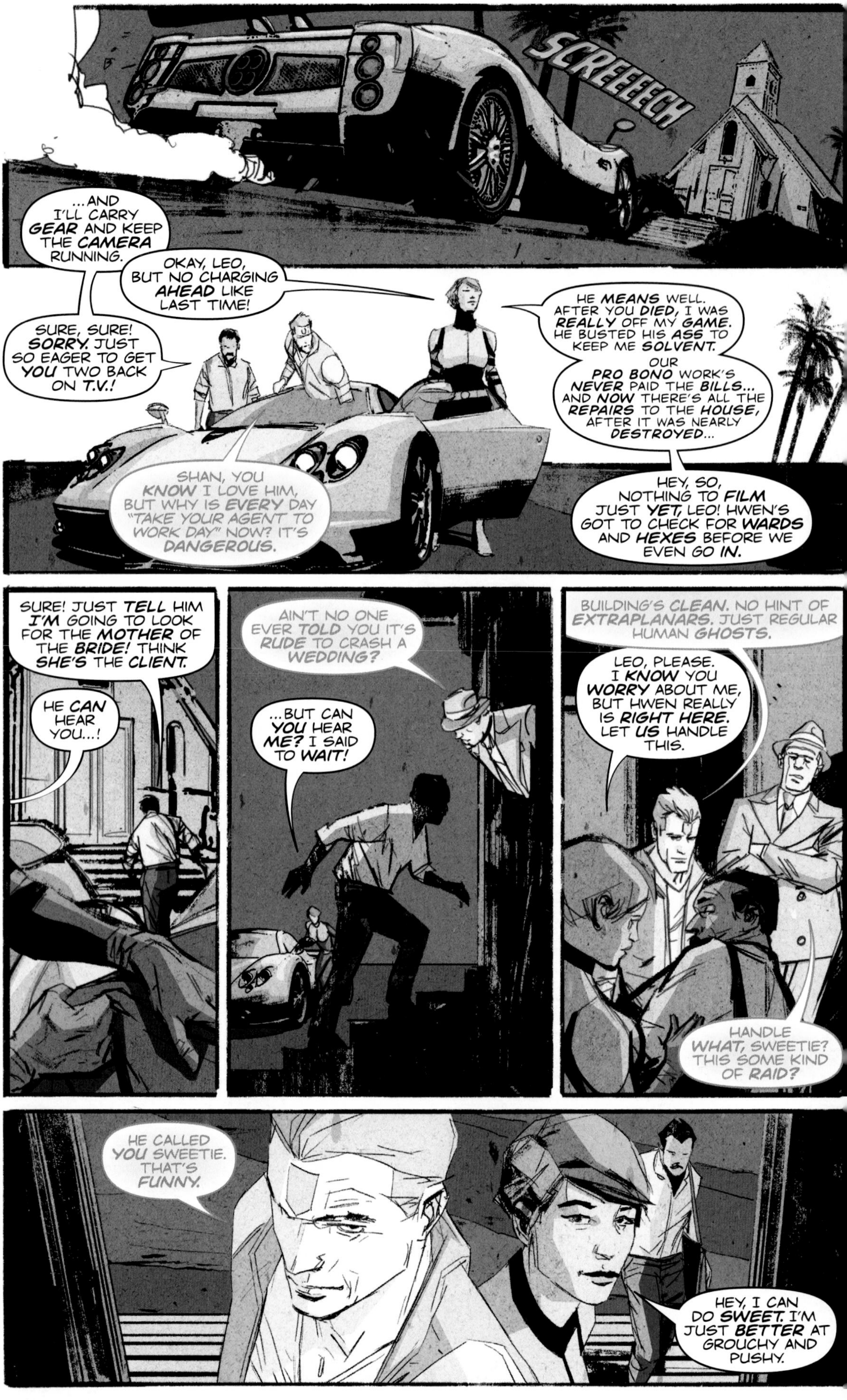
SCREEEEECH
...AND I'LL CARRY GEAR AND KEEP THE CAMERA RUNNING.
OKAY, LEO, BUT NO CHARGING AHEAD LIKE LAST TIME!
SURE, SURE! SORRY. JUST SO EAGER TO GET YOU TWO BACK ON T.V.!
SHAN, YOU KNOW I LOVE HIM, BUT WHY IS EVERY DAY "TAKE YOUR AGENT TO WORK DAY" NOW? IT'S DANGEROUS.
HE MEANS WELL. AFTER YOU DIED, I WAS REALLY OFF MY GAME. HE BUSTED HIS ASS TO KEEP ME SOLVENT.
OUR PRO BONO WORK'S NEVER PAID THE BILLS... AND NOW THERE'S ALL THE REPAIRS TO THE HOUSE, AFTER IT WAS NEARLY DESTROYED...
HEY, SO, NOTHING TO FILM JUST YET, LEO! HWEN'S GOT TO CHECK FOR WARDS AND HEXES BEFORE WE EVEN GO IN.
SURE! JUST TELL HIM I'M GOING TO LOOK FOR THE MOTHER OF THE BRIDE! THINK SHE'S THE CLIENT.
HE CAN HEAR YOU...!
AIN'T NO ONE EVER TOLD YOU IT'S RUDE TO CRASH A WEDDING?
...BUT CAN YOU HEAR ME? I SAID TO WAIT!
BUILDING'S CLEAN. NO HINT OF EXTRAPLANARS. JUST REGULAR HUMAN GHOSTS.
LEO, PLEASE. I KNOW YOU WORRY ABOUT ME, BUT HWEN REALLY IS RIGHT HERE. LET US HANDLE THIS.
HANDLE WHAT, SWEETIE? THIS SOME KIND OF RAID?
HE CALLED YOU SWEETIE. THAT'S FUNNY.
HEY, I CAN DO SWEET. I'M JUST BETTER AT GROUCHY AND PUSHY.

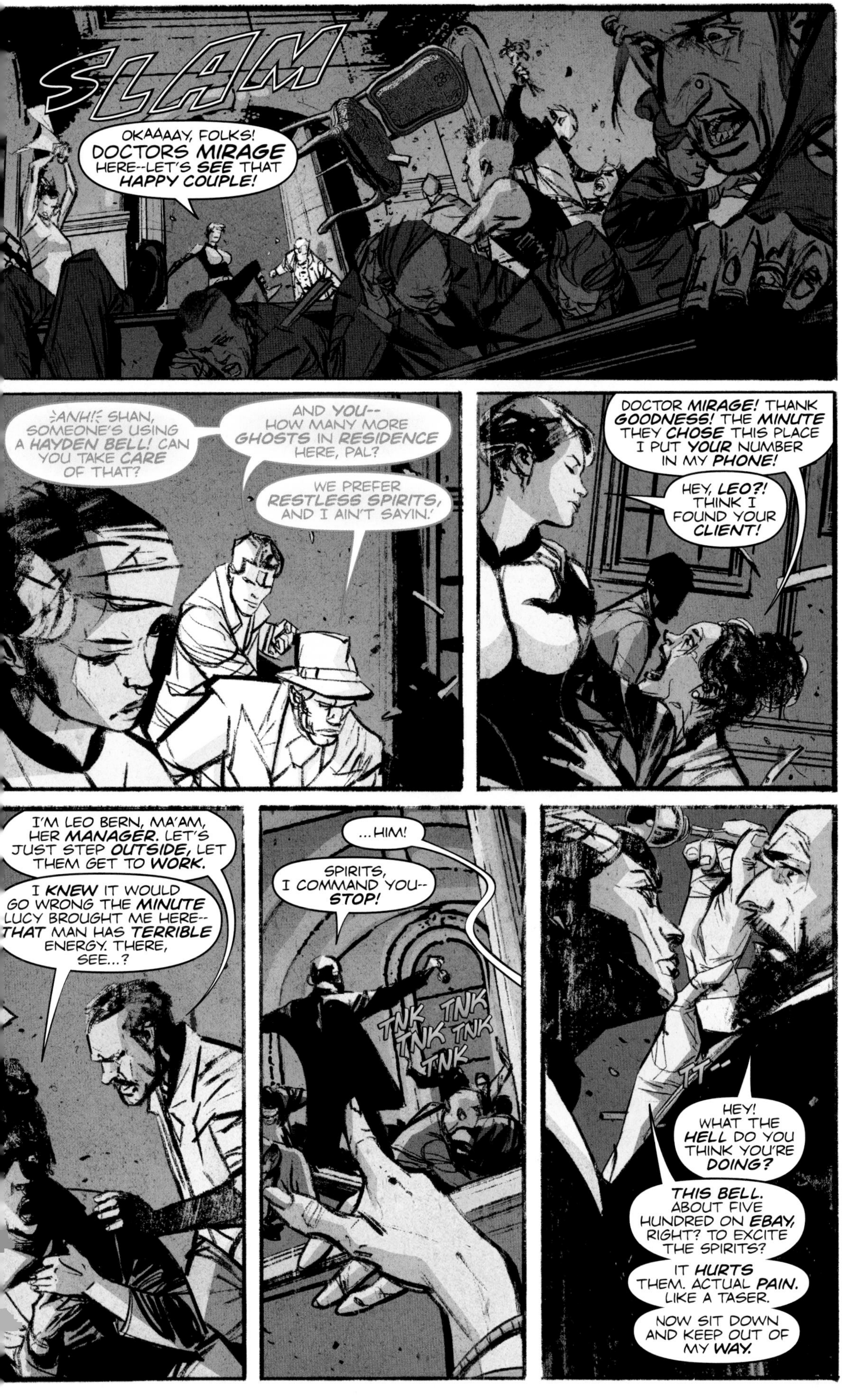
SLAM
OKAAAAY, FOLKS! DOCTORS MIRAGE HERE--LET'S SEE THAT HAPPY COUPLE!
ANH!! SHAN, SOMEONE'S USING A HAYDEN BELL! CAN YOU TAKE CARE OF THAT?
AND YOU-- HOW MANY MORE GHOSTS IN RESIDENCE HERE, PAL?
WE PREFER RESTLESS SPIRITS, AND I AIN'T SAYIN.'
DOCTOR MIRAGE! THANK GOODNESS! THE MINUTE THEY CHOSE THIS PLACE I PUT YOUR NUMBER IN MY PHONE!
HEY, LEO?! THINK I FOUND YOUR CLIENT!
I'M LEO BERN, MA'AM, HER MANAGER. LET'S JUST STEP OUTSIDE, LET THEM GET TO WORK.
I KNEW IT WOULD GO WRONG THE MINUTE LUCY BROUGHT ME HERE--THAT MAN HAS TERRIBLE ENERGY. THERE, SEE...?
...HIM!
SPIRITS, I COMMAND YOU-- STOP!
TNK TNK TNK TNK TNK
IT--
HEY! WHAT THE HELL DO YOU THINK YOU'RE DOING?
THIS BELL. ABOUT FIVE HUNDRED ON EBAY, RIGHT? TO EXCITE THE SPIRITS?
IT HURTS THEM. ACTUAL PAIN. LIKE A TASER.
NOW SIT DOWN AND KEEP OUT OF MY WAY.

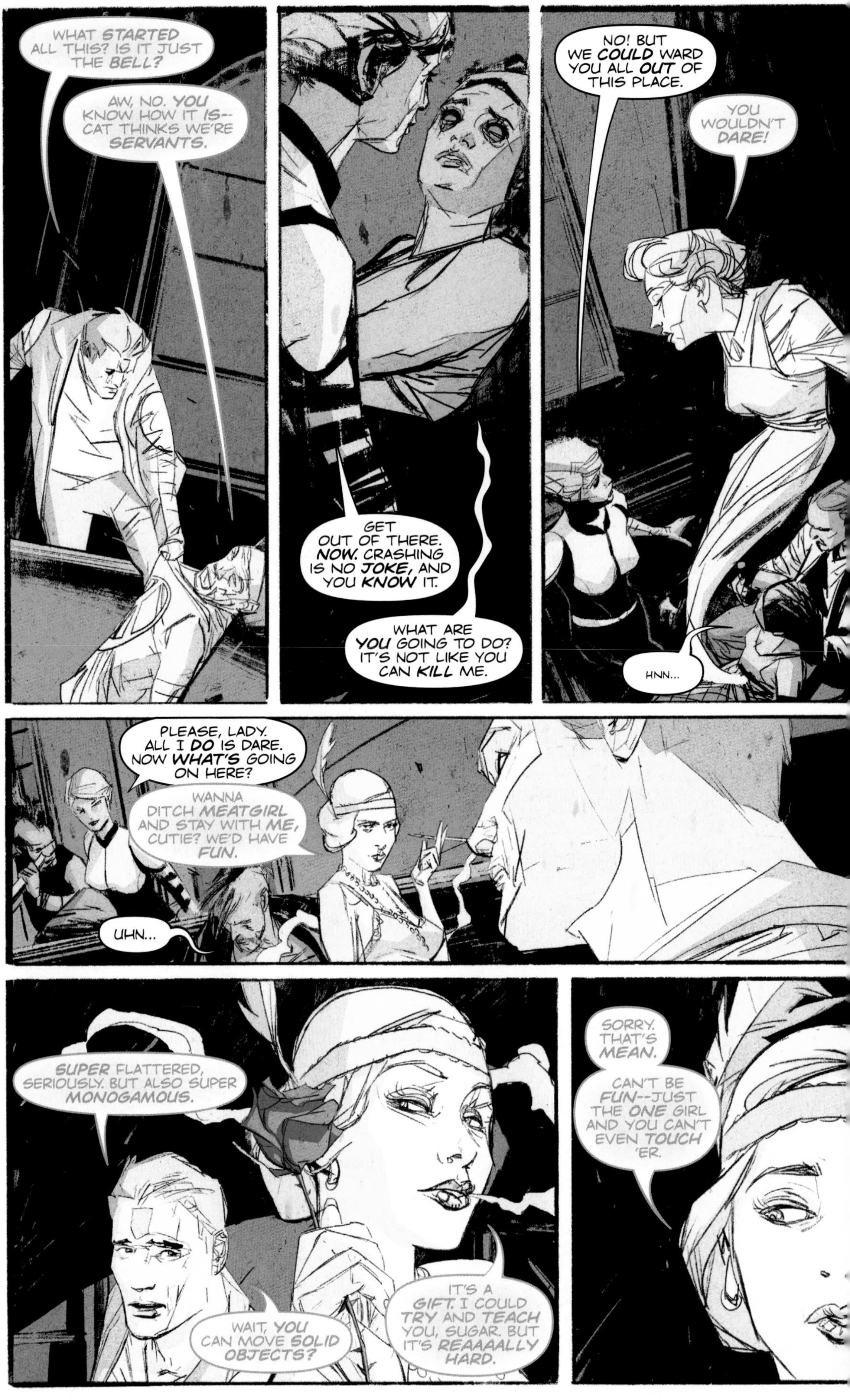
WHAT STARTED ALL THIS? IS IT JUST THE BELL?
AW, NO. YOU KNOW HOW IT IS-- CAT THINKS WE'RE SERVANTS.
GET OUT OF THERE. NOW. CRASHING IS NO JOKE, AND YOU KNOW IT.
WHAT ARE YOU GOING TO DO? IT'S NOT LIKE YOU CAN KILL ME.
NO! BUT WE COULD WARD YOU ALL OUT OF THIS PLACE.
YOU WOULDN'T DARE!
HNN...
PLEASE, LADY. ALL I DO IS DARE. NOW WHAT'S GOING ON HERE?
WANNA DITCH MEATGIRL AND STAY WITH ME, CUTIE? WE'D HAVE FUN.
UHN...
SUPER FLATTERED, SERIOUSLY. BUT ALSO SUPER MONOGAMOUS.
WAIT, YOU CAN MOVE SOLID OBJECTS?
IT'S A GIFT. I COULD TRY AND TEACH YOU, SUGAR. BUT IT'S REAAAALLY HARD.
SORRY. THAT'S MEAN.
CAN'T BE FUN--JUST THE ONE GIRL AND YOU CAN'T EVEN TOUCH 'ER.

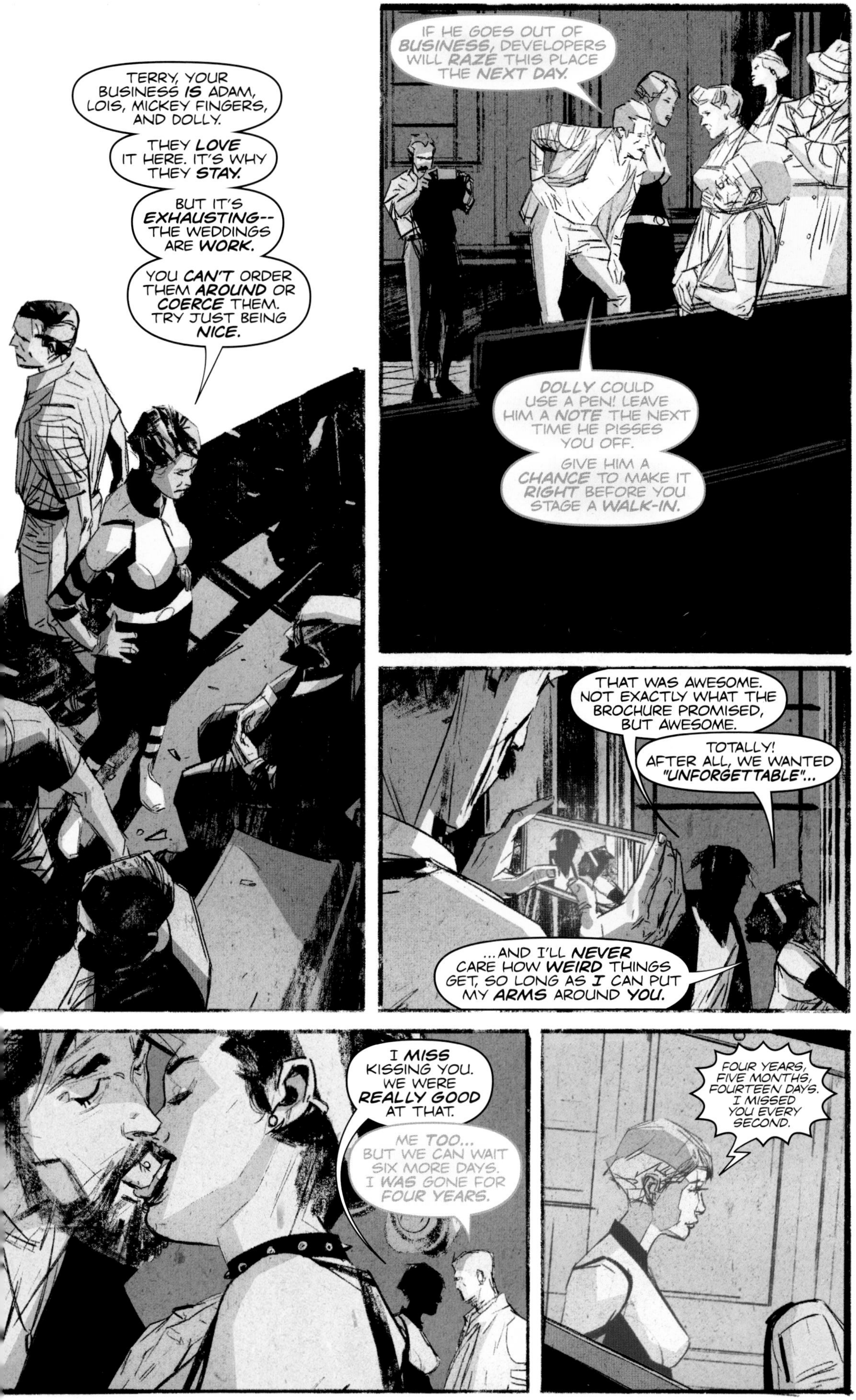

TERRY, YOUR BUSINESS IS ADAM, LOIS, MICKEY FINGERS, AND DOLLY.
THEY LOVE IT HERE. IT'S WHY THEY STAY.
BUT IT'S EXHAUSTING-- THE WEDDINGS ARE WORK.
YOU CAN'T ORDER THEM AROUND OR COERCE THEM. TRY JUST BEING NICE.
IF HE GOES OUT OF BUSINESS, DEVELOPERS WILL RAZE THIS PLACE THE NEXT DAY.
DOLLY COULD USE A PEN! LEAVE HIM A NOTE THE NEXT TIME HE PISSES YOU OFF.
GIVE HIM A CHANCE TO MAKE IT RIGHT BEFORE YOU STAGE A WALK-IN.
THAT WAS AWESOME. NOT EXACTLY WHAT THE BROCHURE PROMISED, BUT AWESOME.
TOTALLY! AFTER ALL, WE WANTED "UNFORGETTABLE"...
...AND I'LL NEVER CARE HOW WEIRD THINGS GET, SO LONG AS I CAN PUT MY ARMS AROUND YOU.
I MISS KISSING YOU. WE WERE REALLY GOOD AT THAT.
ME TOO... BUT WE CAN WAIT SIX MORE DAYS. I WAS GONE FOR FOUR YEARS.
FOUR YEARS, FIVE MONTHS, FOURTEEN DAYS. I MISSED YOU EVERY SECOND.

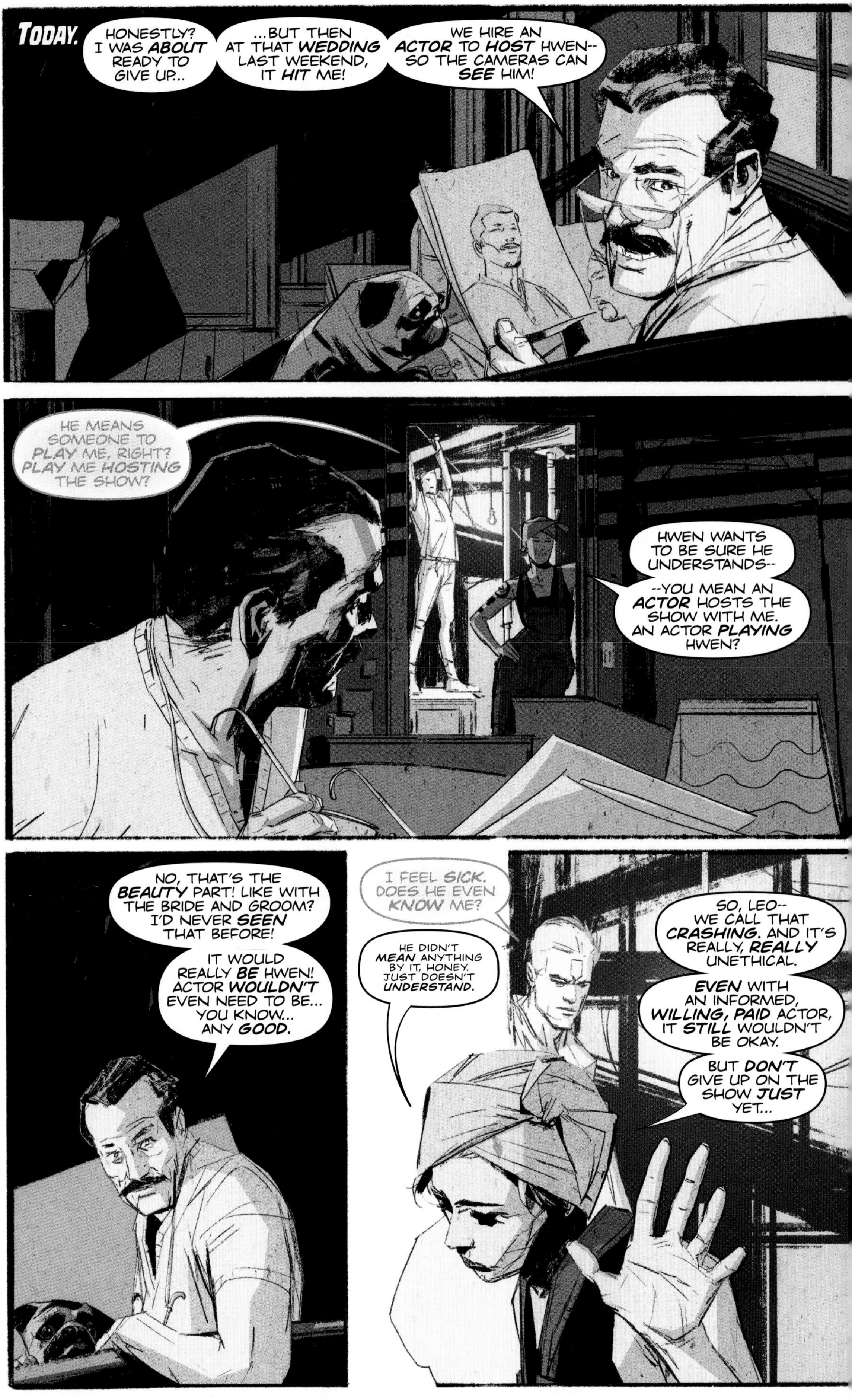
TODAY.
HONESTLY? I WAS ABOUT READY TO GIVE UP...
...BUT THEN AT THAT WEDDING LAST WEEKEND, IT HIT ME!
WE HIRE AN ACTOR TO HOST HWEN-- SO THE CAMERAS CAN SEE HIM!
HE MEANS SOMEONE TO PLAY ME, RIGHT? PLAY ME HOSTING THE SHOW?
HWEN WANTS TO BE SURE HE UNDERSTANDS--
--YOU MEAN AN ACTOR HOSTS THE SHOW WITH ME. AN ACTOR PLAYING HWEN?
NO, THAT'S THE BEAUTY PART! LIKE WITH THE BRIDE AND GROOM? I'D NEVER SEEN THAT BEFORE!
IT WOULD REALLY BE HWEN! ACTOR WOULDN'T EVEN NEED TO BE... YOU KNOW... ANY GOOD.
I FEEL SICK. DOES HE EVEN KNOW ME?
HE DIDN'T MEAN ANYTHING BY IT, HONEY. JUST DOESN'T UNDERSTAND.
SO, LEO-- WE CALL THAT CRASHING. AND IT'S REALLY, REALLY UNETHICAL.
EVEN WITH AN INFORMED, WILLING, PAID ACTOR, IT STILL WOULDN'T BE OKAY.
BUT DON'T GIVE UP ON THE SHOW JUST YET...

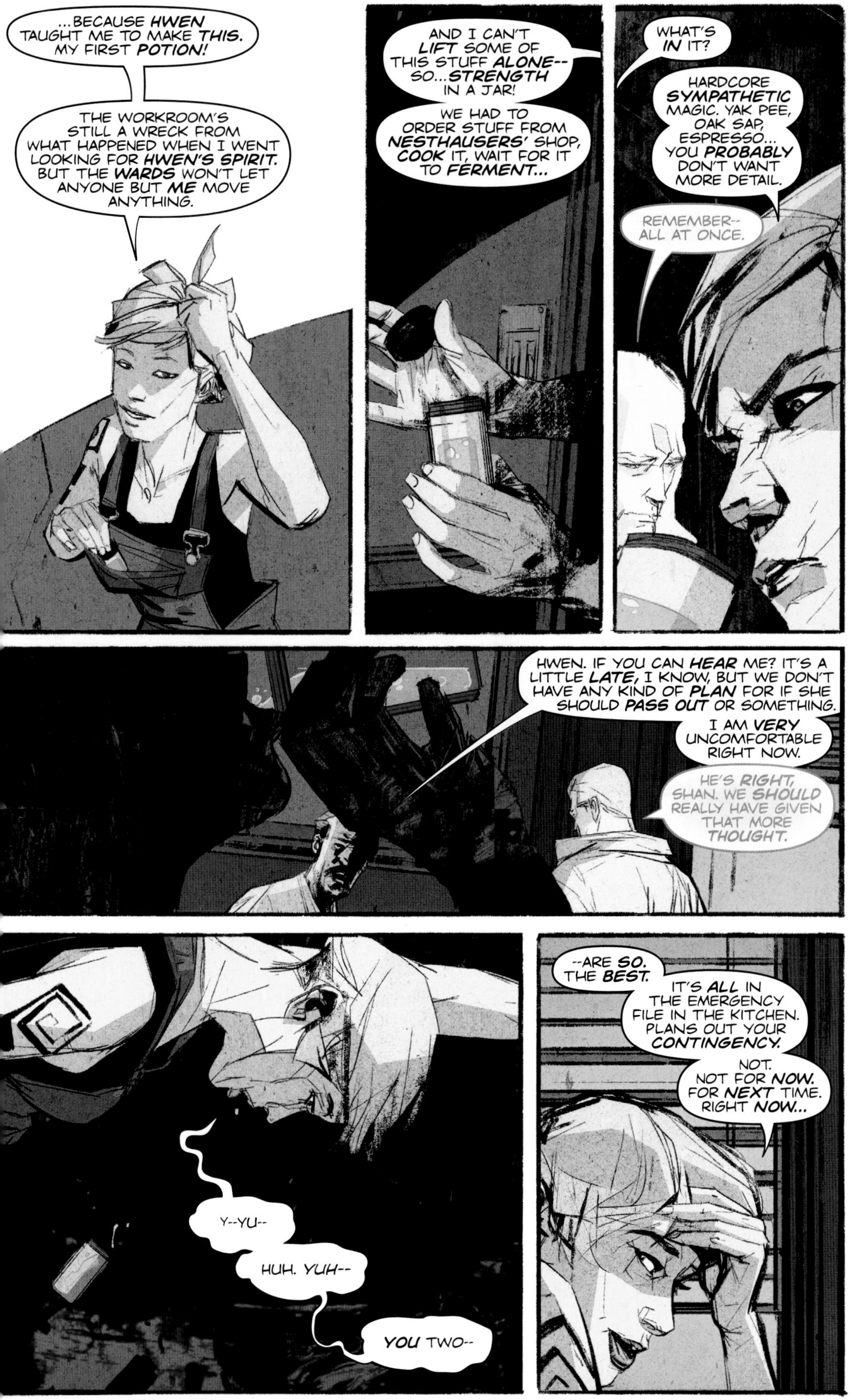
...BECAUSE HWEN TAUGHT ME TO MAKE THIS. MY FIRST POTION!
THE WORKROOM'S STILL A WRECK FROM WHAT HAPPENED WHEN I WENT LOOKING FOR HWEN'S SPIRIT. BUT THE WARDS WON'T LET ANYONE BUT ME MOVE ANYTHING.
AND I CAN'T LIFT SOME OF THIS STUFF ALONE-- SO...STRENGTH IN A JAR!
WE HAD TO ORDER STUFF FROM NESTHAUSERS' SHOP, COOK IT, WAIT FOR IT TO FERMENT...
WHAT'S IN IT?
HARDCORE SYMPATHETIC MAGIC. YAK PEE, OAK SAP, ESPRESSO... YOU PROBABLY DON'T WANT MORE DETAIL.
REMEMBER-- ALL AT ONCE.
HWEN. IF YOU CAN HEAR ME? IT'S A LITTLE LATE, I KNOW, BUT WE DON'T HAVE ANY KIND OF PLAN FOR IF SHE SHOULD PASS OUT OR SOMETHING.
I AM VERY UNCOMFORTABLE RIGHT NOW.
HE'S RIGHT, SHAN. WE SHOULD REALLY HAVE GIVEN THAT MORE THOUGHT.
Y--YU--
HUH. YUH--
YOU TWO--
--ARE SO. THE BEST.
IT'S ALL IN THE EMERGENCY FILE IN THE KITCHEN. PLANS OUT YOUR CONTINGENCY.
NOT. NOT FOR NOW. FOR NEXT TIME. RIGHT NOW...

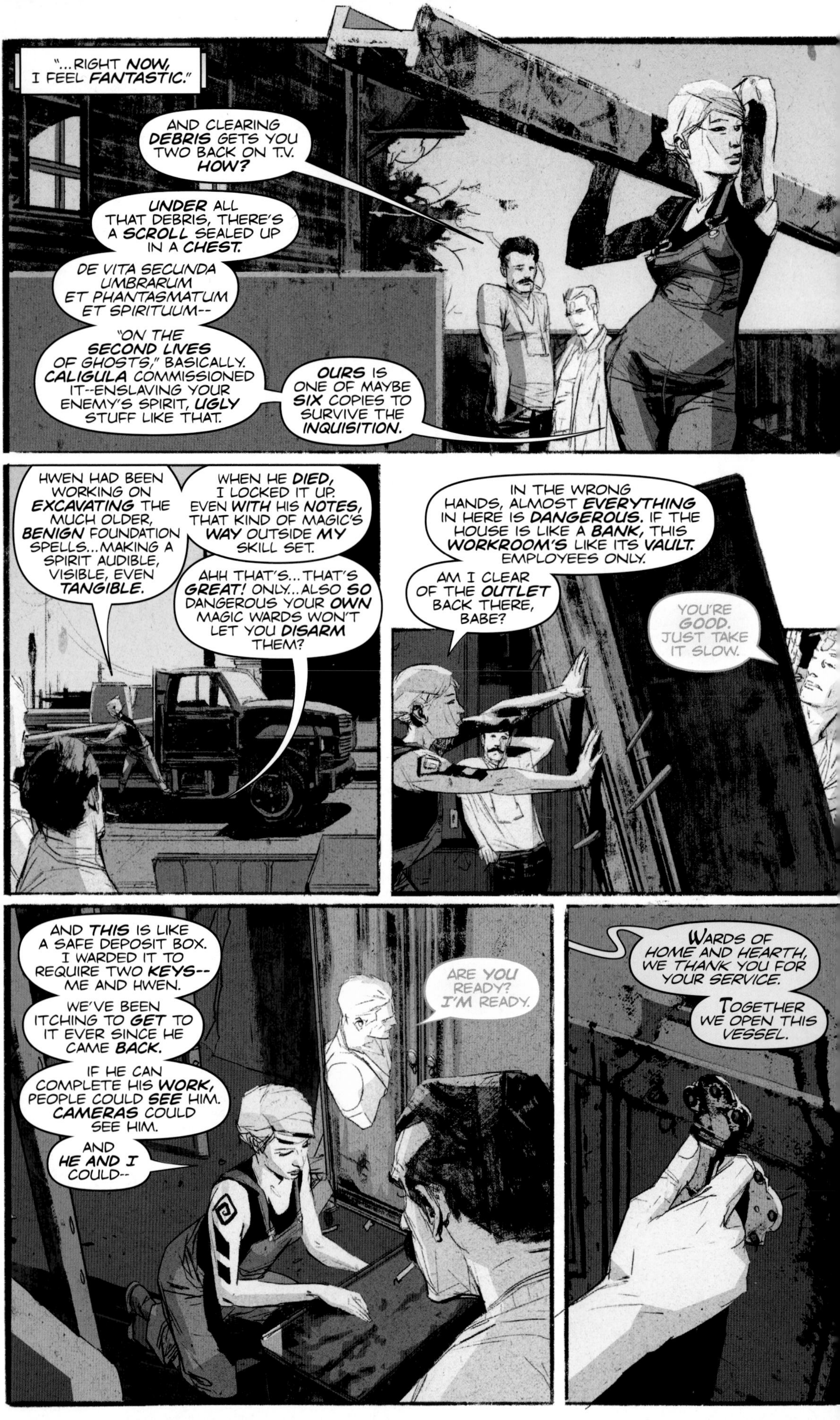
"...RIGHT NOW, I FEEL FANTASTIC."
AND CLEARING DEBRIS GETS YOU TWO BACK ON T.V. HOW?
UNDER ALL THAT DEBRIS, THERE'S A SCROLL SEALED UP IN A CHEST.
DE VITA SECUNDA UMBRARUM ET PHANTASMATUM ET SPIRITUUM--
"ON THE SECOND LIVES OF GHOSTS," BASICALLY. CALIGULA COMMISSIONED IT--ENSLAVING YOUR ENEMY'S SPIRIT, UGLY STUFF LIKE THAT.
OURS IS ONE OF MAYBE SIX COPIES TO SURVIVE THE INQUISITION.
HWEN HAD BEEN WORKING ON EXCAVATING THE MUCH OLDER, BENIGN FOUNDATION SPELLS...MAKING A SPIRIT AUDIBLE, VISIBLE, EVEN TANGIBLE.
WHEN HE DIED, I LOCKED IT UP. EVEN WITH HIS NOTES, THAT KIND OF MAGIC'S WAY OUTSIDE MY SKILL SET.
AHH THAT'S...THAT'S GREAT! ONLY...ALSO SO DANGEROUS YOUR OWN MAGIC WARDS WON'T LET YOU DISARM THEM?
IN THE WRONG HANDS, ALMOST EVERYTHING IN HERE IS DANGEROUS. IF THE HOUSE IS LIKE A BANK, THIS WORKROOM'S LIKE ITS VAULT. EMPLOYEES ONLY.
AM I CLEAR OF THE OUTLET BACK THERE, BABE?
YOU'RE GOOD. JUST TAKE IT SLOW.
AND THIS IS LIKE A SAFE DEPOSIT BOX. I WARDED IT TO REQUIRE TWO KEYS-- ME AND HWEN.
WE'VE BEEN ITCHING TO GET TO IT EVER SINCE HE CAME BACK.
IF HE CAN COMPLETE HIS WORK, PEOPLE COULD SEE HIM. CAMERAS COULD SEE HIM.
AND HE AND I COULD--
ARE YOU READY? I'M READY.
WARDS OF HOME AND HEARTH, WE THANK YOU FOR YOUR SERVICE.
TOGETHER WE OPEN THIS VESSEL.

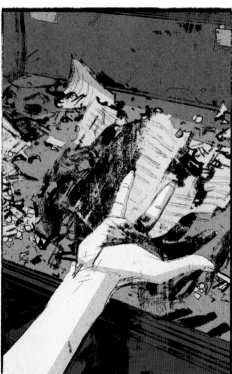

WHAT'S THE **MATTER**, KID? WHAT **HAPPENED?**

MAYBE WHEN **LINTON MARCH'S** GUYS KIDNAPPED YOU AND THE **HOUSE** BERSERKED, SOMETHING WENT HAYWIRE.

MAYBE. OR THERE COULD HAVE BEEN A MOMENT WHEN THE CHEST'S WARDS THOUGHT WE WERE **BOTH** DEAD.

OR MAYBE I **SCREWED** SOMETHING UP WHEN I **SET** THEM.

THE **POTION** SHOULD BE OUT OF YOUR **SYSTEM** BY NOW. HOW'RE YOU **FEELING?**

WRECKED. I AM BECOME **BRUISE,** DESTROYER OF DELTOIDS.

AND I **JUST**... WE WERE **SO** CLOSE... TO BEING **CLOSE** AGAIN.

I AM SO **GRATEFUL** YOU'RE BACK. **EVERY** DAY.

I FEEL **GUILTY,** WANTING MORE.

I KNOW. ME TOO. BUT IT'S A PRETTY **NORMAL** WANT.

TRY AND GET SOME REST. I CAN'T USE A **KEYBOARD**--

--SO STARTING TOMORROW IT'LL BE ALL **YOU** TRYING TO TRACK DOWN ONE OF THE **OTHER** COPIES. MAYBE WE'LL GET **LUCKY**...

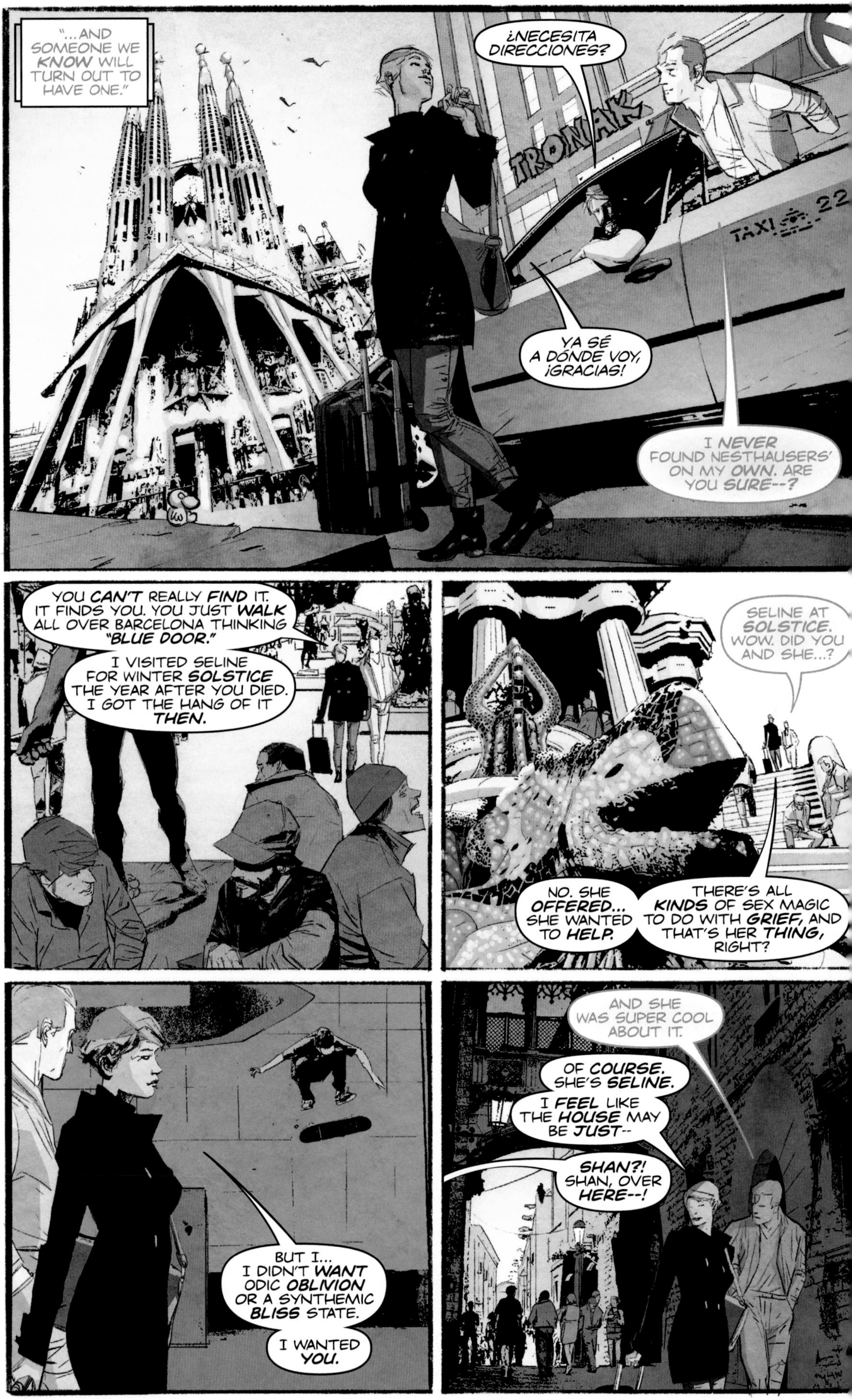
"...AND SOMEONE WE KNOW WILL TURN OUT TO HAVE ONE."
¿NECESITA DIRECCIONES?
TRONAK
TAXI 22
YA SÉ A DÓNDE VOY, ¡GRACIAS!
I NEVER FOUND NESTHAUSERS' ON MY OWN. ARE YOU SURE--?
YOU CAN'T REALLY FIND IT. IT FINDS YOU. YOU JUST WALK ALL OVER BARCELONA THINKING "BLUE DOOR."
I VISITED SELINE FOR WINTER SOLSTICE THE YEAR AFTER YOU DIED. I GOT THE HANG OF IT THEN.
SELINE AT SOLSTICE. WOW. DID YOU AND SHE...?
NO. SHE OFFERED... SHE WANTED TO HELP.
THERE'S ALL KINDS OF SEX MAGIC TO DO WITH GRIEF, AND THAT'S HER THING, RIGHT?
BUT I... I DIDN'T WANT ODIC OBLIVION OR A SYNTHEMIC BLISS STATE.
I WANTED YOU.
AND SHE WAS SUPER COOL ABOUT IT.
OF COURSE. SHE'S SELINE.
I FEEL LIKE THE HOUSE MAY BE JUST--
SHAN?! SHAN, OVER HERE--!

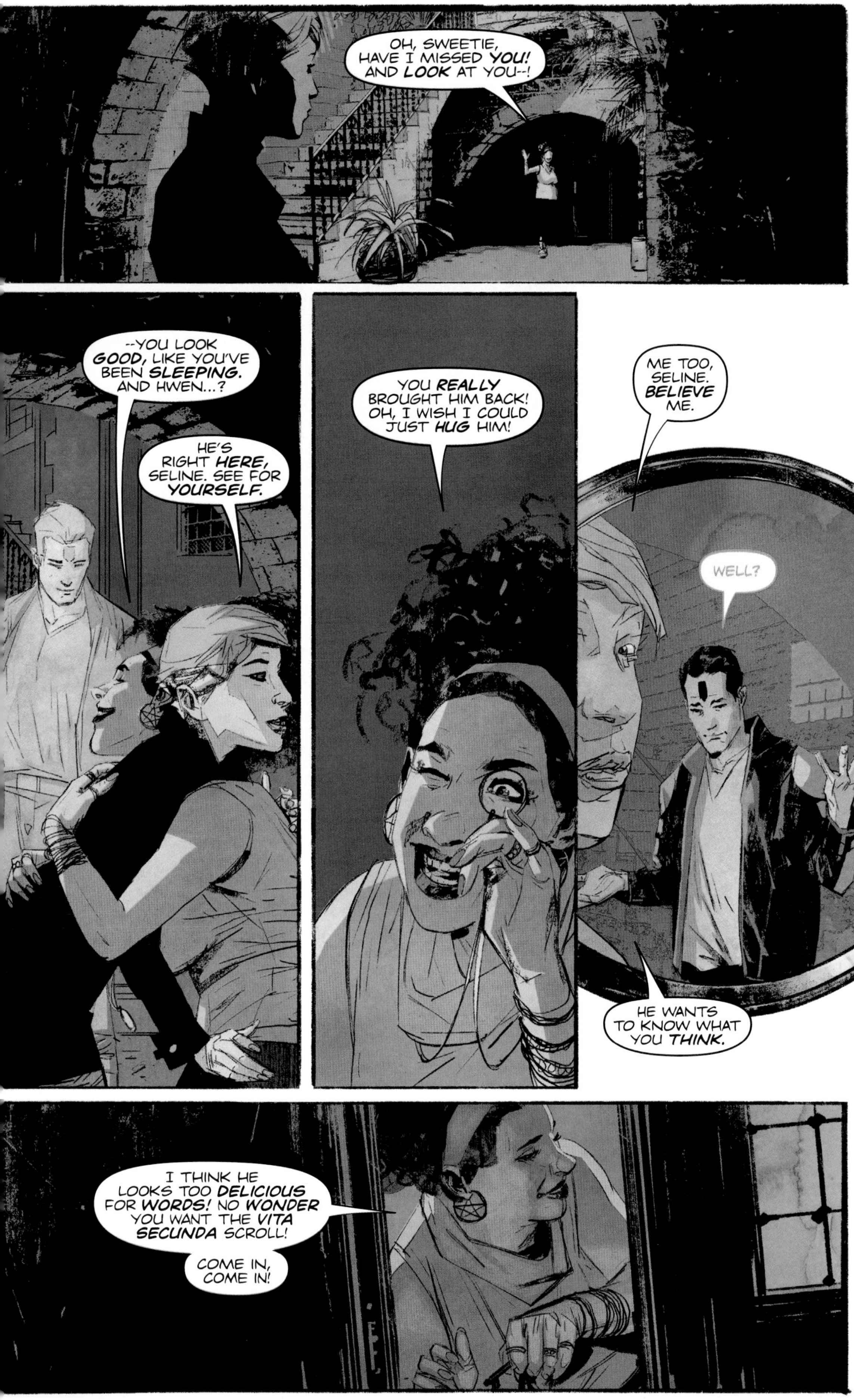
OH, SWEETIE, HAVE I MISSED YOU! AND LOOK AT YOU--!
--YOU LOOK GOOD, LIKE YOU'VE BEEN SLEEPING. AND HWEN...?
HE'S RIGHT HERE, SELINE. SEE FOR YOURSELF.
YOU REALLY BROUGHT HIM BACK! OH, I WISH I COULD JUST HUG HIM!
ME TOO, SELINE. BELIEVE ME.
WELL?
HE WANTS TO KNOW WHAT YOU THINK.
I THINK HE LOOKS TOO DELICIOUS FOR WORDS! NO WONDER YOU WANT THE VITA SECUNDA SCROLL!
COME IN, COME IN!

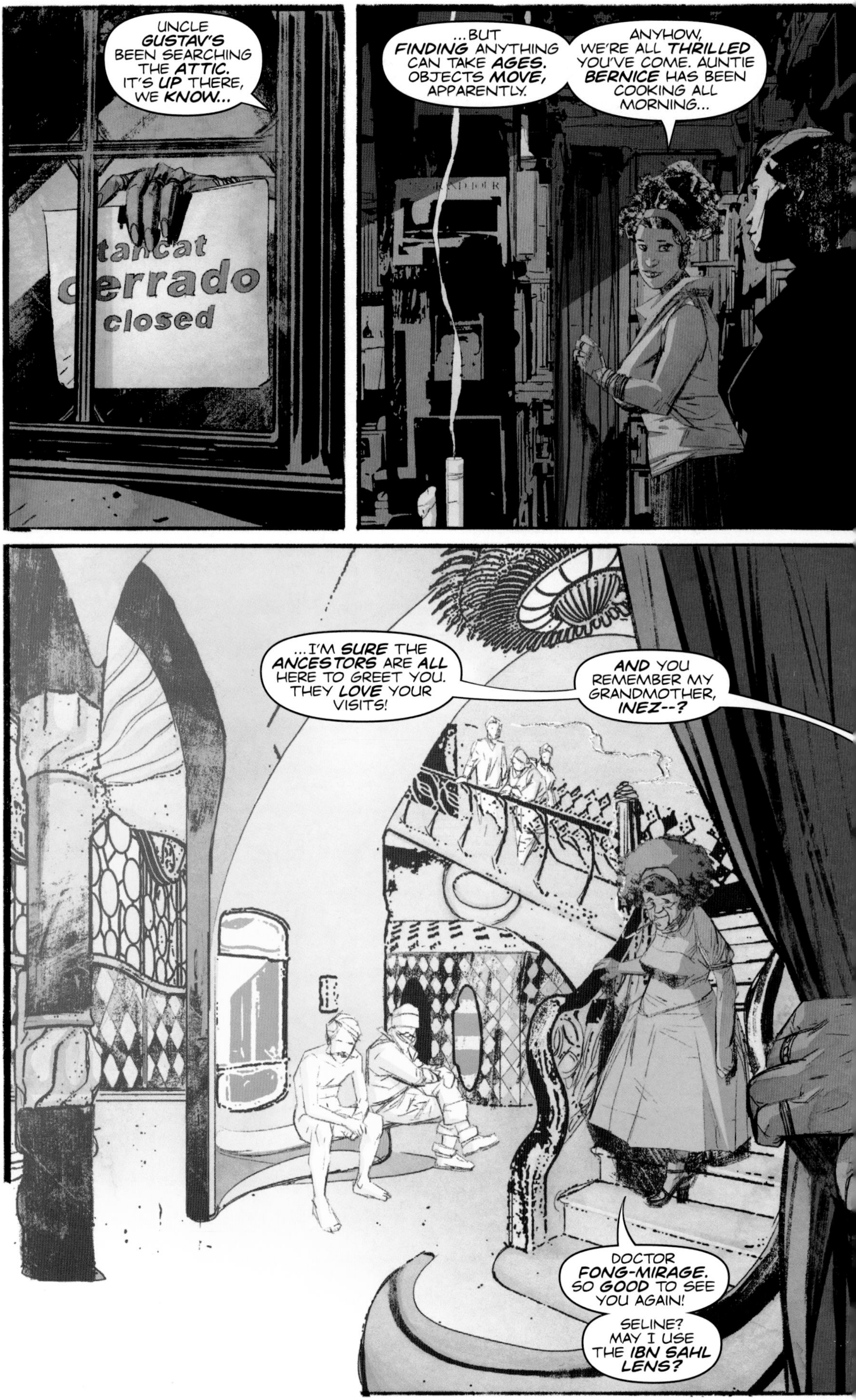
UNCLE GUSTAV'S BEEN SEARCHING THE ATTIC. IT'S UP THERE, WE KNOW...
tancat
cerrado
closed
...BUT FINDING ANYTHING CAN TAKE AGES. OBJECTS MOVE, APPARENTLY.
ANYHOW, WE'RE ALL THRILLED YOU'VE COME. AUNTIE BERNICE HAS BEEN COOKING ALL MORNING...
...I'M SURE THE ANCESTORS ARE ALL HERE TO GREET YOU. THEY LOVE YOUR VISITS!
AND YOU REMEMBER MY GRANDMOTHER, INEZ--?
DOCTOR FONG-MIRAGE. SO GOOD TO SEE YOU AGAIN!
SELINE? MAY I USE THE IBN SAHL LENS?

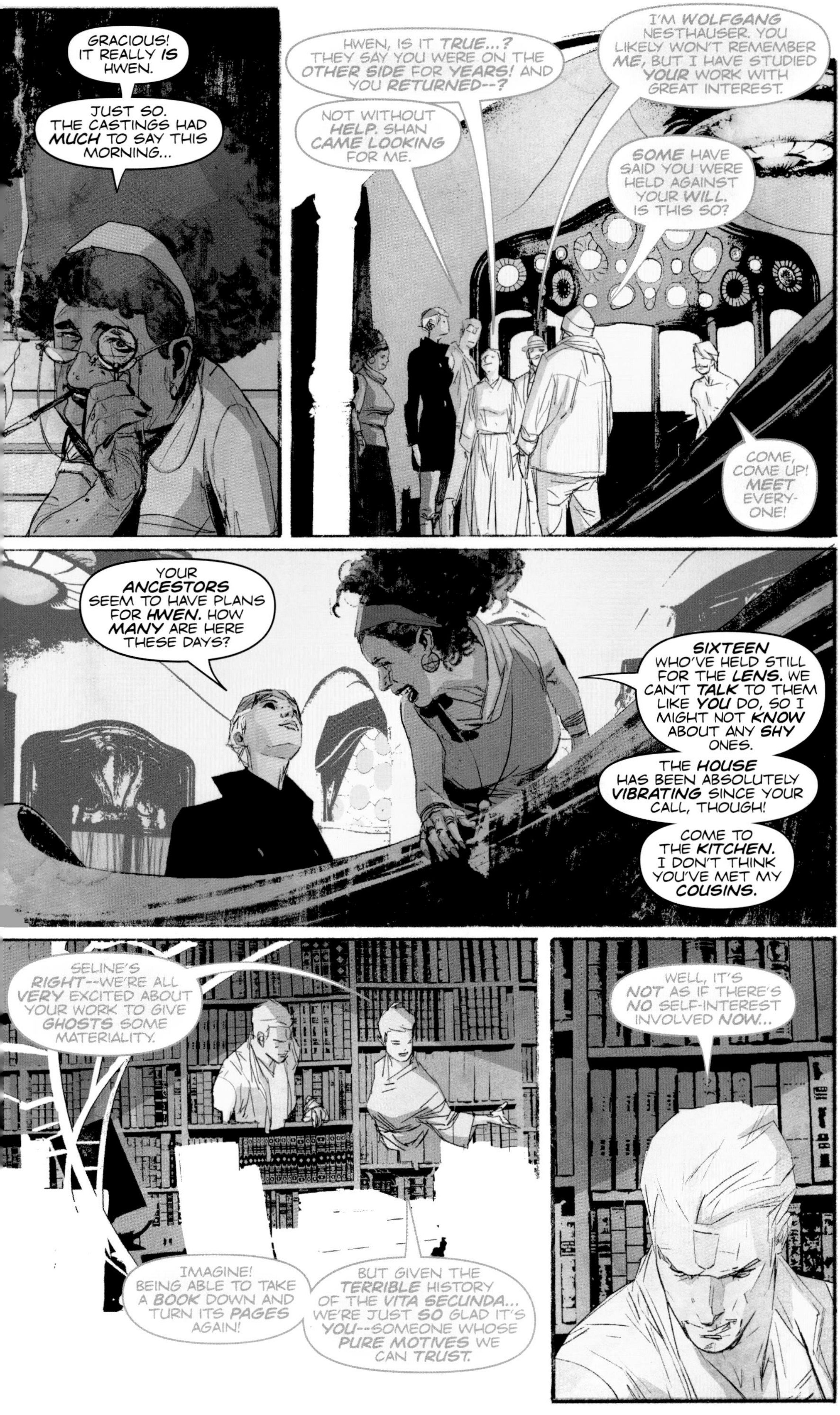
GRACIOUS! IT REALLY IS HWEN.
JUST SO. THE CASTINGS HAD MUCH TO SAY THIS MORNING...
HWEN, IS IT TRUE...? THEY SAY YOU WERE ON THE OTHER SIDE FOR YEARS! AND YOU RETURNED--?
NOT WITHOUT HELP. SHAN CAME LOOKING FOR ME.
I'M WOLFGANG NESTHAUSER. YOU LIKELY WON'T REMEMBER ME, BUT I HAVE STUDIED YOUR WORK WITH GREAT INTEREST.
SOME HAVE SAID YOU WERE HELD AGAINST YOUR WILL. IS THIS SO?
COME, COME UP! MEET EVERY-ONE!
YOUR ANCESTORS SEEM TO HAVE PLANS FOR HWEN. HOW MANY ARE HERE THESE DAYS?
SIXTEEN WHO'VE HELD STILL FOR THE LENS. WE CAN'T TALK TO THEM LIKE YOU DO, SO I MIGHT NOT KNOW ABOUT ANY SHY ONES.
THE HOUSE HAS BEEN ABSOLUTELY VIBRATING SINCE YOUR CALL, THOUGH!
COME TO THE KITCHEN. I DON'T THINK YOU'VE MET MY COUSINS.
SELINE'S RIGHT--WE'RE ALL VERY EXCITED ABOUT YOUR WORK TO GIVE GHOSTS SOME MATERIALITY.
IMAGINE! BEING ABLE TO TAKE A BOOK DOWN AND TURN ITS PAGES AGAIN!
BUT GIVEN THE TERRIBLE HISTORY OF THE VITA SECUNDA... WE'RE JUST SO GLAD IT'S YOU--SOMEONE WHOSE PURE MOTIVES WE CAN TRUST.
WELL, IT'S NOT AS IF THERE'S NO SELF-INTEREST INVOLVED NOW...

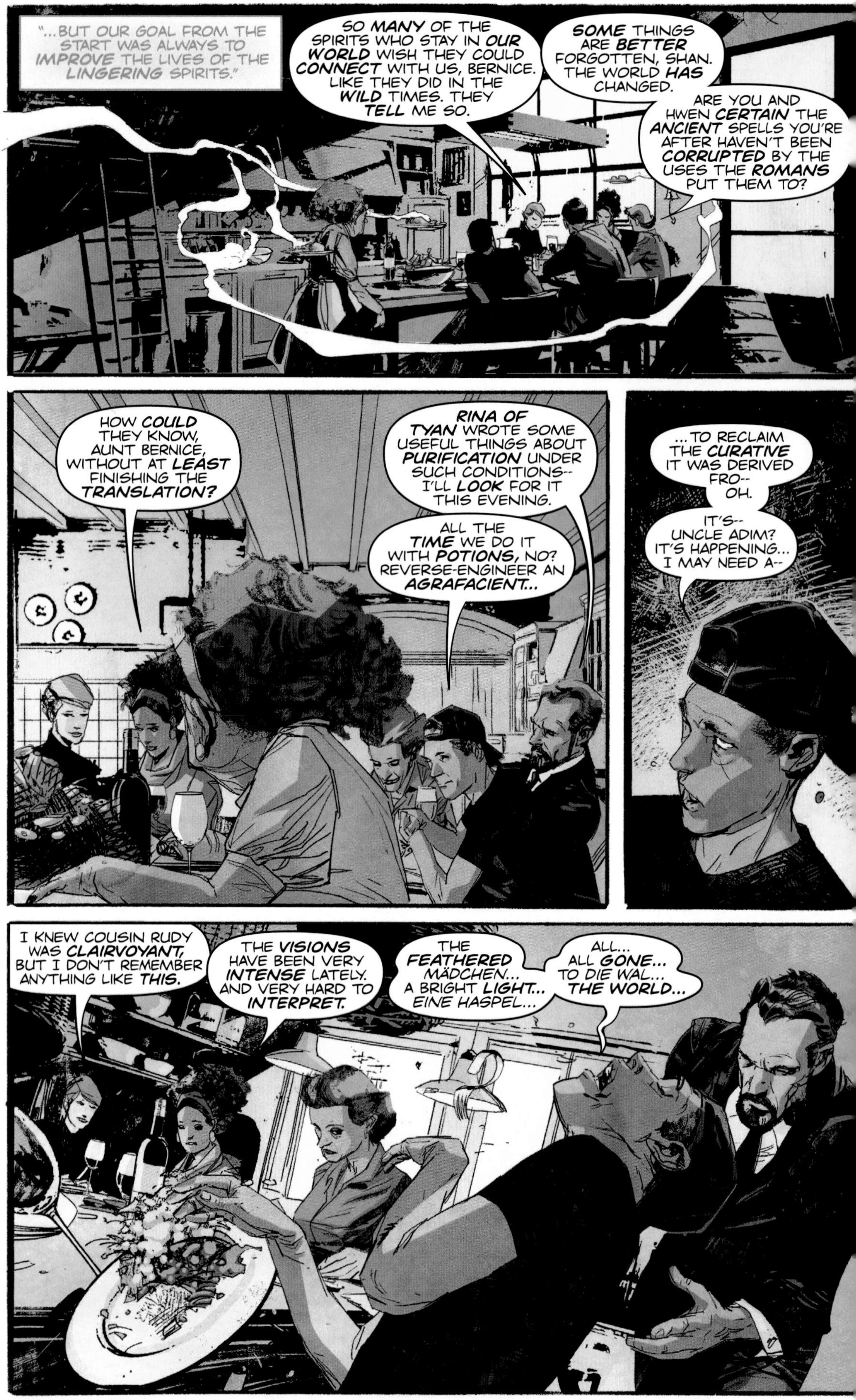
"...BUT OUR GOAL FROM THE START WAS ALWAYS TO IMPROVE THE LIVES OF THE LINGERING SPIRITS."
SO MANY OF THE SPIRITS WHO STAY IN OUR WORLD WISH THEY COULD CONNECT WITH US, BERNICE. LIKE THEY DID IN THE WILD TIMES. THEY TELL ME SO.
SOME THINGS ARE BETTER FORGOTTEN, SHAN. THE WORLD HAS CHANGED.
ARE YOU AND HWEN CERTAIN THE ANCIENT SPELLS YOU'RE AFTER HAVEN'T BEEN CORRUPTED BY THE USES THE ROMANS PUT THEM TO?
HOW COULD THEY KNOW, AUNT BERNICE, WITHOUT AT LEAST FINISHING THE TRANSLATION?
RINA OF TYAN WROTE SOME USEFUL THINGS ABOUT PURIFICATION UNDER SUCH CONDITIONS-- I'LL LOOK FOR IT THIS EVENING.
ALL THE TIME WE DO IT WITH POTIONS, NO? REVERSE-ENGINEER AN AGRAFACIENT...
...TO RECLAIM THE CURATIVE IT WAS DERIVED FRO-- OH.
IT'S-- UNCLE ADIM? IT'S HAPPENING... I MAY NEED A--
I KNEW COUSIN RUDY WAS CLAIRVOYANT, BUT I DON'T REMEMBER ANYTHING LIKE THIS.
THE VISIONS HAVE BEEN VERY INTENSE LATELY. AND VERY HARD TO INTERPRET.
THE FEATHERED MÄDCHEN... A BRIGHT LIGHT... EINE HASPEL...
ALL... ALL GONE... TO DIE WAL... THE WORLD...

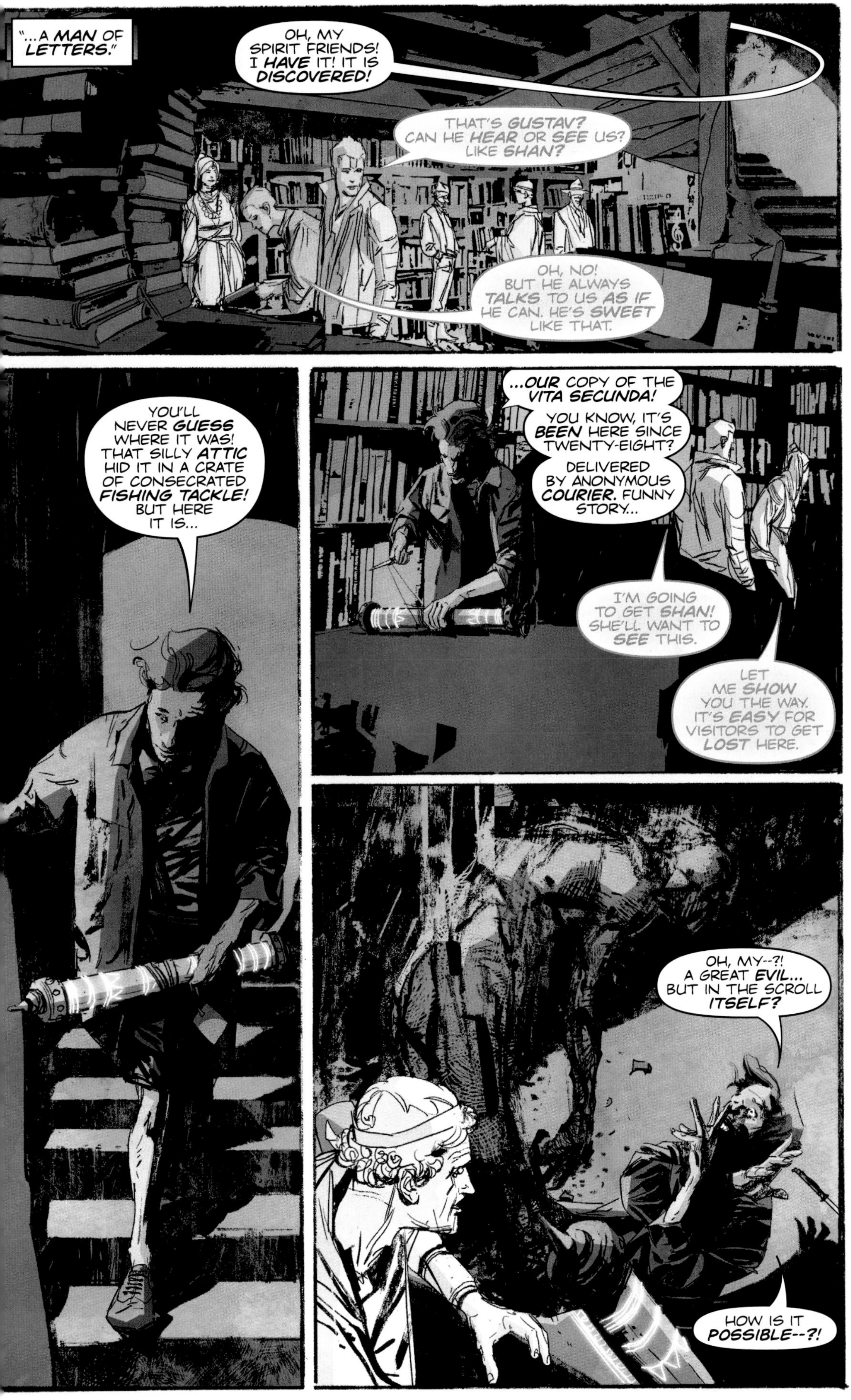

"...A MAN OF LETTERS."
OH, MY SPIRIT FRIENDS! I HAVE IT! IT IS DISCOVERED!
THAT'S GUSTAV? CAN HE HEAR OR SEE US? LIKE SHAN?
OH, NO! BUT HE ALWAYS TALKS TO US AS IF HE CAN. HE'S SWEET LIKE THAT.
YOU'LL NEVER GUESS WHERE IT WAS! THAT SILLY ATTIC HID IT IN A CRATE OF CONSECRATED FISHING TACKLE! BUT HERE IT IS...
...OUR COPY OF THE VITA SECUNDA!
YOU KNOW, IT'S BEEN HERE SINCE TWENTY-EIGHT?
DELIVERED BY ANONYMOUS COURIER. FUNNY STORY...
I'M GOING TO GET SHAN! SHE'LL WANT TO SEE THIS.
LET ME SHOW YOU THE WAY. IT'S EASY FOR VISITORS TO GET LOST HERE.
OH, MY--?! A GREAT EVIL... BUT IN THE SCROLL ITSELF?
HOW IS IT POSSIBLE--?!

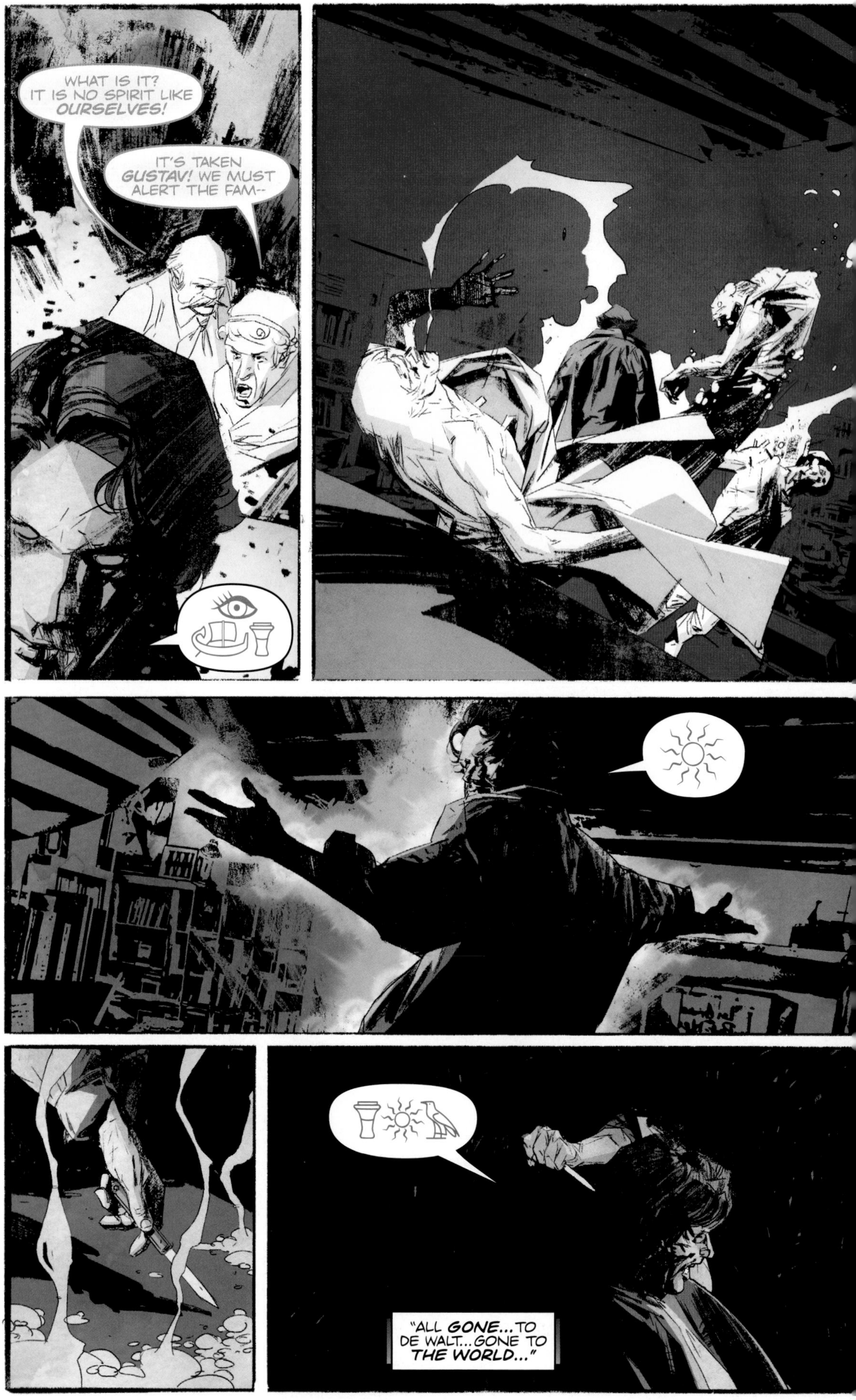
WHAT IS IT? IT IS NO SPIRIT LIKE OURSELVES!
IT'S TAKEN GUSTAV! WE MUST ALERT THE FAM--
"ALL GONE...TO DE WALT...GONE TO THE WORLD..."

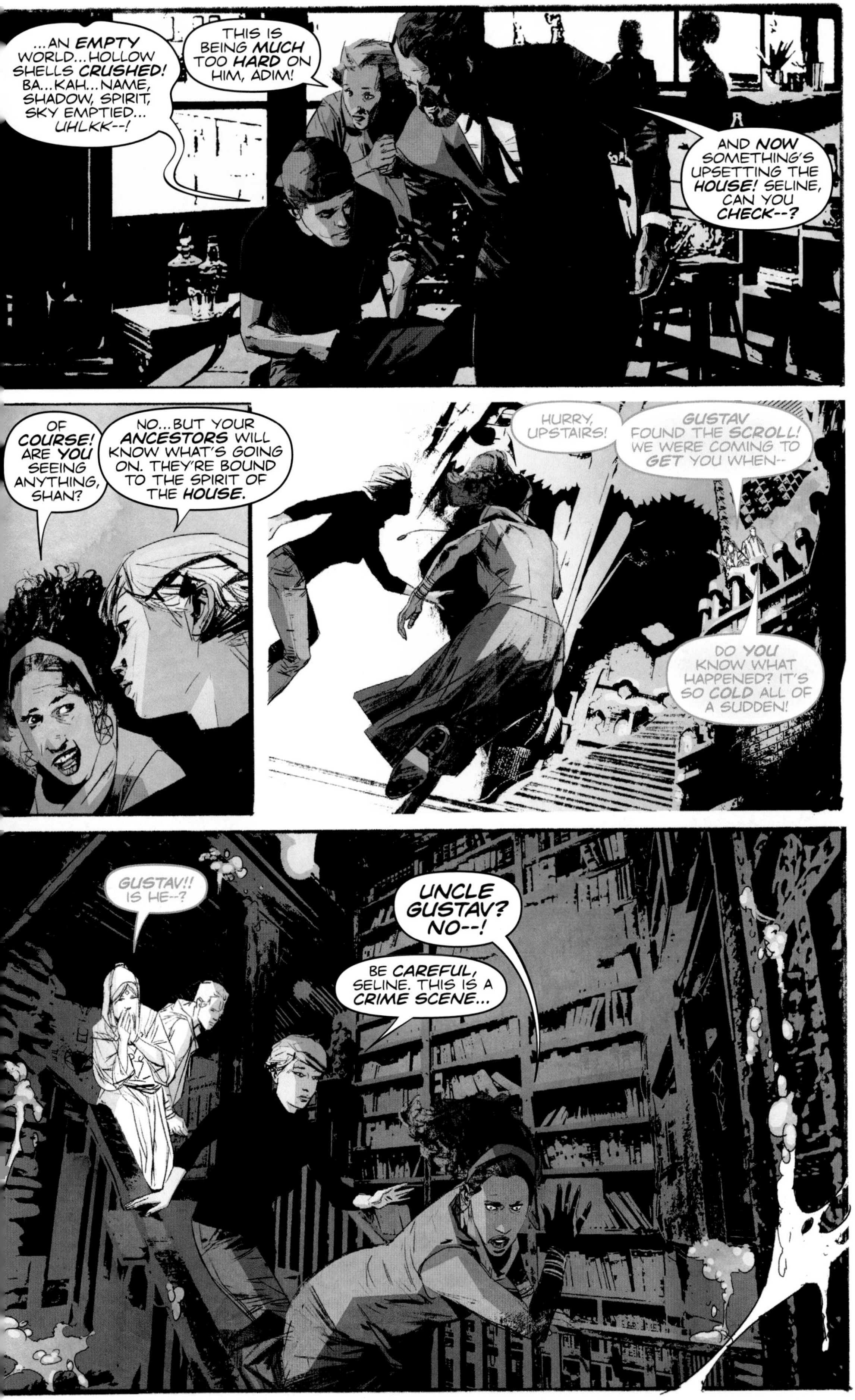
...AN EMPTY WORLD...HOLLOW SHELLS CRUSHED! BA...KAH...NAME, SHADOW, SPIRIT, SKY EMPTIED... UHLKK--!
THIS IS BEING MUCH TOO HARD ON HIM, ADIM!
AND NOW SOMETHING'S UPSETTING THE HOUSE! SELINE, CAN YOU CHECK--?
OF COURSE! ARE YOU SEEING ANYTHING, SHAN?
NO...BUT YOUR ANCESTORS WILL KNOW WHAT'S GOING ON. THEY'RE BOUND TO THE SPIRIT OF THE HOUSE.
HURRY, UPSTAIRS!
GUSTAV FOUND THE SCROLL! WE WERE COMING TO GET YOU WHEN--
DO YOU KNOW WHAT HAPPENED? IT'S SO COLD ALL OF A SUDDEN!
GUSTAV!! IS HE--?
UNCLE GUSTAV? NO--!
BE CAREFUL, SELINE. THIS IS A CRIME SCENE...

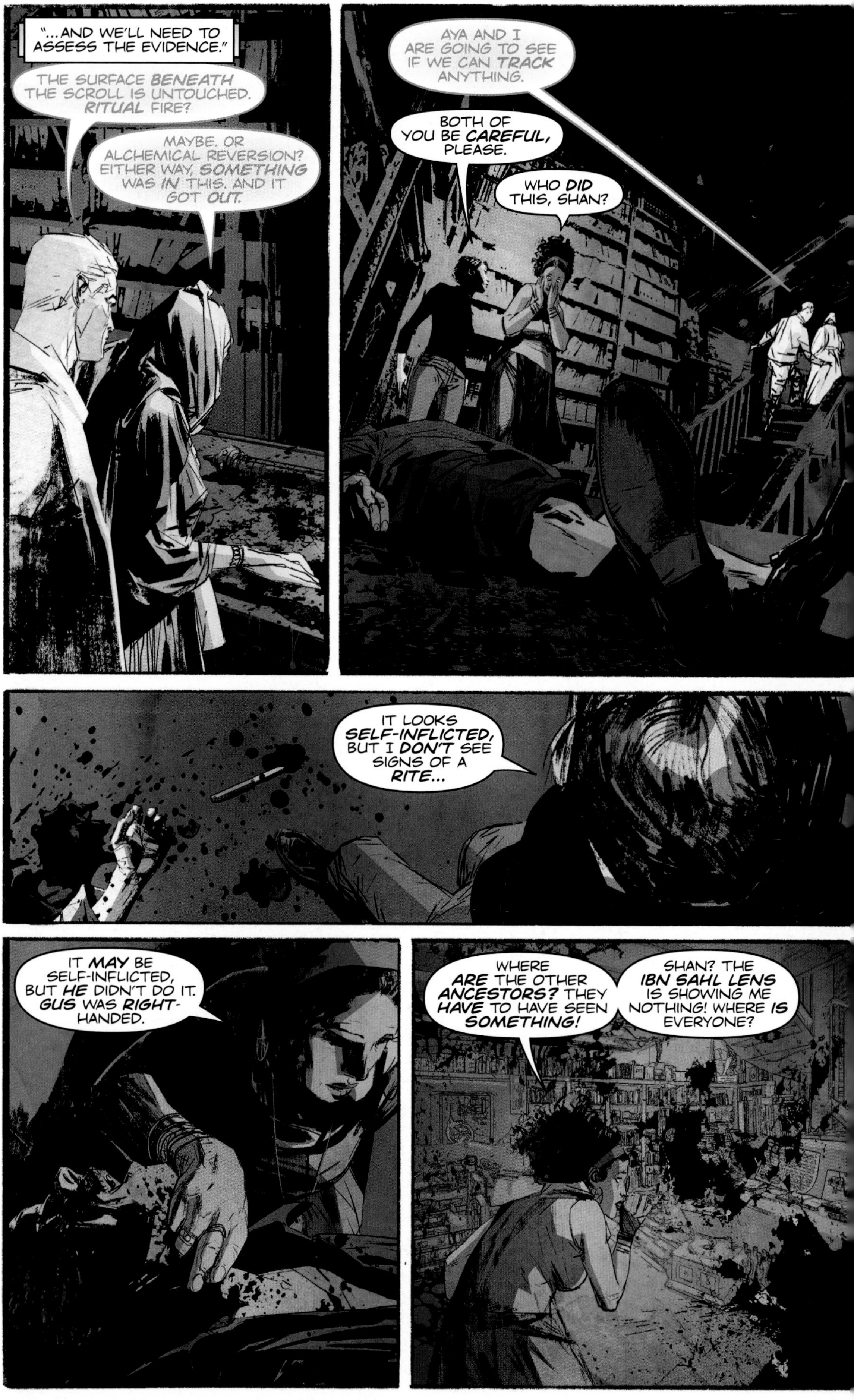
"...AND WE'LL NEED TO ASSESS THE EVIDENCE."
THE SURFACE BENEATH THE SCROLL IS UNTOUCHED. RITUAL FIRE?
MAYBE. OR ALCHEMICAL REVERSION? EITHER WAY, SOMETHING WAS IN THIS. AND IT GOT OUT.
AYA AND I ARE GOING TO SEE IF WE CAN TRACK ANYTHING.
BOTH OF YOU BE CAREFUL, PLEASE.
WHO DID THIS, SHAN?
IT LOOKS SELF-INFLICTED, BUT I DON'T SEE SIGNS OF A RITE...
IT MAY BE SELF-INFLICTED, BUT HE DIDN'T DO IT. GUS WAS RIGHT-HANDED.
WHERE ARE THE OTHER ANCESTORS? THEY HAVE TO HAVE SEEN SOMETHING!
SHAN? THE IBN SAHL LENS IS SHOWING ME NOTHING! WHERE IS EVERYONE?

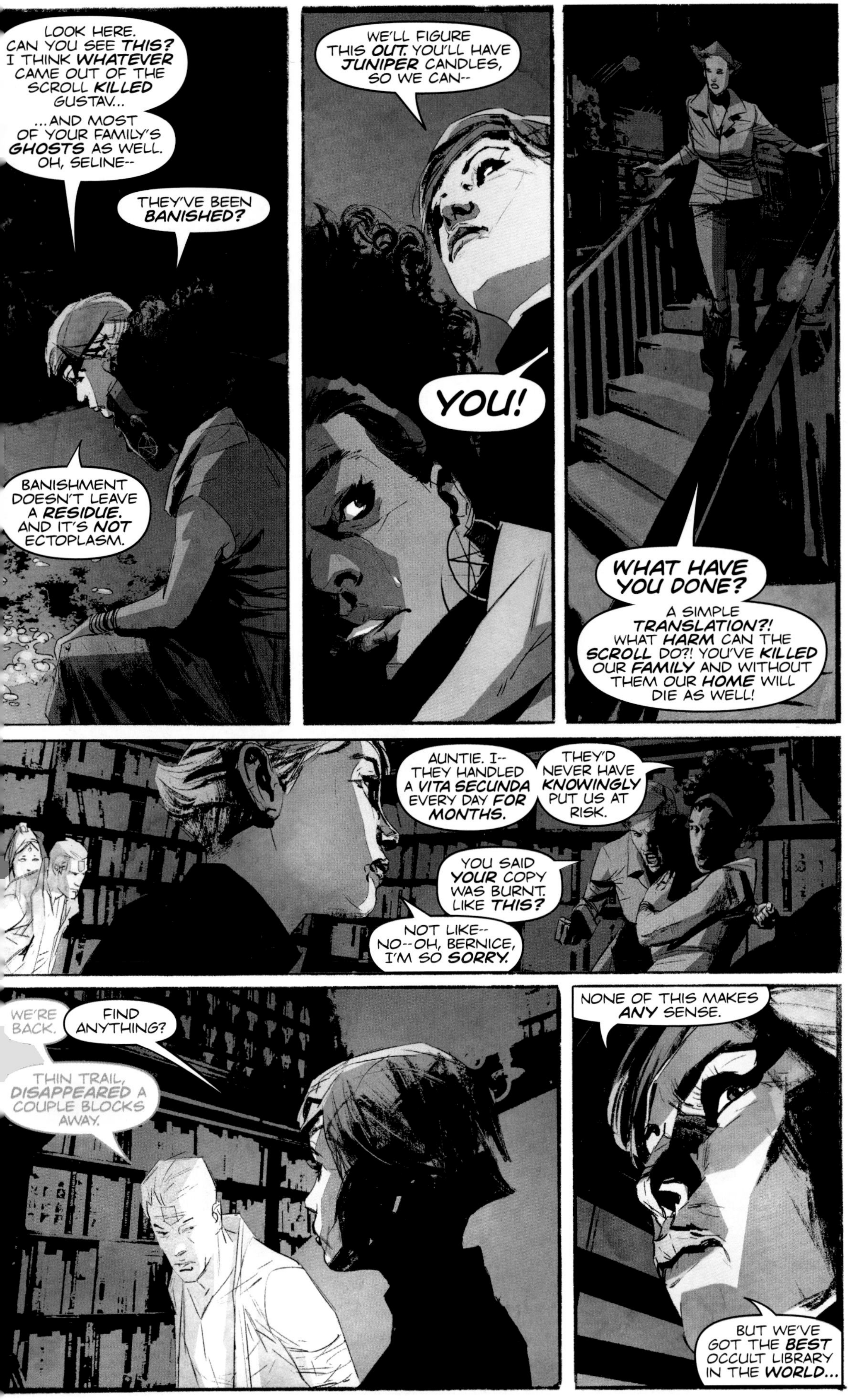

LOOK HERE. CAN YOU SEE **THIS?** I THINK **WHATEVER** CAME OUT OF THE SCROLL **KILLED** GUSTAV...
...AND MOST OF YOUR FAMILY'S **GHOSTS** AS WELL. OH, SELINE--
THEY'VE BEEN **BANISHED?**
BANISHMENT DOESN'T LEAVE A **RESIDUE.** AND IT'S **NOT** ECTOPLASM.
WE'LL FIGURE THIS **OUT.** YOU'LL HAVE **JUNIPER** CANDLES, SO WE CAN--
YOU!
WHAT HAVE YOU DONE?
A SIMPLE **TRANSLATION?!** WHAT **HARM** CAN THE **SCROLL** DO?! YOU'VE **KILLED** OUR **FAMILY** AND WITHOUT THEM OUR **HOME** WILL DIE AS WELL!
AUNTIE. I-- THEY HANDLED A **VITA SECUNDA** EVERY DAY **FOR MONTHS.**
THEY'D NEVER HAVE **KNOWINGLY** PUT US AT RISK.
YOU SAID **YOUR** COPY WAS BURNT. LIKE **THIS?**
NOT LIKE-- NO--OH, BERNICE, I'M SO **SORRY.**
WE'RE BACK.
FIND ANYTHING?
THIN TRAIL, **DISAPPEARED** A COUPLE BLOCKS AWAY.
NONE OF THIS MAKES **ANY** SENSE.
BUT WE'VE GOT THE **BEST** OCCULT LIBRARY IN THE **WORLD...**

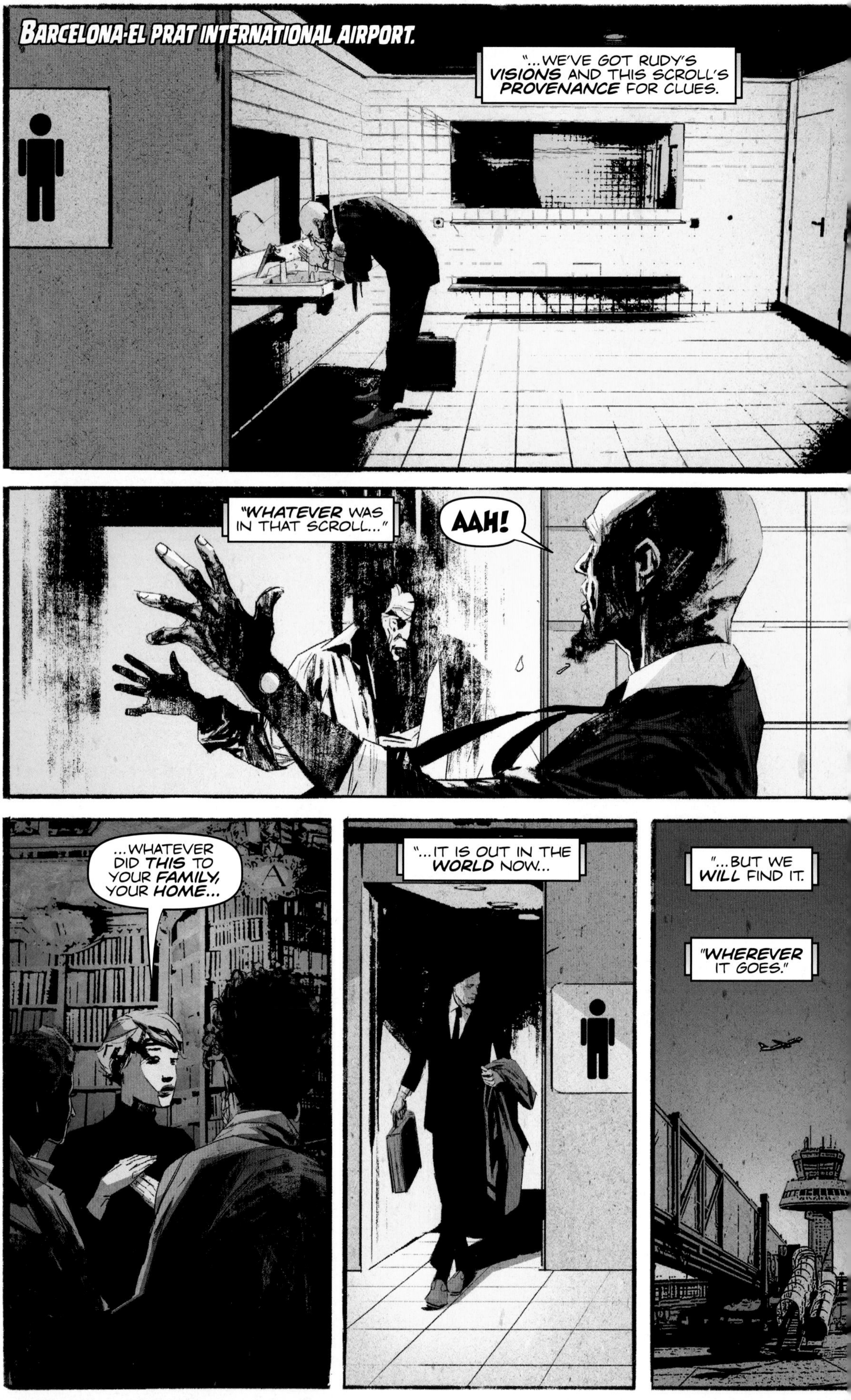
BARCELONA-EL PRAT INTERNATIONAL AIRPORT.
"...WE'VE GOT RUDY'S VISIONS AND THIS SCROLL'S PROVENANCE FOR CLUES.
"WHATEVER WAS IN THAT SCROLL..."
AAH!
...WHATEVER DID THIS TO YOUR FAMILY, YOUR HOME...
"...IT IS OUT IN THE WORLD NOW...
"...BUT WE WILL FIND IT.
"WHEREVER IT GOES."

VALIANT | DAVID BARON | DAVE LANPHEAR

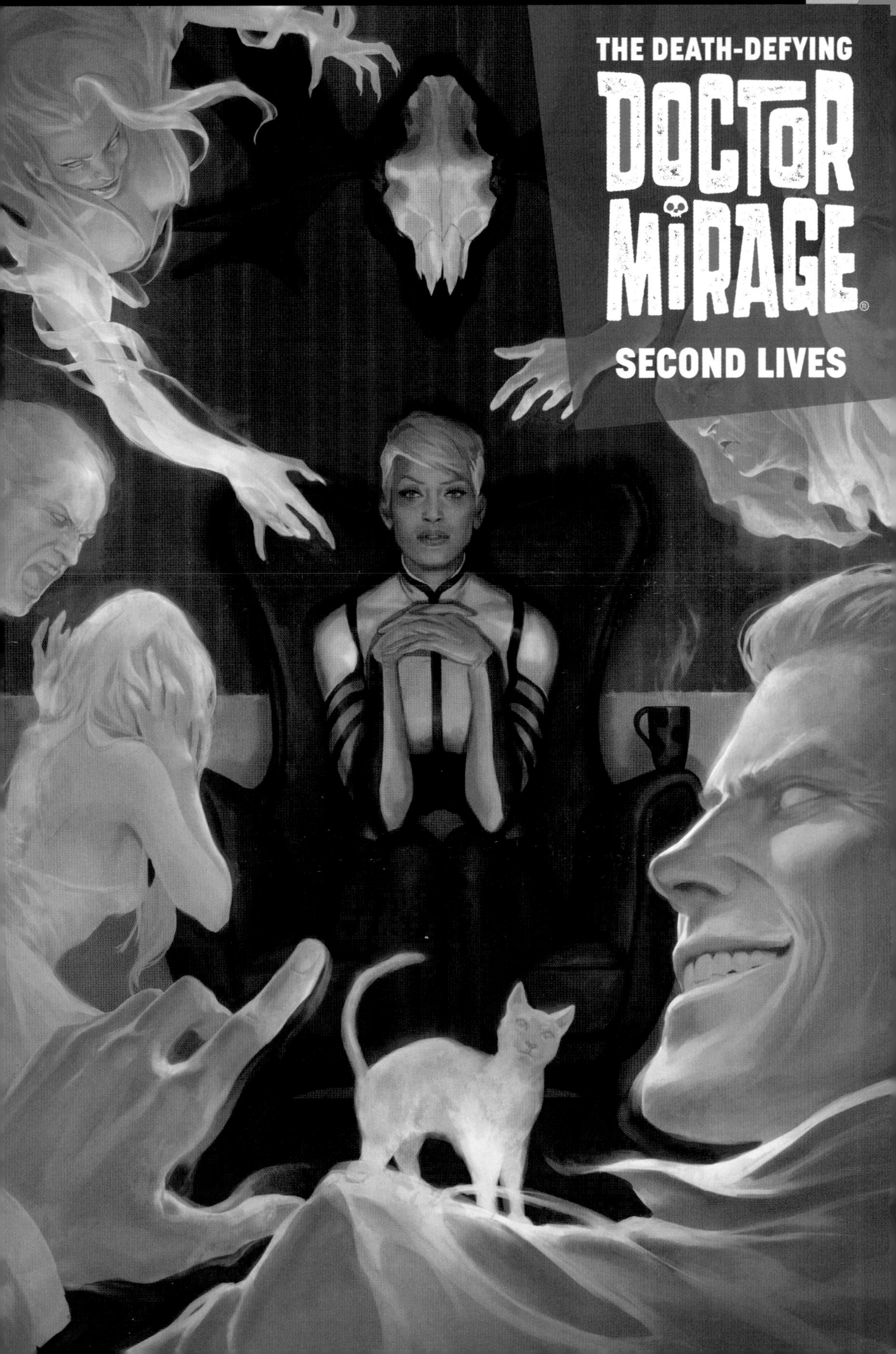
THE DEATH-DEFYING
DOCTOR MIRAGE®
SECOND LIVES

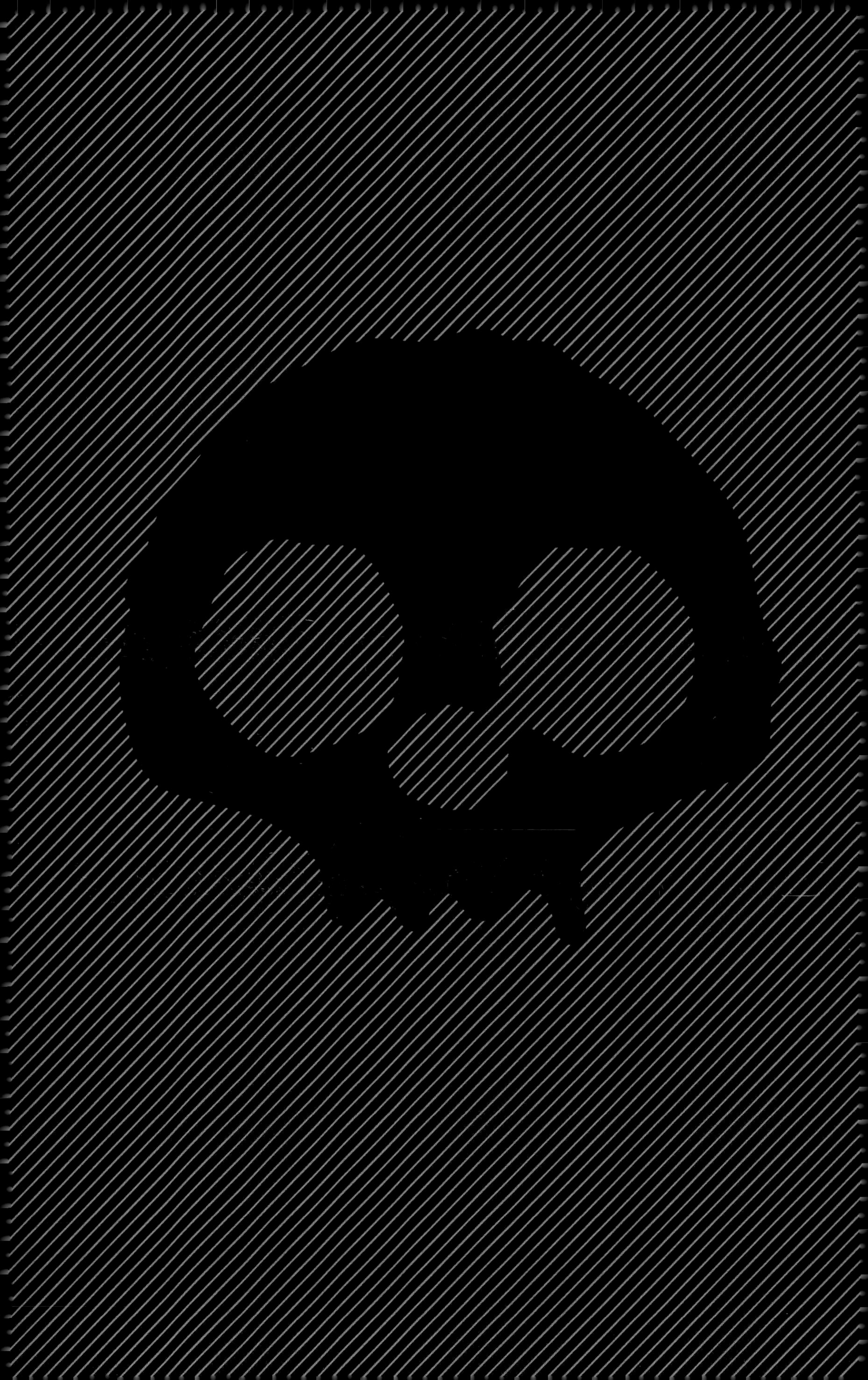

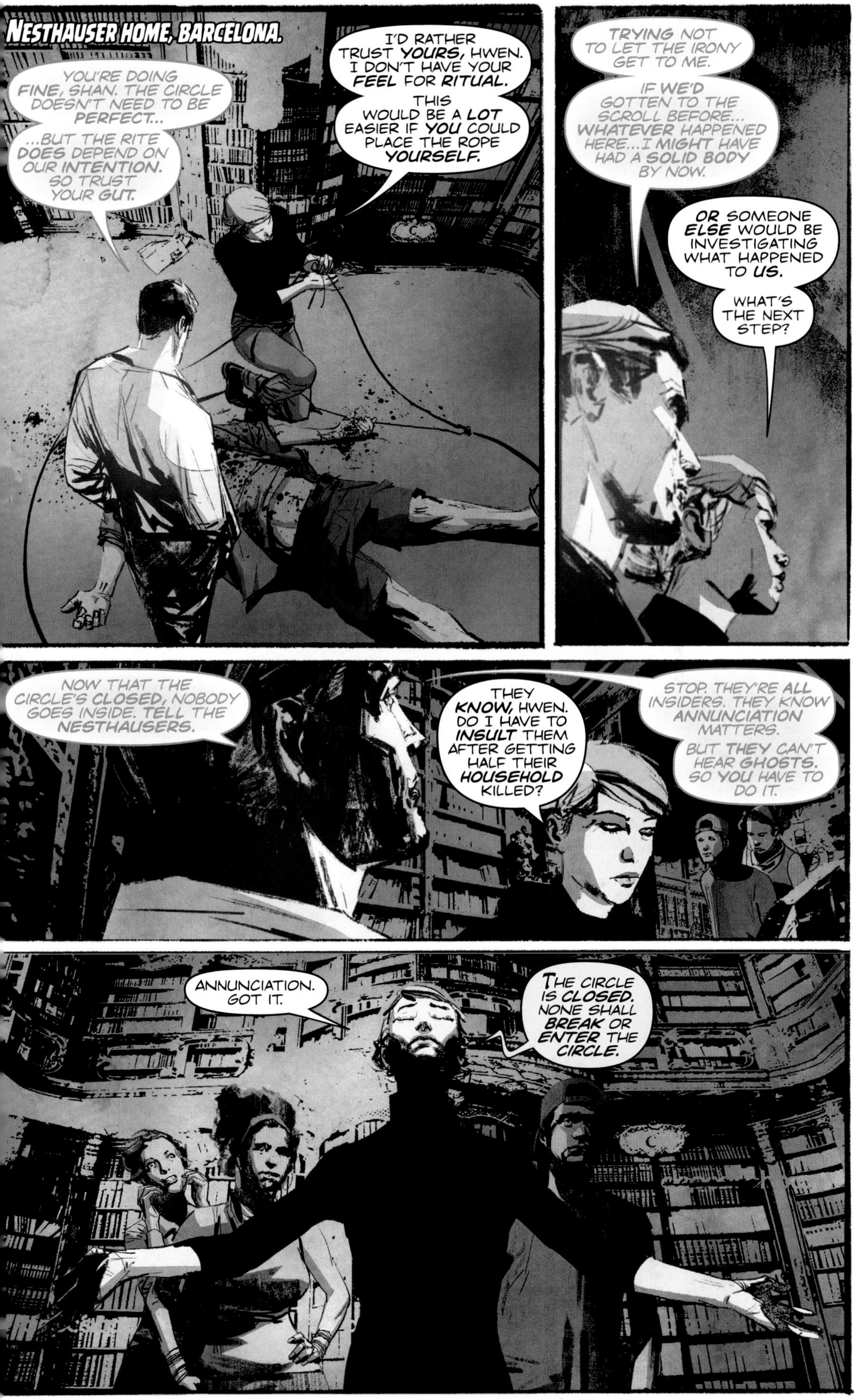
NESTHAUSER HOME, BARCELONA.
YOU'RE DOING FINE, SHAN. THE CIRCLE DOESN'T NEED TO BE PERFECT...
...BUT THE RITE DOES DEPEND ON OUR INTENTION. SO TRUST YOUR GUT.
I'D RATHER TRUST YOURS, HWEN. I DON'T HAVE YOUR FEEL FOR RITUAL.
THIS WOULD BE A LOT EASIER IF YOU COULD PLACE THE ROPE YOURSELF.
TRYING NOT TO LET THE IRONY GET TO ME.
IF WE'D GOTTEN TO THE SCROLL BEFORE... WHATEVER HAPPENED HERE...I MIGHT HAVE HAD A SOLID BODY BY NOW.
OR SOMEONE ELSE WOULD BE INVESTIGATING WHAT HAPPENED TO US.
WHAT'S THE NEXT STEP?
NOW THAT THE CIRCLE'S CLOSED, NOBODY GOES INSIDE. TELL THE NESTHAUSERS.
THEY KNOW, HWEN. DO I HAVE TO INSULT THEM AFTER GETTING HALF THEIR HOUSEHOLD KILLED?
STOP. THEY'RE ALL INSIDERS. THEY KNOW ANNUNCIATION MATTERS.
BUT THEY CAN'T HEAR GHOSTS. SO YOU HAVE TO DO IT.
ANNUNCIATION. GOT IT.
THE CIRCLE IS CLOSED. NONE SHALL BREAK OR ENTER THE CIRCLE.

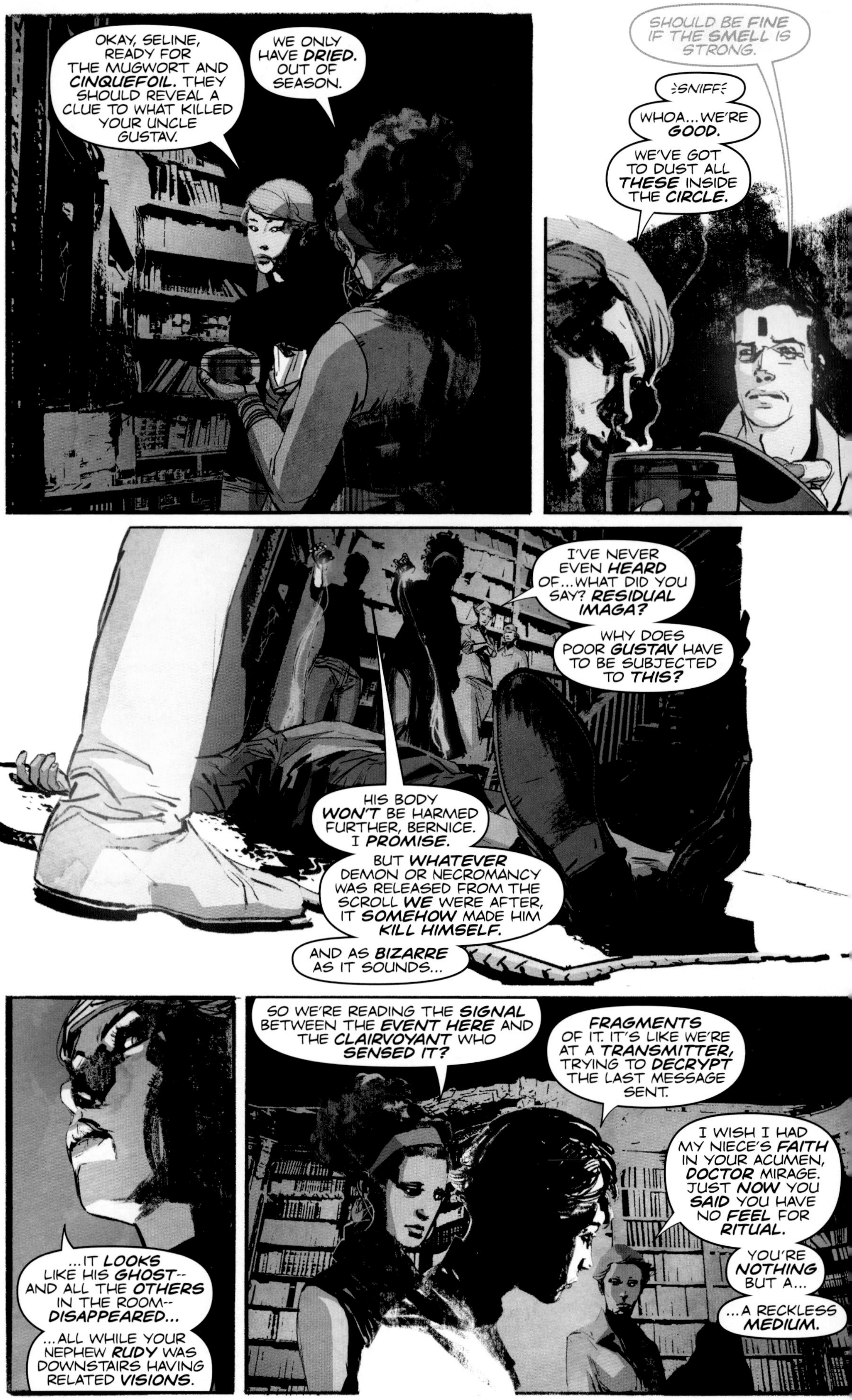
OKAY, SELINE, READY FOR THE MUGWORT AND CINQUEFOIL. THEY SHOULD REVEAL A CLUE TO WHAT KILLED YOUR UNCLE GUSTAV.
WE ONLY HAVE DRIED. OUT OF SEASON.
SHOULD BE FINE IF THE SMELL IS STRONG.
SNIFF
WHOA...WE'RE GOOD.
WE'VE GOT TO DUST ALL THESE INSIDE THE CIRCLE.
I'VE NEVER EVEN HEARD OF...WHAT DID YOU SAY? RESIDUAL IMAGA?
WHY DOES POOR GUSTAV HAVE TO BE SUBJECTED TO THIS?
HIS BODY WON'T BE HARMED FURTHER, BERNICE. I PROMISE.
BUT WHATEVER DEMON OR NECROMANCY WAS RELEASED FROM THE SCROLL WE WERE AFTER, IT SOMEHOW MADE HIM KILL HIMSELF.
AND AS BIZARRE AS IT SOUNDS...
...IT LOOKS LIKE HIS GHOST-- AND ALL THE OTHERS IN THE ROOM-- DISAPPEARED...
...ALL WHILE YOUR NEPHEW RUDY WAS DOWNSTAIRS HAVING RELATED VISIONS.
SO WE'RE READING THE SIGNAL BETWEEN THE EVENT HERE AND THE CLAIRVOYANT WHO SENSED IT?
FRAGMENTS OF IT. IT'S LIKE WE'RE AT A TRANSMITTER, TRYING TO DECRYPT THE LAST MESSAGE SENT.
I WISH I HAD MY NIECE'S FAITH IN YOUR ACUMEN, DOCTOR MIRAGE. JUST NOW YOU SAID YOU HAVE NO FEEL FOR RITUAL.
YOU'RE NOTHING BUT A...
...A RECKLESS MEDIUM.

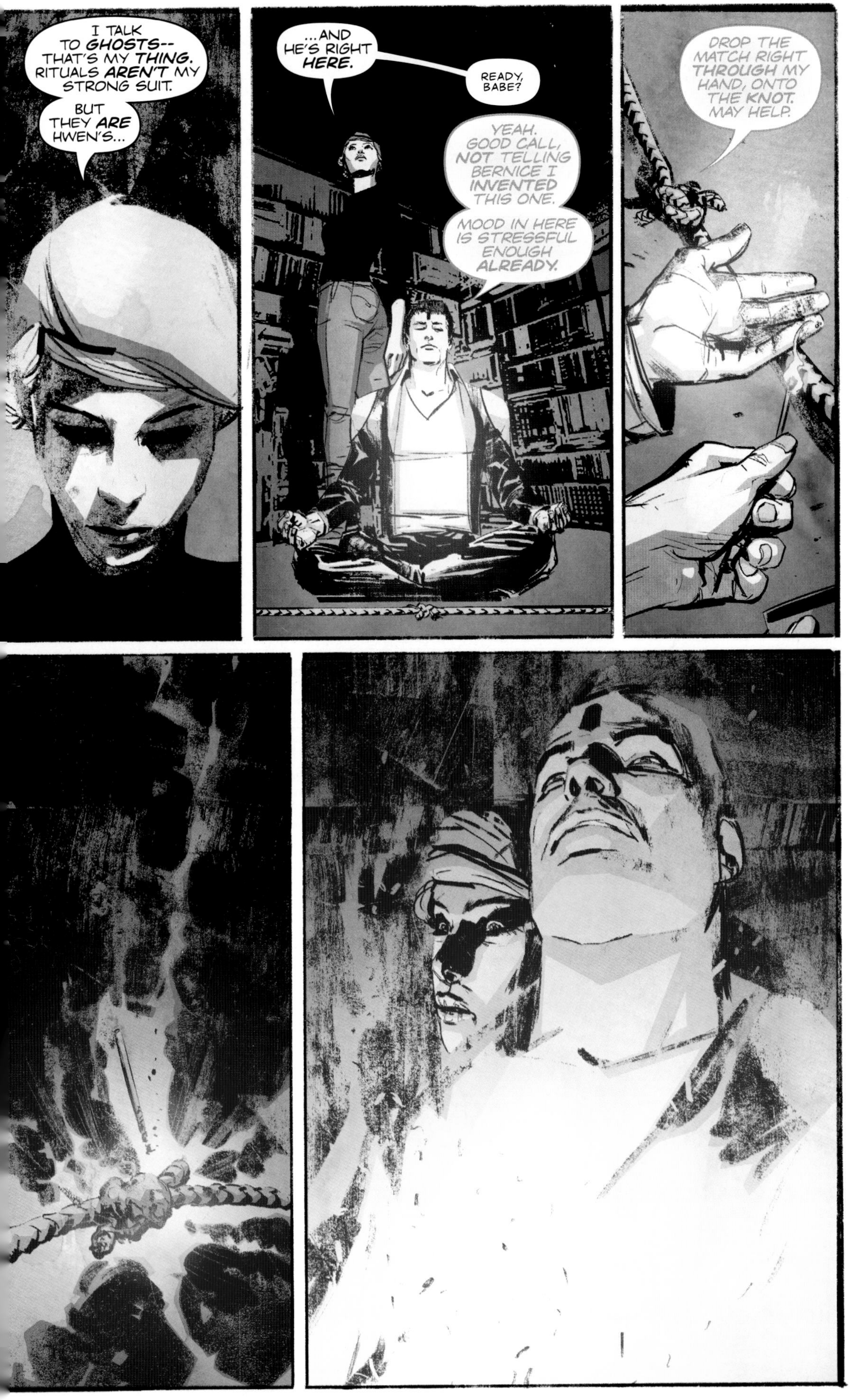
I TALK TO GHOSTS-- THAT'S MY THING. RITUALS AREN'T MY STRONG SUIT.
BUT THEY ARE HWEN'S...
...AND HE'S RIGHT HERE.
READY, BABE?
YEAH. GOOD CALL, NOT TELLING BERNICE I INVENTED THIS ONE.
MOOD IN HERE IS STRESSFUL ENOUGH ALREADY.
DROP THE MATCH RIGHT THROUGH MY HAND, ONTO THE KNOT. MAY HELP.

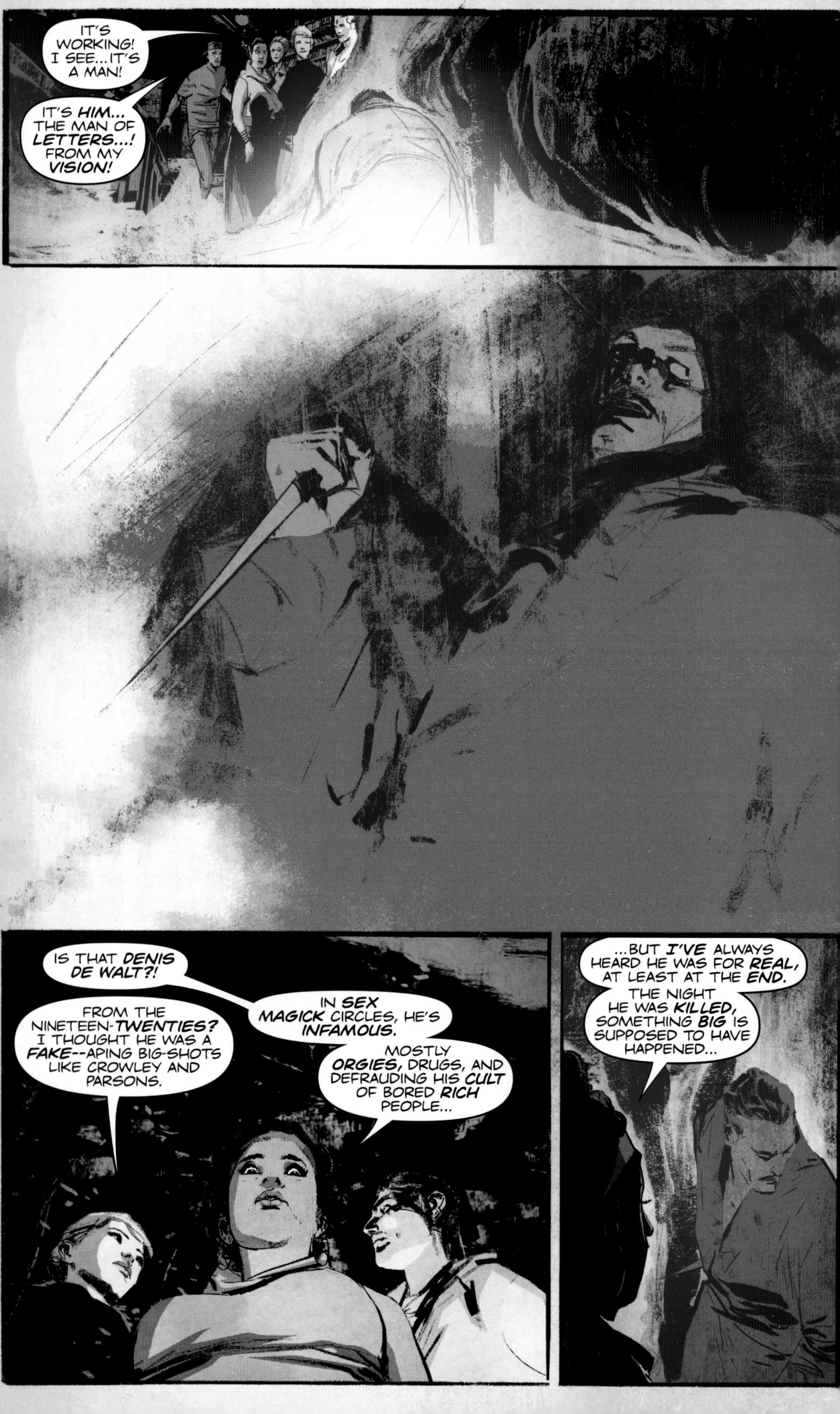
IT'S WORKING! I SEE...IT'S A MAN!
IT'S HIM... THE MAN OF LETTERS...! FROM MY VISION!
IS THAT DENIS DE WALT?!
FROM THE NINETEEN-TWENTIES? I THOUGHT HE WAS A FAKE--APING BIG-SHOTS LIKE CROWLEY AND PARSONS.
IN SEX MAGICK CIRCLES, HE'S INFAMOUS.
MOSTLY ORGIES, DRUGS, AND DEFRAUDING HIS CULT OF BORED RICH PEOPLE...
...BUT I'VE ALWAYS HEARD HE WAS FOR REAL, AT LEAST AT THE END.
THE NIGHT HE WAS KILLED, SOMETHING BIG IS SUPPOSED TO HAVE HAPPENED...

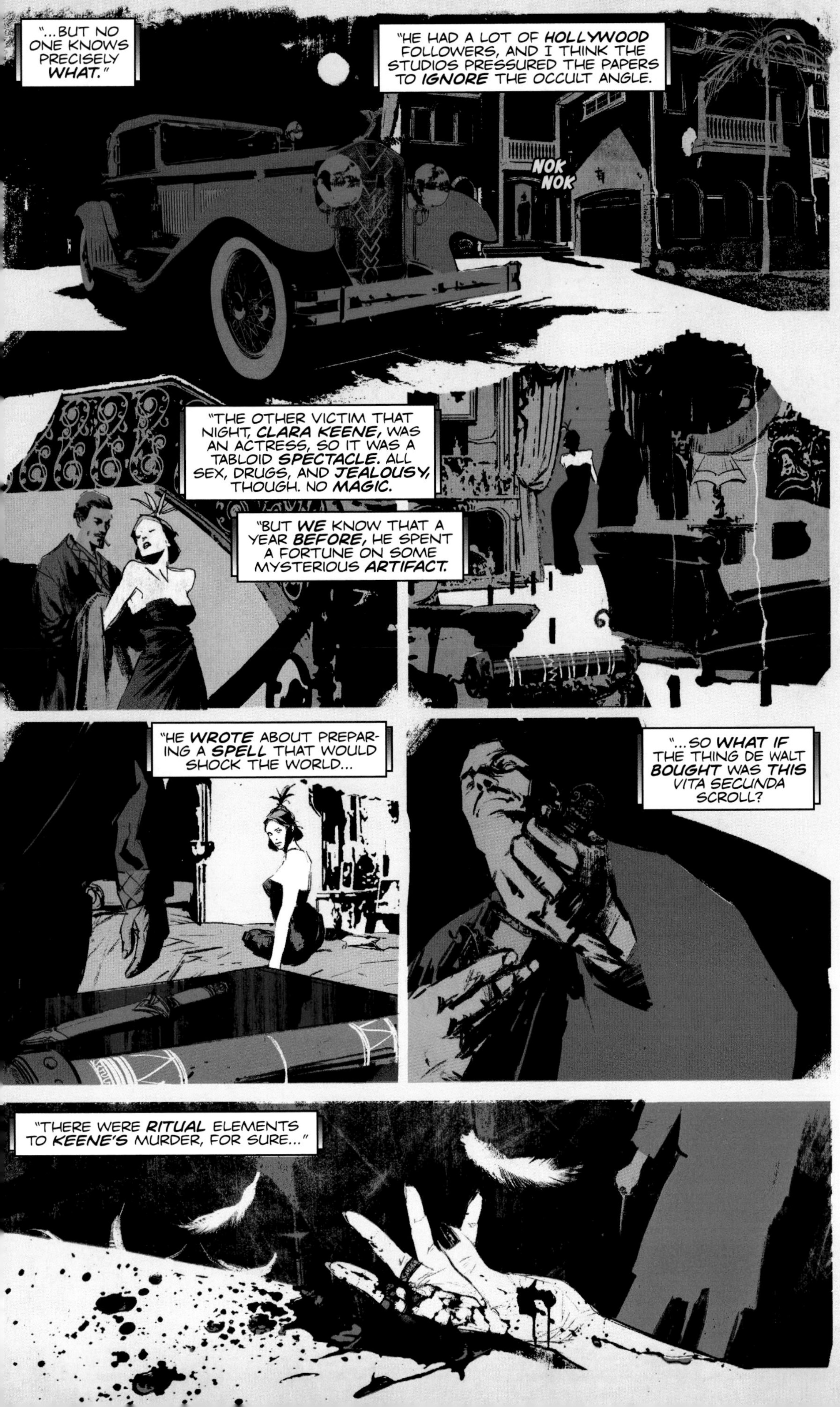
"...BUT NO ONE KNOWS PRECISELY WHAT."
"HE HAD A LOT OF HOLLYWOOD FOLLOWERS, AND I THINK THE STUDIOS PRESSURED THE PAPERS TO IGNORE THE OCCULT ANGLE.
NOK NOK
"THE OTHER VICTIM THAT NIGHT, CLARA KEENE, WAS AN ACTRESS, SO IT WAS A TABLOID SPECTACLE. ALL SEX, DRUGS, AND JEALOUSY, THOUGH. NO MAGIC.
"BUT WE KNOW THAT A YEAR BEFORE, HE SPENT A FORTUNE ON SOME MYSTERIOUS ARTIFACT.
"HE WROTE ABOUT PREPARING A SPELL THAT WOULD SHOCK THE WORLD...
"...SO WHAT IF THE THING DE WALT BOUGHT WAS THIS VITA SECUNDA SCROLL?
"THERE WERE RITUAL ELEMENTS TO KEENE'S MURDER, FOR SURE..."

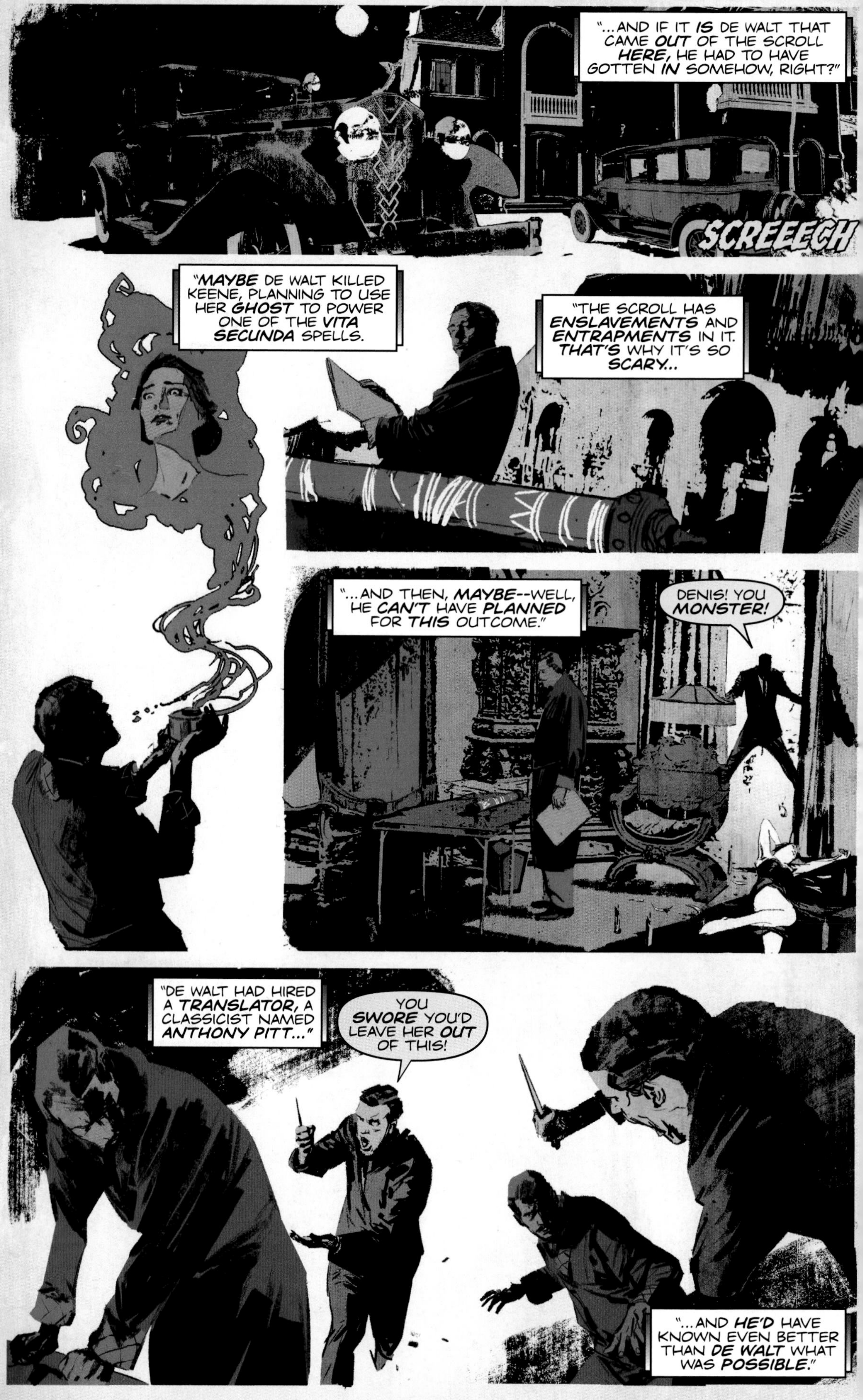
"...AND IF IT IS DE WALT THAT CAME OUT OF THE SCROLL HERE, HE HAD TO HAVE GOTTEN IN SOMEHOW, RIGHT?"
SCREEECH
"MAYBE DE WALT KILLED KEENE, PLANNING TO USE HER GHOST TO POWER ONE OF THE VITA SECUNDA SPELLS.
"THE SCROLL HAS ENSLAVEMENTS AND ENTRAPMENTS IN IT. THAT'S WHY IT'S SO SCARY...
"...AND THEN, MAYBE--WELL, HE CAN'T HAVE PLANNED FOR THIS OUTCOME."
DENIS! YOU MONSTER!
"DE WALT HAD HIRED A TRANSLATOR, A CLASSICIST NAMED ANTHONY PITT..."
YOU SWORE YOU'D LEAVE HER OUT OF THIS!
"...AND HE'D HAVE KNOWN EVEN BETTER THAN DE WALT WHAT WAS POSSIBLE."

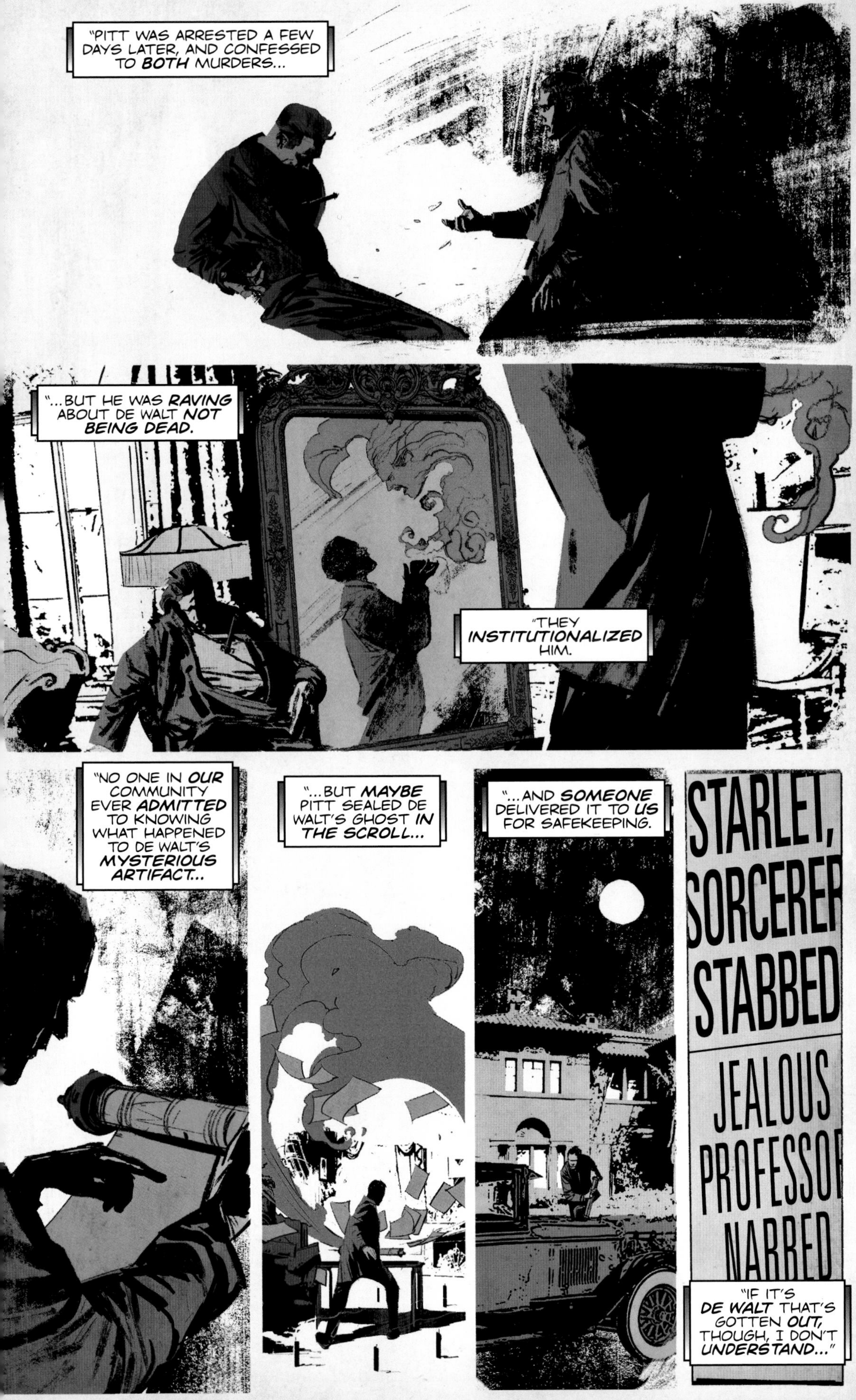
"PITT WAS ARRESTED A FEW DAYS LATER, AND CONFESSED TO BOTH MURDERS...
"...BUT HE WAS RAVING ABOUT DE WALT NOT BEING DEAD.
"THEY INSTITUTIONALIZED HIM.
"NO ONE IN OUR COMMUNITY EVER ADMITTED TO KNOWING WHAT HAPPENED TO DE WALT'S MYSTERIOUS ARTIFACT...
"...BUT MAYBE PITT SEALED DE WALT'S GHOST IN THE SCROLL...
"...AND SOMEONE DELIVERED IT TO US FOR SAFEKEEPING.
STARLET, SORCERER STABBED
JEALOUS PROFESSOR NABBED
"IF IT'S DE WALT THAT'S GOTTEN OUT, THOUGH, I DON'T UNDERSTAND..."

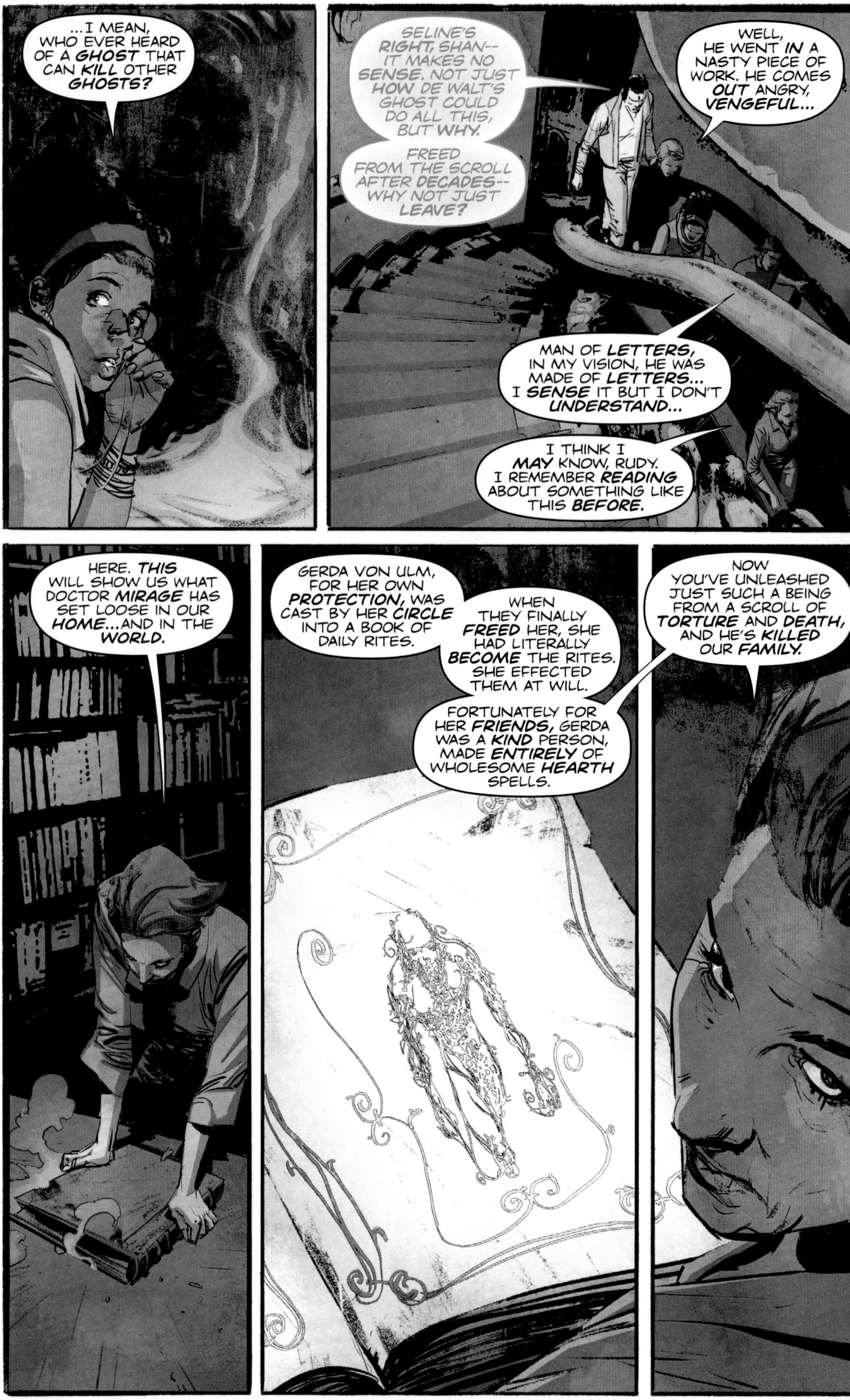
...I MEAN, WHO EVER HEARD OF A GHOST THAT CAN KILL OTHER GHOSTS?
SELINE'S RIGHT, SHAN-- IT MAKES NO SENSE. NOT JUST HOW DE WALT'S GHOST COULD DO ALL THIS, BUT WHY.
FREED FROM THE SCROLL AFTER DECADES-- WHY NOT JUST LEAVE?
WELL, HE WENT IN A NASTY PIECE OF WORK. HE COMES OUT ANGRY, VENGEFUL...
MAN OF LETTERS, IN MY VISION, HE WAS MADE OF LETTERS... I SENSE IT BUT I DON'T UNDERSTAND...
I THINK I MAY KNOW, RUDY. I REMEMBER READING ABOUT SOMETHING LIKE THIS BEFORE.
HERE. THIS WILL SHOW US WHAT DOCTOR MIRAGE HAS SET LOOSE IN OUR HOME...AND IN THE WORLD.
GERDA VON ULM, FOR HER OWN PROTECTION, WAS CAST BY HER CIRCLE INTO A BOOK OF DAILY RITES.
WHEN THEY FINALLY FREED HER, SHE HAD LITERALLY BECOME THE RITES. SHE EFFECTED THEM AT WILL.
FORTUNATELY FOR HER FRIENDS, GERDA WAS A KIND PERSON, MADE ENTIRELY OF WHOLESOME HEARTH SPELLS.
NOW YOU'VE UNLEASHED JUST SUCH A BEING FROM A SCROLL OF TORTURE AND DEATH, AND HE'S KILLED OUR FAMILY.

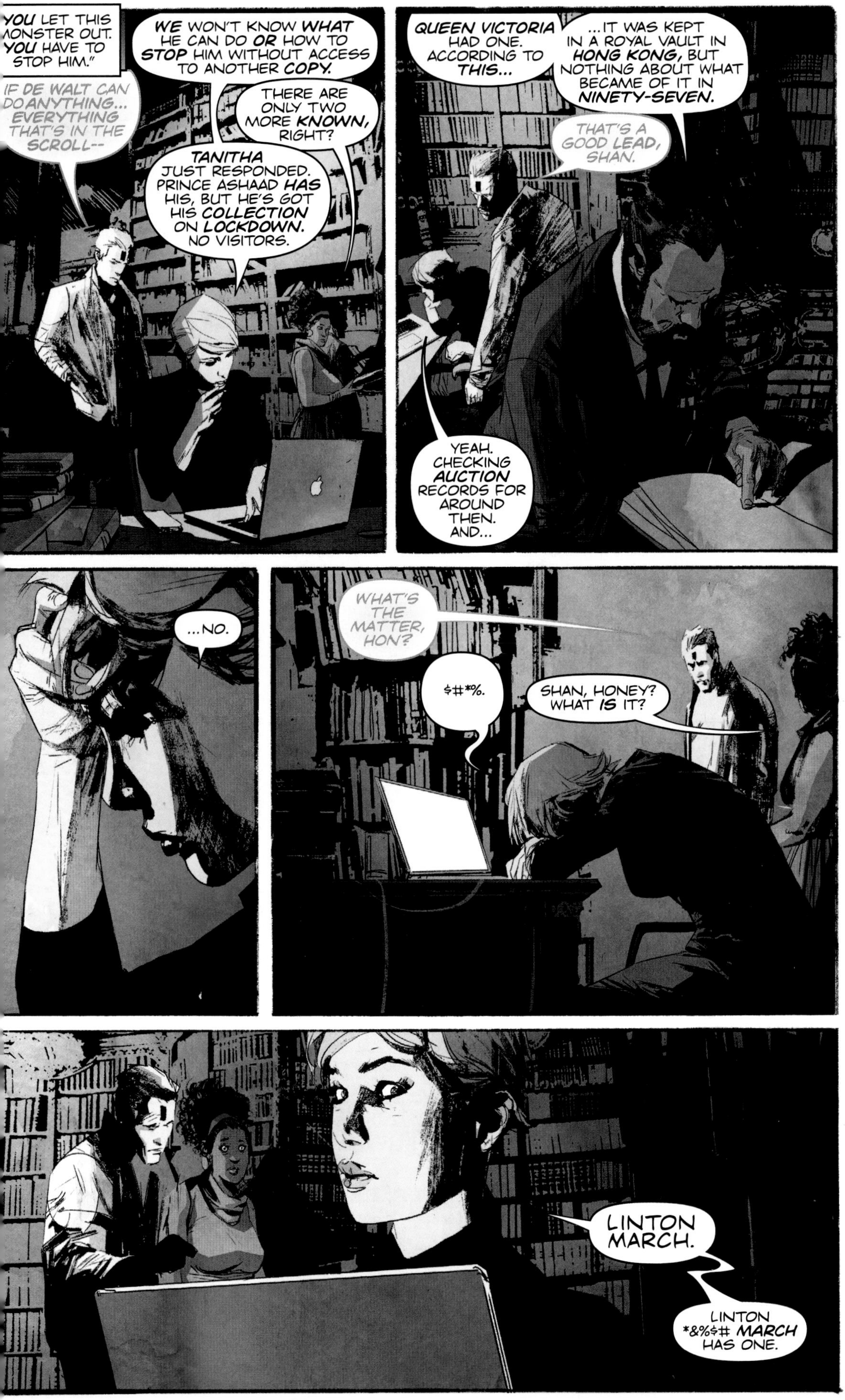
YOU LET THIS MONSTER OUT. YOU HAVE TO STOP HIM."
IF DE WALT CAN DO ANYTHING... EVERYTHING THAT'S IN THE SCROLL--
WE WON'T KNOW WHAT HE CAN DO OR HOW TO STOP HIM WITHOUT ACCESS TO ANOTHER COPY.
THERE ARE ONLY TWO MORE KNOWN, RIGHT?
TANITHA JUST RESPONDED. PRINCE ASHAAD HAS HIS, BUT HE'S GOT HIS COLLECTION ON LOCKDOWN. NO VISITORS.
QUEEN VICTORIA HAD ONE. ACCORDING TO THIS...
...IT WAS KEPT IN A ROYAL VAULT IN HONG KONG, BUT NOTHING ABOUT WHAT BECAME OF IT IN NINETY-SEVEN.
THAT'S A GOOD LEAD, SHAN.
YEAH. CHECKING AUCTION RECORDS FOR AROUND THEN. AND...
...NO.
WHAT'S THE MATTER, HON?
$#*%.
SHAN, HONEY? WHAT IS IT?
LINTON MARCH.
LINTON *&%$# MARCH HAS ONE.

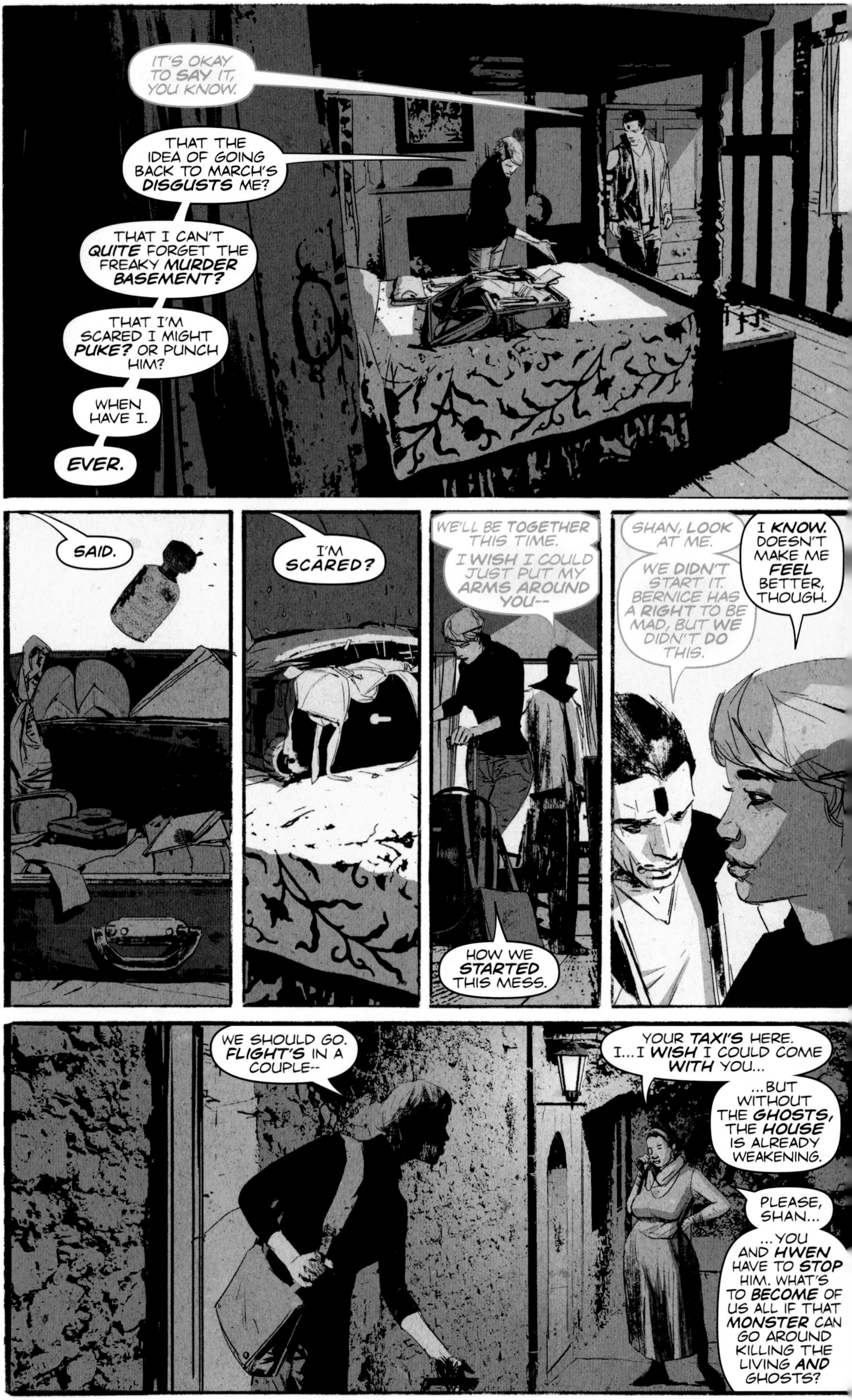
IT'S OKAY TO SAY IT, YOU KNOW.
THAT THE IDEA OF GOING BACK TO MARCH'S DISGUSTS ME?
THAT I CAN'T QUITE FORGET THE FREAKY MURDER BASEMENT?
THAT I'M SCARED I MIGHT PUKE? OR PUNCH HIM?
WHEN HAVE I.
EVER.
SAID.
I'M SCARED?
WE'LL BE TOGETHER THIS TIME.
I WISH I COULD JUST PUT MY ARMS AROUND YOU--
HOW WE STARTED THIS MESS.
SHAN, LOOK AT ME.
WE DIDN'T START IT. BERNICE HAS A RIGHT TO BE MAD, BUT WE DIDN'T DO THIS.
I KNOW. DOESN'T MAKE ME FEEL BETTER, THOUGH.
WE SHOULD GO. FLIGHT'S IN A COUPLE--
YOUR TAXI'S HERE. I...I WISH I COULD COME WITH YOU...
...BUT WITHOUT THE GHOSTS, THE HOUSE IS ALREADY WEAKENING.
PLEASE, SHAN...
...YOU AND HWEN HAVE TO STOP HIM. WHAT'S TO BECOME OF US ALL IF THAT MONSTER CAN GO AROUND KILLING THE LIVING AND GHOSTS?

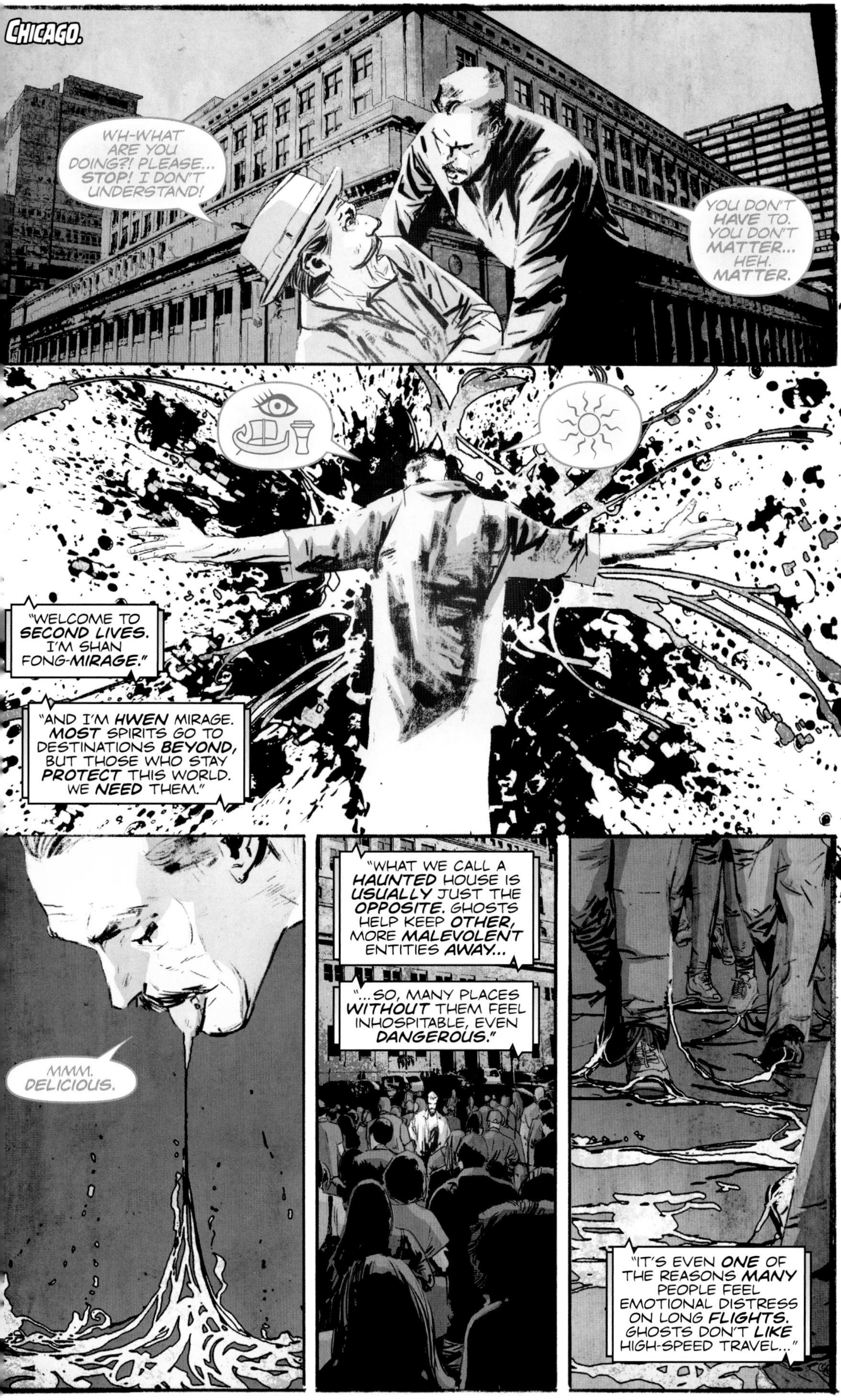
CHICAGO.
WH-WHAT ARE YOU DOING?! PLEASE... STOP! I DON'T UNDERSTAND!
YOU DON'T HAVE TO. YOU DON'T MATTER... HEH. MATTER.
"WELCOME TO SECOND LIVES. I'M SHAN FONG-MIRAGE."
"AND I'M HWEN MIRAGE. MOST SPIRITS GO TO DESTINATIONS BEYOND, BUT THOSE WHO STAY PROTECT THIS WORLD. WE NEED THEM."
MMM. DELICIOUS.
"WHAT WE CALL A HAUNTED HOUSE IS USUALLY JUST THE OPPOSITE. GHOSTS HELP KEEP OTHER, MORE MALEVOLENT ENTITIES AWAY...
"...SO, MANY PLACES WITHOUT THEM FEEL INHOSPITABLE, EVEN DANGEROUS."
"IT'S EVEN ONE OF THE REASONS MANY PEOPLE FEEL EMOTIONAL DISTRESS ON LONG FLIGHTS. GHOSTS DON'T LIKE HIGH-SPEED TRAVEL..."

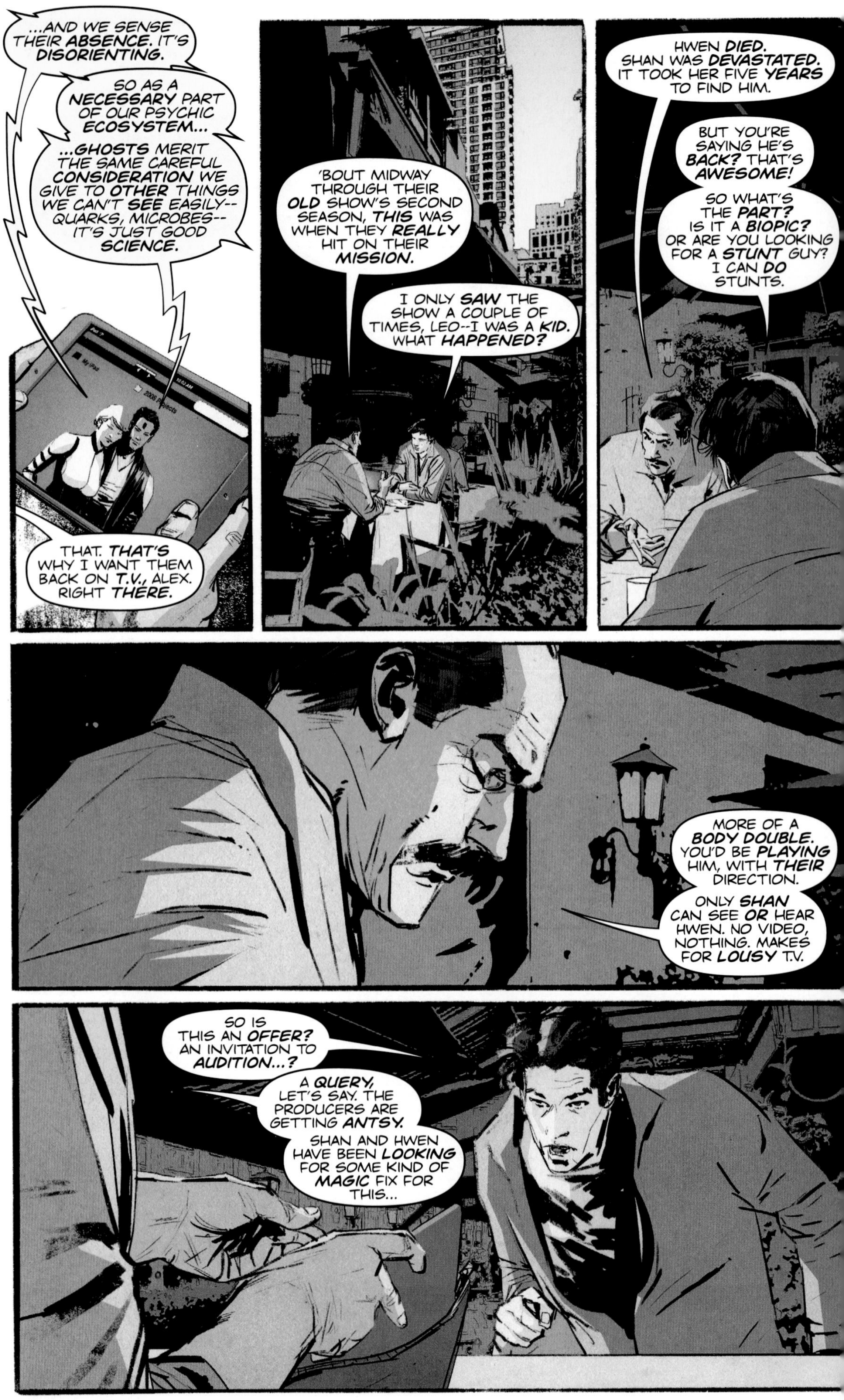

...AND WE SENSE THEIR ABSENCE. IT'S DISORIENTING.
SO AS A NECESSARY PART OF OUR PSYCHIC ECOSYSTEM...
...GHOSTS MERIT THE SAME CAREFUL CONSIDERATION WE GIVE TO OTHER THINGS WE CAN'T SEE EASILY--QUARKS, MICROBES--IT'S JUST GOOD SCIENCE.
THAT. THAT'S WHY I WANT THEM BACK ON T.V., ALEX. RIGHT THERE.
'BOUT MIDWAY THROUGH THEIR OLD SHOW'S SECOND SEASON, THIS WAS WHEN THEY REALLY HIT ON THEIR MISSION.
I ONLY SAW THE SHOW A COUPLE OF TIMES, LEO--I WAS A KID. WHAT HAPPENED?
HWEN DIED. SHAN WAS DEVASTATED. IT TOOK HER FIVE YEARS TO FIND HIM.
BUT YOU'RE SAYING HE'S BACK? THAT'S AWESOME!
SO WHAT'S THE PART? IS IT A BIOPIC? OR ARE YOU LOOKING FOR A STUNT GUY? I CAN DO STUNTS.
MORE OF A BODY DOUBLE. YOU'D BE PLAYING HIM, WITH THEIR DIRECTION.
ONLY SHAN CAN SEE OR HEAR HWEN. NO VIDEO, NOTHING. MAKES FOR LOUSY T.V.
SO IS THIS AN OFFER? AN INVITATION TO AUDITION...?
A QUERY, LET'S SAY. THE PRODUCERS ARE GETTING ANTSY.
SHAN AND HWEN HAVE BEEN LOOKING FOR SOME KIND OF MAGIC FIX FOR THIS...

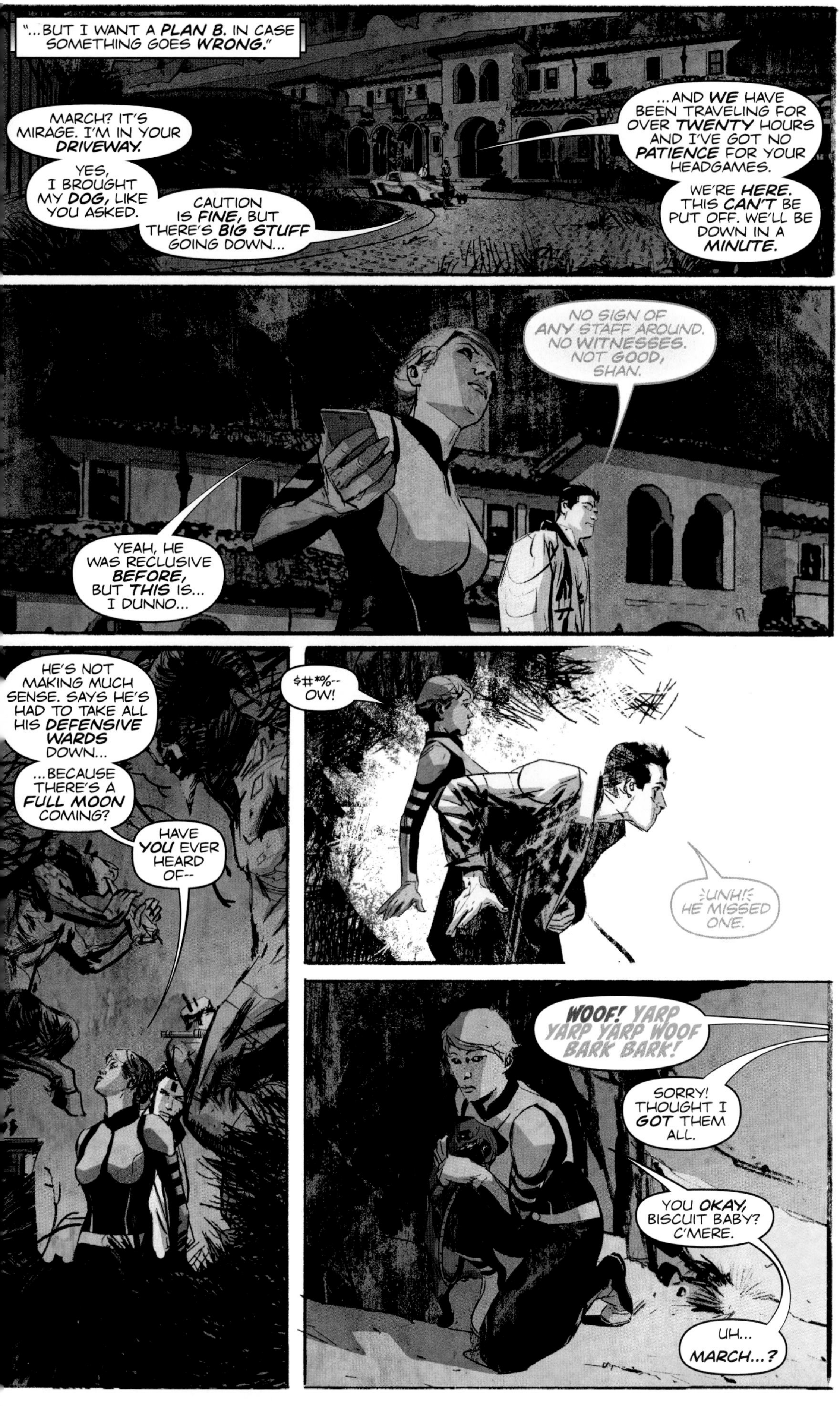
"...BUT I WANT A PLAN B. IN CASE SOMETHING GOES WRONG."
MARCH? IT'S MIRAGE. I'M IN YOUR DRIVEWAY.
YES, I BROUGHT MY DOG, LIKE YOU ASKED.
CAUTION IS FINE, BUT THERE'S BIG STUFF GOING DOWN...
...AND WE HAVE BEEN TRAVELING FOR OVER TWENTY HOURS AND I'VE GOT NO PATIENCE FOR YOUR HEADGAMES.
WE'RE HERE. THIS CAN'T BE PUT OFF. WE'LL BE DOWN IN A MINUTE.
NO SIGN OF ANY STAFF AROUND. NO WITNESSES. NOT GOOD, SHAN.
YEAH, HE WAS RECLUSIVE BEFORE, BUT THIS IS... I DUNNO...
HE'S NOT MAKING MUCH SENSE. SAYS HE'S HAD TO TAKE ALL HIS DEFENSIVE WARDS DOWN...
...BECAUSE THERE'S A FULL MOON COMING?
HAVE YOU EVER HEARD OF--
$#*%-- OW!
UNH! HE MISSED ONE.
WOOF! YARP YARP YARP WOOF BARK BARK!
SORRY! THOUGHT I GOT THEM ALL.
YOU OKAY, BISCUIT BABY? C'MERE.
UH... MARCH...?

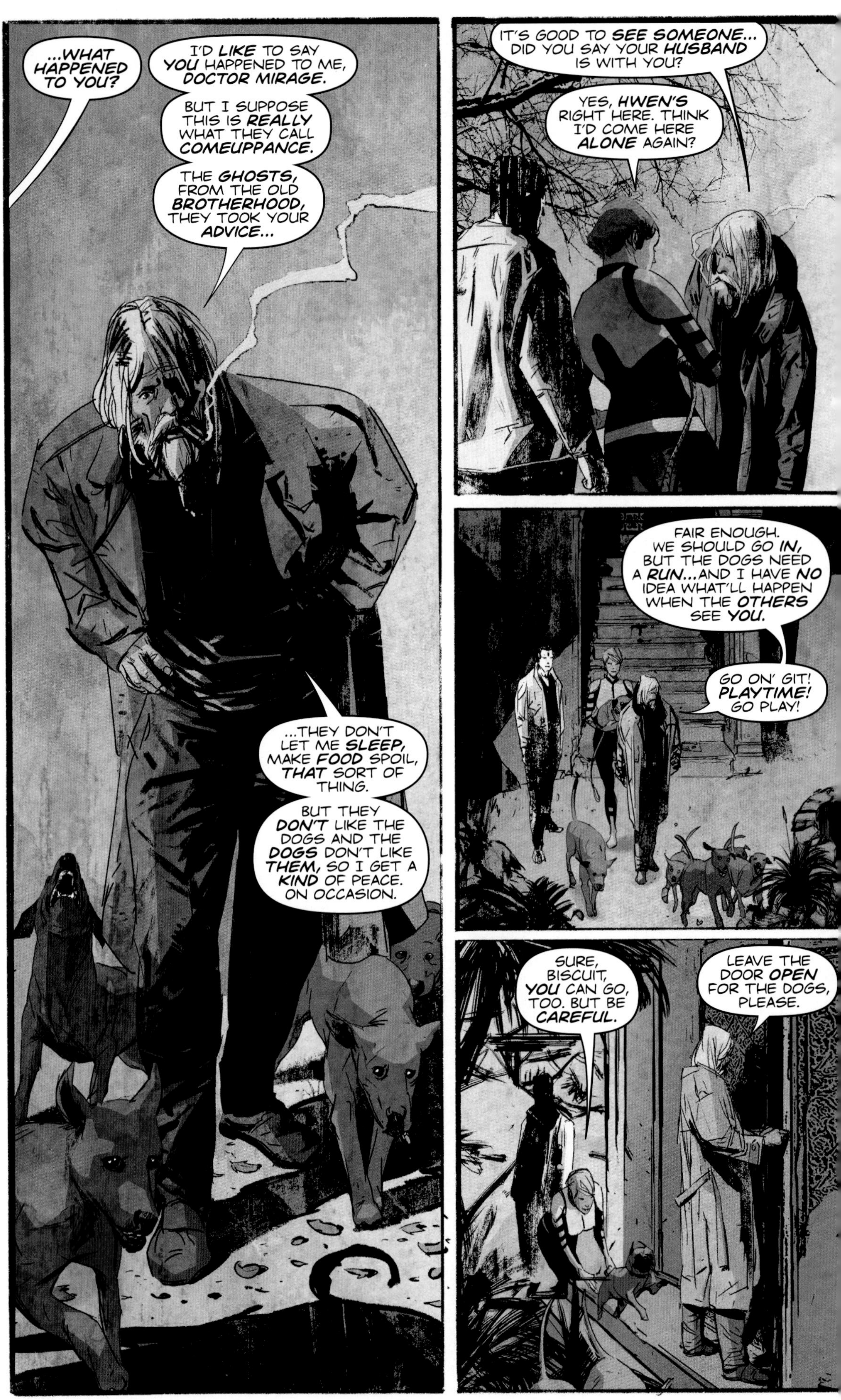

...WHAT HAPPENED TO YOU?
I'D LIKE TO SAY YOU HAPPENED TO ME, DOCTOR MIRAGE.
BUT I SUPPOSE THIS IS REALLY WHAT THEY CALL COMEUPPANCE.
THE GHOSTS, FROM THE OLD BROTHERHOOD, THEY TOOK YOUR ADVICE...
...THEY DON'T LET ME SLEEP, MAKE FOOD SPOIL, THAT SORT OF THING.
BUT THEY DON'T LIKE THE DOGS AND THE DOGS DON'T LIKE THEM, SO I GET A KIND OF PEACE. ON OCCASION.
IT'S GOOD TO SEE SOMEONE... DID YOU SAY YOUR HUSBAND IS WITH YOU?
YES, HWEN'S RIGHT HERE. THINK I'D COME HERE ALONE AGAIN?
FAIR ENOUGH. WE SHOULD GO IN, BUT THE DOGS NEED A RUN...AND I HAVE NO IDEA WHAT'LL HAPPEN WHEN THE OTHERS SEE YOU.
GO ON' GIT! PLAYTIME! GO PLAY!
SURE, BISCUIT, YOU CAN GO, TOO. BUT BE CAREFUL.
LEAVE THE DOOR OPEN FOR THE DOGS, PLEASE.

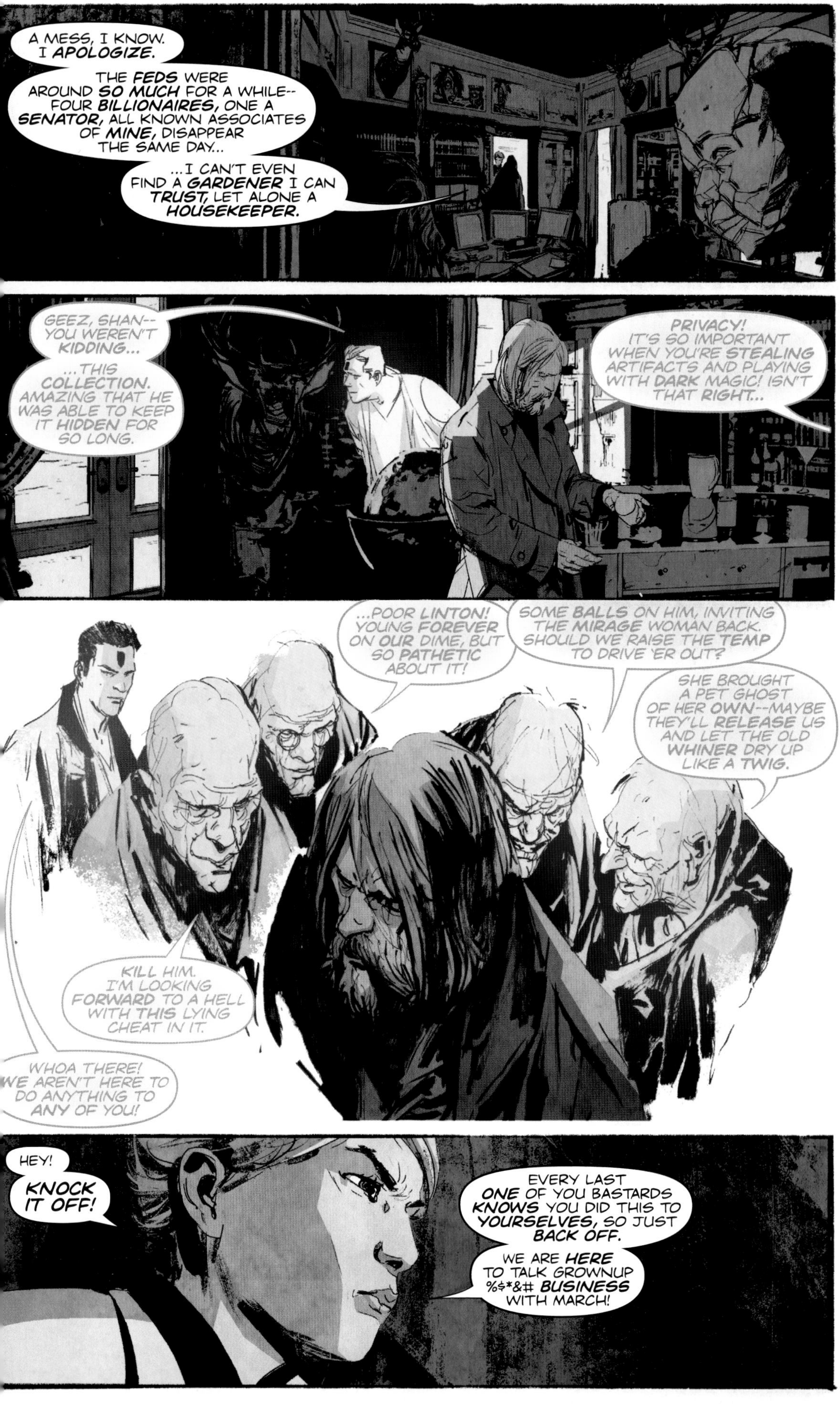
A MESS, I KNOW. I APOLOGIZE.
THE FEDS WERE AROUND SO MUCH FOR A WHILE-- FOUR BILLIONAIRES, ONE A SENATOR, ALL KNOWN ASSOCIATES OF MINE, DISAPPEAR THE SAME DAY...
...I CAN'T EVEN FIND A GARDENER I CAN TRUST, LET ALONE A HOUSEKEEPER.
GEEZ, SHAN-- YOU WEREN'T KIDDING...
...THIS COLLECTION. AMAZING THAT HE WAS ABLE TO KEEP IT HIDDEN FOR SO LONG.
PRIVACY! IT'S SO IMPORTANT WHEN YOU'RE STEALING ARTIFACTS AND PLAYING WITH DARK MAGIC! ISN'T THAT RIGHT...
...POOR LINTON! YOUNG FOREVER ON OUR DIME, BUT SO PATHETIC ABOUT IT!
SOME BALLS ON HIM, INVITING THE MIRAGE WOMAN BACK. SHOULD WE RAISE THE TEMP TO DRIVE 'ER OUT?
SHE BROUGHT A PET GHOST OF HER OWN--MAYBE THEY'LL RELEASE US AND LET THE OLD WHINER DRY UP LIKE A TWIG.
KILL HIM. I'M LOOKING FORWARD TO A HELL WITH THIS LYING CHEAT IN IT.
WHOA THERE! WE AREN'T HERE TO DO ANYTHING TO ANY OF YOU!
HEY! KNOCK IT OFF!
EVERY LAST ONE OF YOU BASTARDS KNOWS YOU DID THIS TO YOURSELVES, SO JUST BACK OFF.
WE ARE HERE TO TALK GROWNUP %$*&# BUSINESS WITH MARCH!

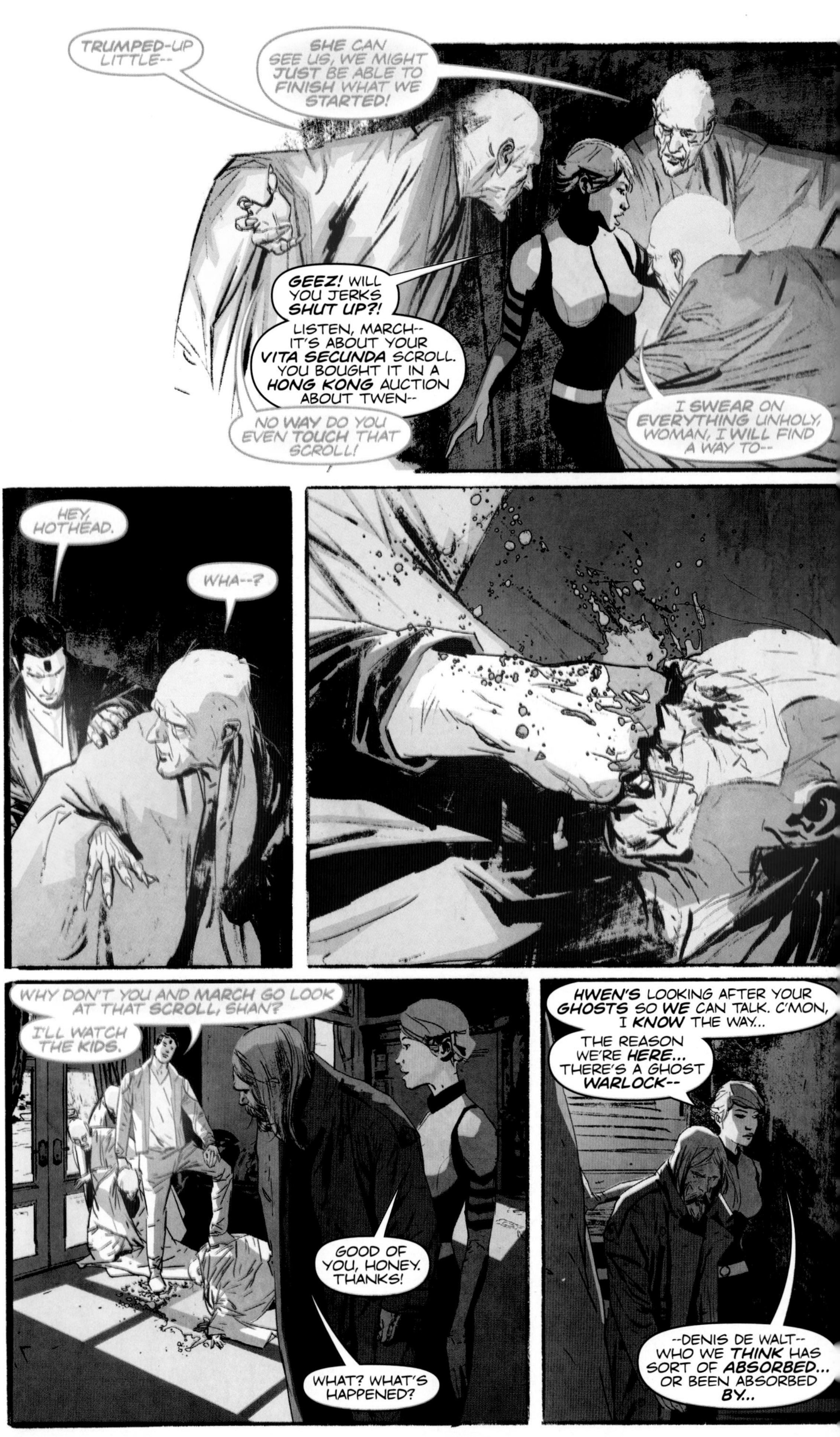
TRUMPED-UP LITTLE--
SHE CAN SEE US, WE MIGHT JUST BE ABLE TO FINISH WHAT WE STARTED!
GEEZ! WILL YOU JERKS SHUT UP?!
LISTEN, MARCH-- IT'S ABOUT YOUR VITA SECUNDA SCROLL. YOU BOUGHT IT IN A HONG KONG AUCTION ABOUT TWEN--
NO WAY DO YOU EVEN TOUCH THAT SCROLL!
I SWEAR ON EVERYTHING UNHOLY, WOMAN, I WILL FIND A WAY TO--
HEY, HOTHEAD.
WHA--?
WHY DON'T YOU AND MARCH GO LOOK AT THAT SCROLL, SHAN?
I'LL WATCH THE KIDS.
GOOD OF YOU, HONEY. THANKS!
WHAT? WHAT'S HAPPENED?
HWEN'S LOOKING AFTER YOUR GHOSTS SO WE CAN TALK. C'MON, I KNOW THE WAY...
THE REASON WE'RE HERE... THERE'S A GHOST WARLOCK--
--DENIS DE WALT-- WHO WE THINK HAS SORT OF ABSORBED... OR BEEN ABSORBED BY...

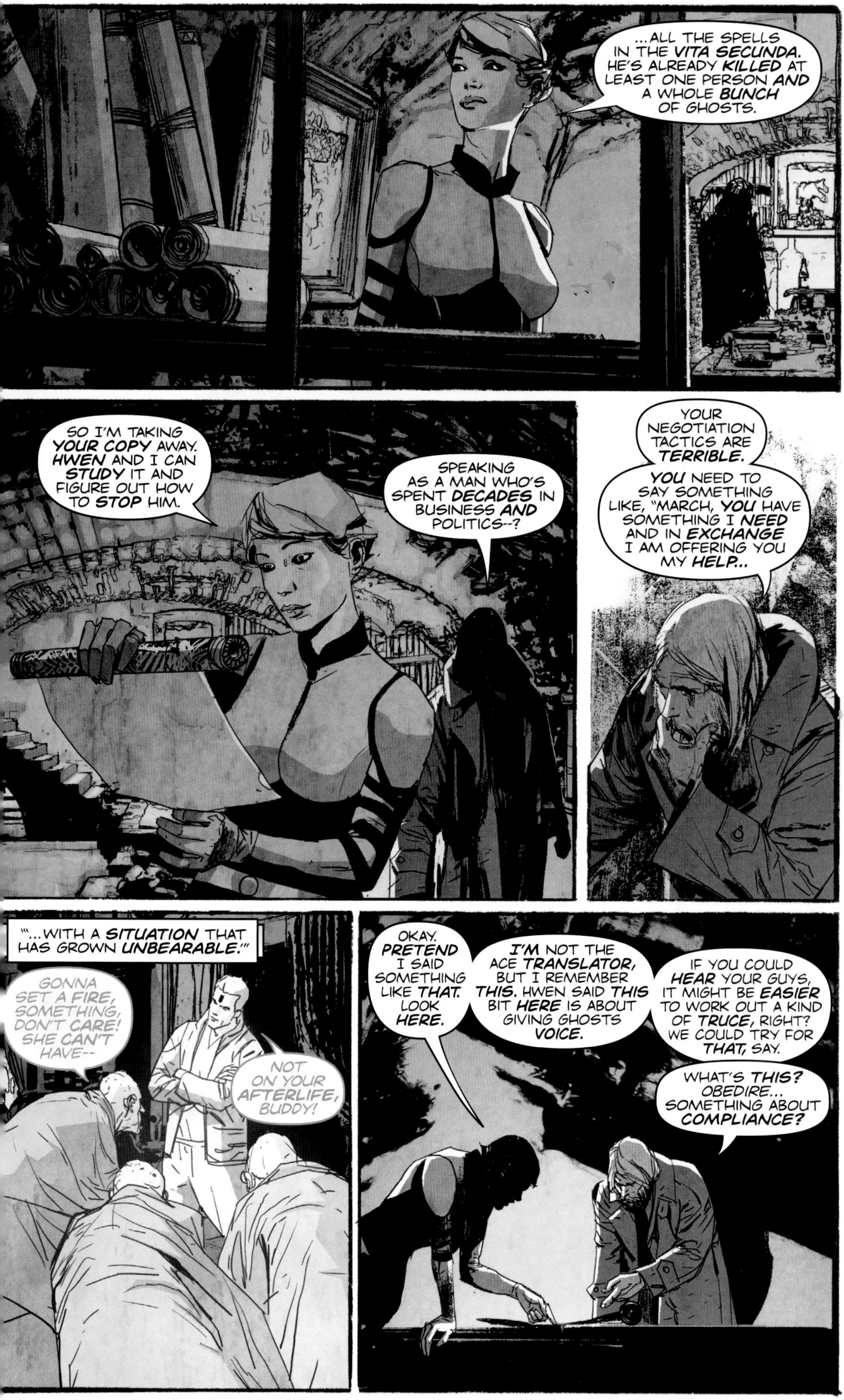
...ALL THE SPELLS IN THE VITA SECUNDA. HE'S ALREADY KILLED AT LEAST ONE PERSON AND A WHOLE BUNCH OF GHOSTS.
SO I'M TAKING YOUR COPY AWAY. HWEN AND I CAN STUDY IT AND FIGURE OUT HOW TO STOP HIM.
SPEAKING AS A MAN WHO'S SPENT DECADES IN BUSINESS AND POLITICS--?
YOUR NEGOTIATION TACTICS ARE TERRIBLE.
YOU NEED TO SAY SOMETHING LIKE, "MARCH, YOU HAVE SOMETHING I NEED AND IN EXCHANGE I AM OFFERING YOU MY HELP...
"...WITH A SITUATION THAT HAS GROWN UNBEARABLE."
GONNA SET A FIRE, SOMETHING, DON'T CARE! SHE CAN'T HAVE--
NOT ON YOUR AFTERLIFE, BUDDY!
OKAY. PRETEND I SAID SOMETHING LIKE THAT. LOOK HERE.
I'M NOT THE ACE TRANSLATOR, BUT I REMEMBER THIS. HWEN SAID THIS BIT HERE IS ABOUT GIVING GHOSTS VOICE.
IF YOU COULD HEAR YOUR GUYS, IT MIGHT BE EASIER TO WORK OUT A KIND OF TRUCE, RIGHT? WE COULD TRY FOR THAT, SAY.
WHAT'S THIS? OBEDIRE... SOMETHING ABOUT COMPLIANCE?

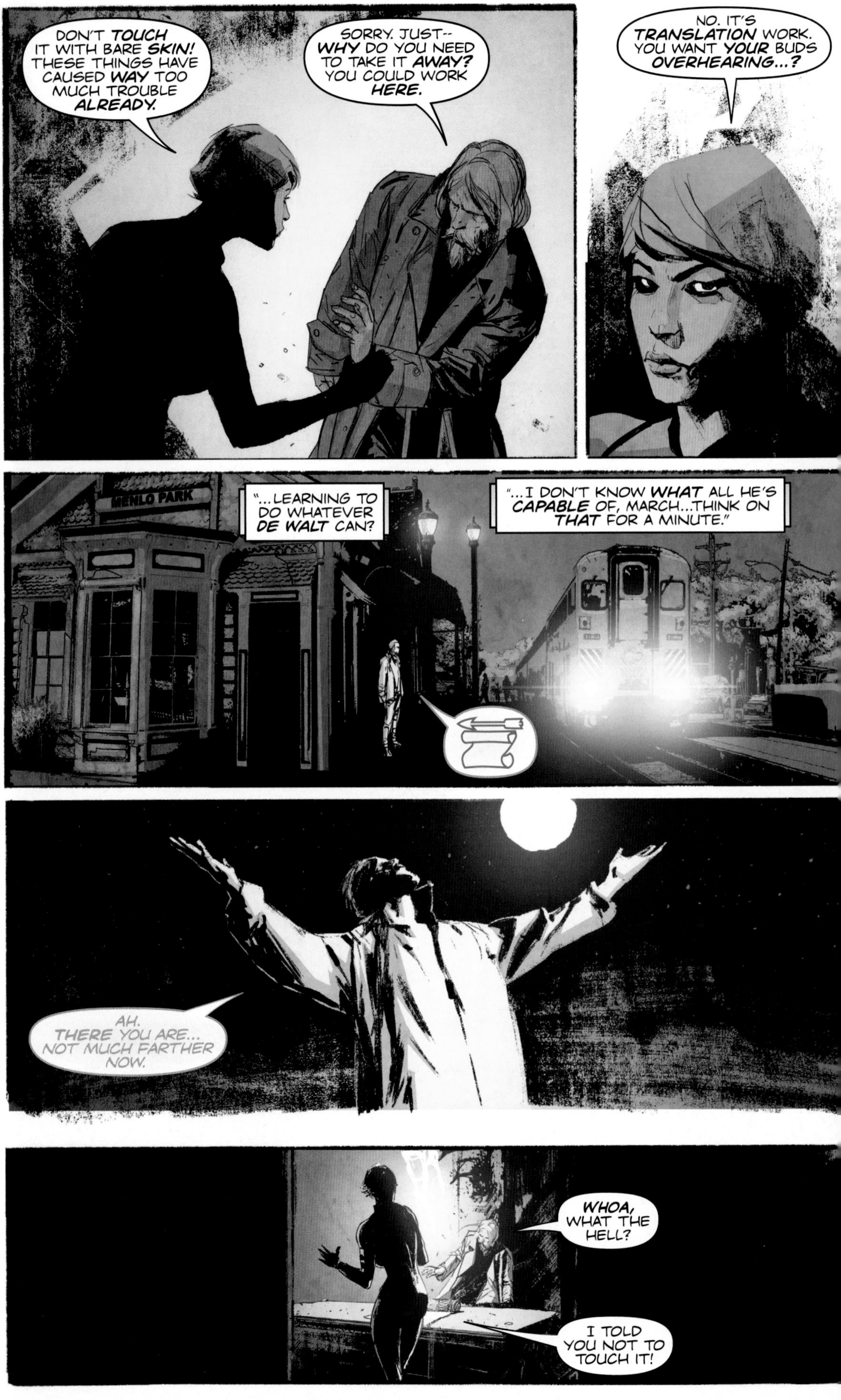
DON'T TOUCH IT WITH BARE SKIN! THESE THINGS HAVE CAUSED WAY TOO MUCH TROUBLE ALREADY.
SORRY. JUST-- WHY DO YOU NEED TO TAKE IT AWAY? YOU COULD WORK HERE.
NO. IT'S TRANSLATION WORK. YOU WANT YOUR BUDS OVERHEARING...?
MENLO PARK
"...LEARNING TO DO WHATEVER DE WALT CAN?
"...I DON'T KNOW WHAT ALL HE'S CAPABLE OF, MARCH...THINK ON THAT FOR A MINUTE."
AH. THERE YOU ARE... NOT MUCH FARTHER NOW.
WHOA, WHAT THE HELL?
I TOLD YOU NOT TO TOUCH IT!

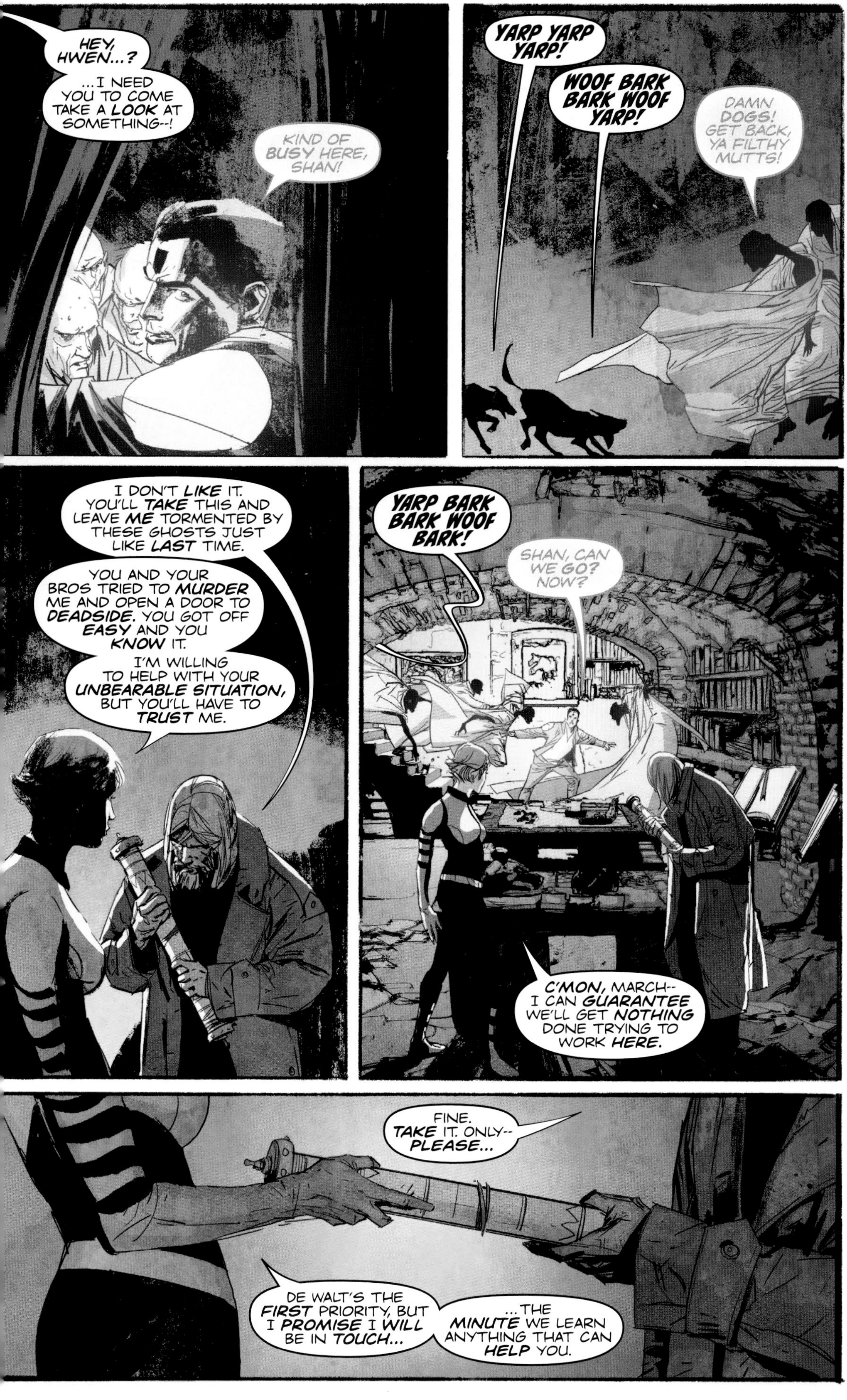
HEY, HWEN...?
...I NEED YOU TO COME TAKE A LOOK AT SOMETHING--!
KIND OF BUSY HERE, SHAN!
YARP YARP YARP!
WOOF BARK BARK WOOF YARP!
DAMN DOGS! GET BACK, YA FILTHY MUTTS!
I DON'T LIKE IT. YOU'LL TAKE THIS AND LEAVE ME TORMENTED BY THESE GHOSTS JUST LIKE LAST TIME.
YOU AND YOUR BROS TRIED TO MURDER ME AND OPEN A DOOR TO DEADSIDE. YOU GOT OFF EASY AND YOU KNOW IT.
I'M WILLING TO HELP WITH YOUR UNBEARABLE SITUATION, BUT YOU'LL HAVE TO TRUST ME.
YARP BARK BARK WOOF BARK!
SHAN, CAN WE GO? NOW?
C'MON, MARCH-- I CAN GUARANTEE WE'LL GET NOTHING DONE TRYING TO WORK HERE.
FINE. TAKE IT. ONLY-- PLEASE...
DE WALT'S THE FIRST PRIORITY, BUT I PROMISE I WILL BE IN TOUCH...
...THE MINUTE WE LEARN ANYTHING THAT CAN HELP YOU.

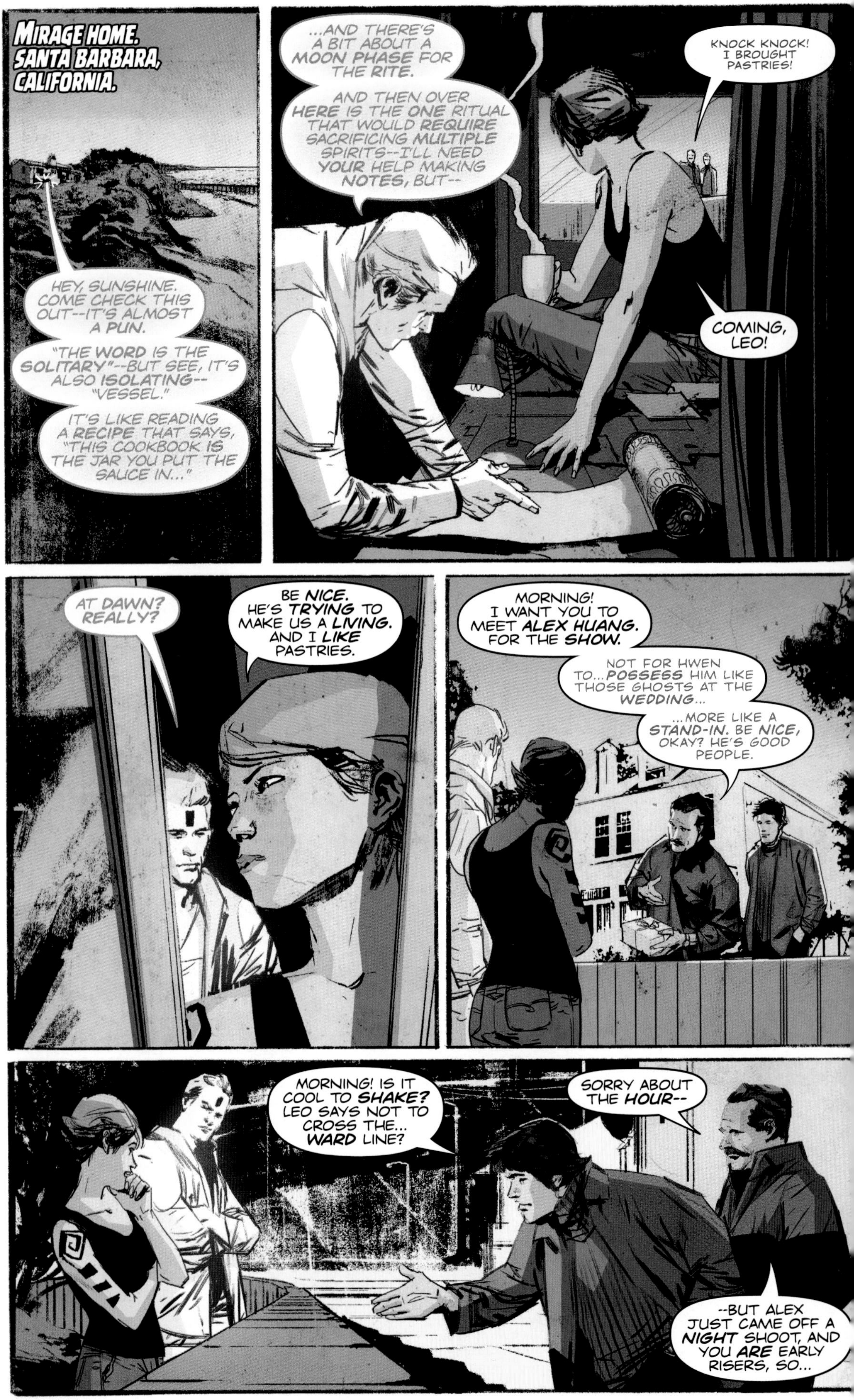
MIRAGE HOME. SANTA BARBARA, CALIFORNIA.
HEY, SUNSHINE. COME CHECK THIS OUT--IT'S ALMOST A PUN.
"THE WORD IS THE SOLITARY"--BUT SEE, IT'S ALSO ISOLATING--"VESSEL."
IT'S LIKE READING A RECIPE THAT SAYS, "THIS COOKBOOK IS THE JAR YOU PUT THE SAUCE IN..."
...AND THERE'S A BIT ABOUT A MOON PHASE FOR THE RITE.
AND THEN OVER HERE IS THE ONE RITUAL THAT WOULD REQUIRE SACRIFICING MULTIPLE SPIRITS--I'LL NEED YOUR HELP MAKING NOTES, BUT--
KNOCK KNOCK! I BROUGHT PASTRIES!
COMING, LEO!
AT DAWN? REALLY?
BE NICE. HE'S TRYING TO MAKE US A LIVING. AND I LIKE PASTRIES.
MORNING! I WANT YOU TO MEET ALEX HUANG. FOR THE SHOW.
NOT FOR HWEN TO...POSSESS HIM LIKE THOSE GHOSTS AT THE WEDDING...
...MORE LIKE A STAND-IN. BE NICE, OKAY? HE'S GOOD PEOPLE.
MORNING! IS IT COOL TO SHAKE? LEO SAYS NOT TO CROSS THE... WARD LINE?
SORRY ABOUT THE HOUR--
--BUT ALEX JUST CAME OFF A NIGHT SHOOT, AND YOU ARE EARLY RISERS, SO...

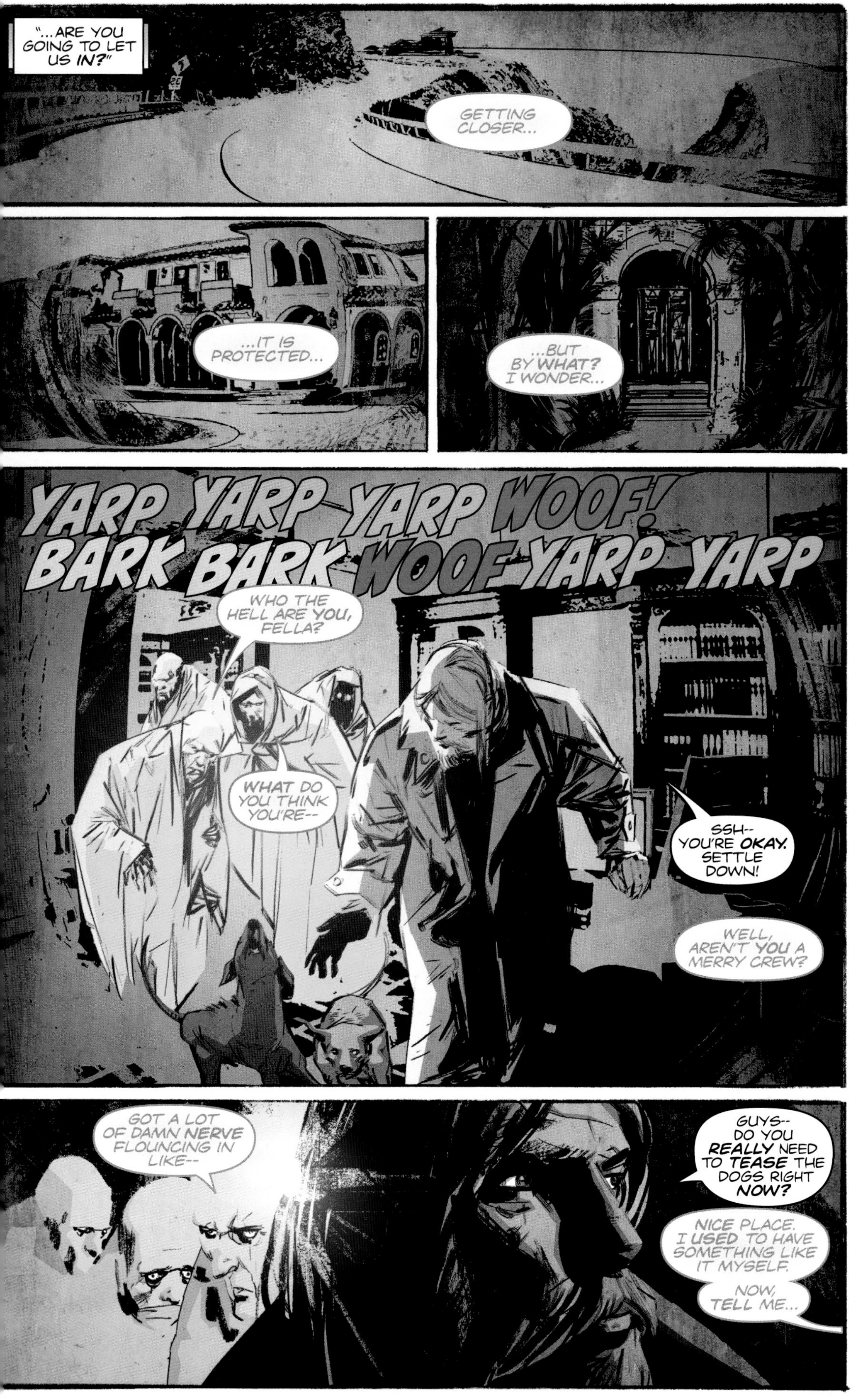

"...ARE YOU GOING TO LET US IN?"
GETTING CLOSER...
...IT IS PROTECTED...
...BUT BY WHAT? I WONDER...
YARP YARP YARP WOOF! BARK BARK WOOF YARP YARP
WHO THE HELL ARE YOU, FELLA?
WHAT DO YOU THINK YOU'RE--
SSH-- YOU'RE OKAY. SETTLE DOWN!
WELL, AREN'T YOU A MERRY CREW?
GOT A LOT OF DAMN NERVE FLOUNCING IN LIKE--
GUYS-- DO YOU REALLY NEED TO TEASE THE DOGS RIGHT NOW?
NICE PLACE. I USED TO HAVE SOMETHING LIKE IT MYSELF.
NOW, TELL ME...

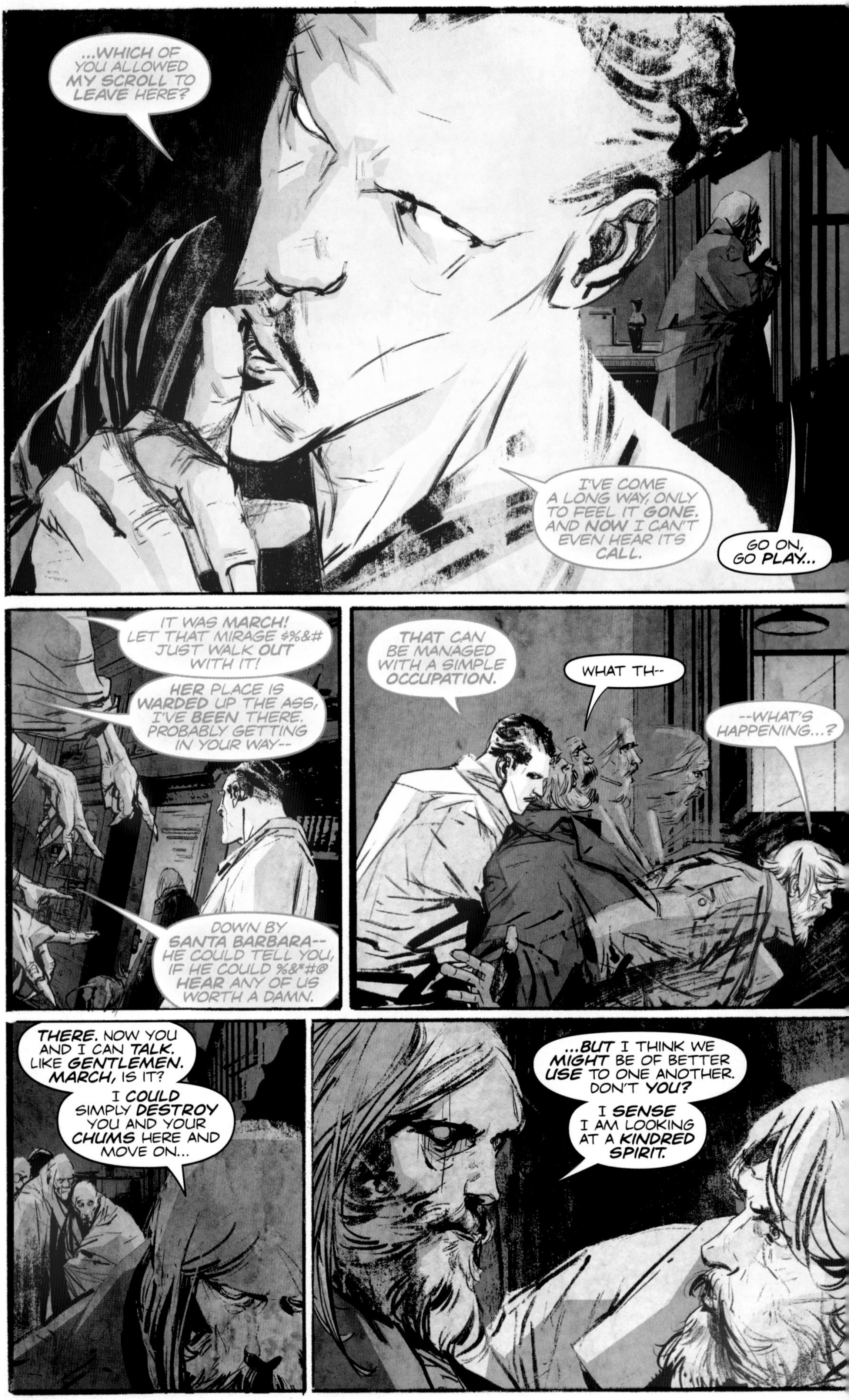
...WHICH OF YOU ALLOWED MY SCROLL TO LEAVE HERE?
I'VE COME A LONG WAY, ONLY TO FEEL IT GONE. AND NOW I CAN'T EVEN HEAR ITS CALL.
GO ON, GO PLAY...
IT WAS MARCH! LET THAT MIRAGE $%&# JUST WALK OUT WITH IT!
HER PLACE IS WARDED UP THE ASS, I'VE BEEN THERE. PROBABLY GETTING IN YOUR WAY--
DOWN BY SANTA BARBARA-- HE COULD TELL YOU, IF HE COULD %&*#@ HEAR ANY OF US WORTH A DAMN.
THAT CAN BE MANAGED WITH A SIMPLE OCCUPATION.
WHAT TH--
--WHAT'S HAPPENING...?
THERE. NOW YOU AND I CAN TALK. LIKE GENTLEMEN. MARCH, IS IT?
I COULD SIMPLY DESTROY YOU AND YOUR CHUMS HERE AND MOVE ON...
...BUT I THINK WE MIGHT BE OF BETTER USE TO ONE ANOTHER. DON'T YOU?
I SENSE I AM LOOKING AT A KINDRED SPIRIT.

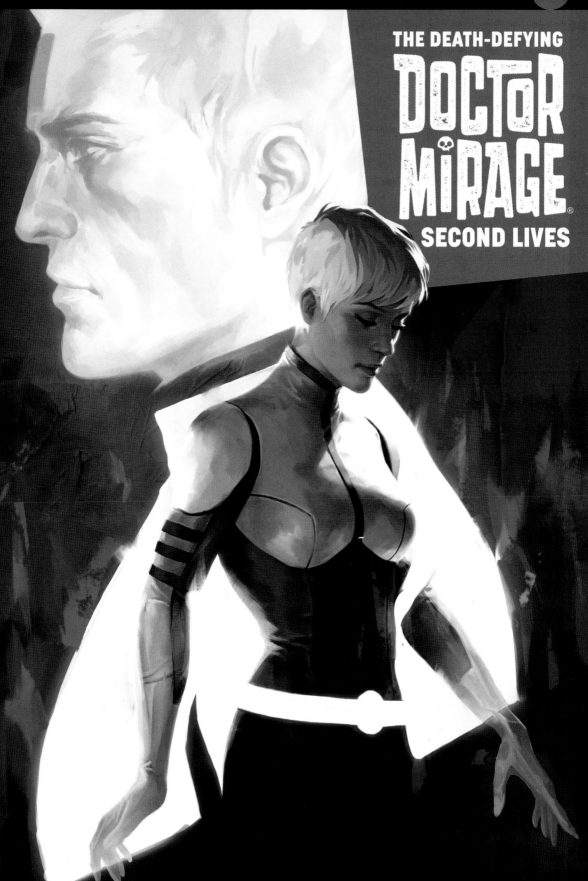

VALIANT

JEN VAN METER | ROBERTO DE LA TORRE
DIEGO BERNARD | TOM PALMER | DAVID BARON

#3

THE DEATH-DEFYING

DOCTOR
MIRAGE

SECOND LIVES

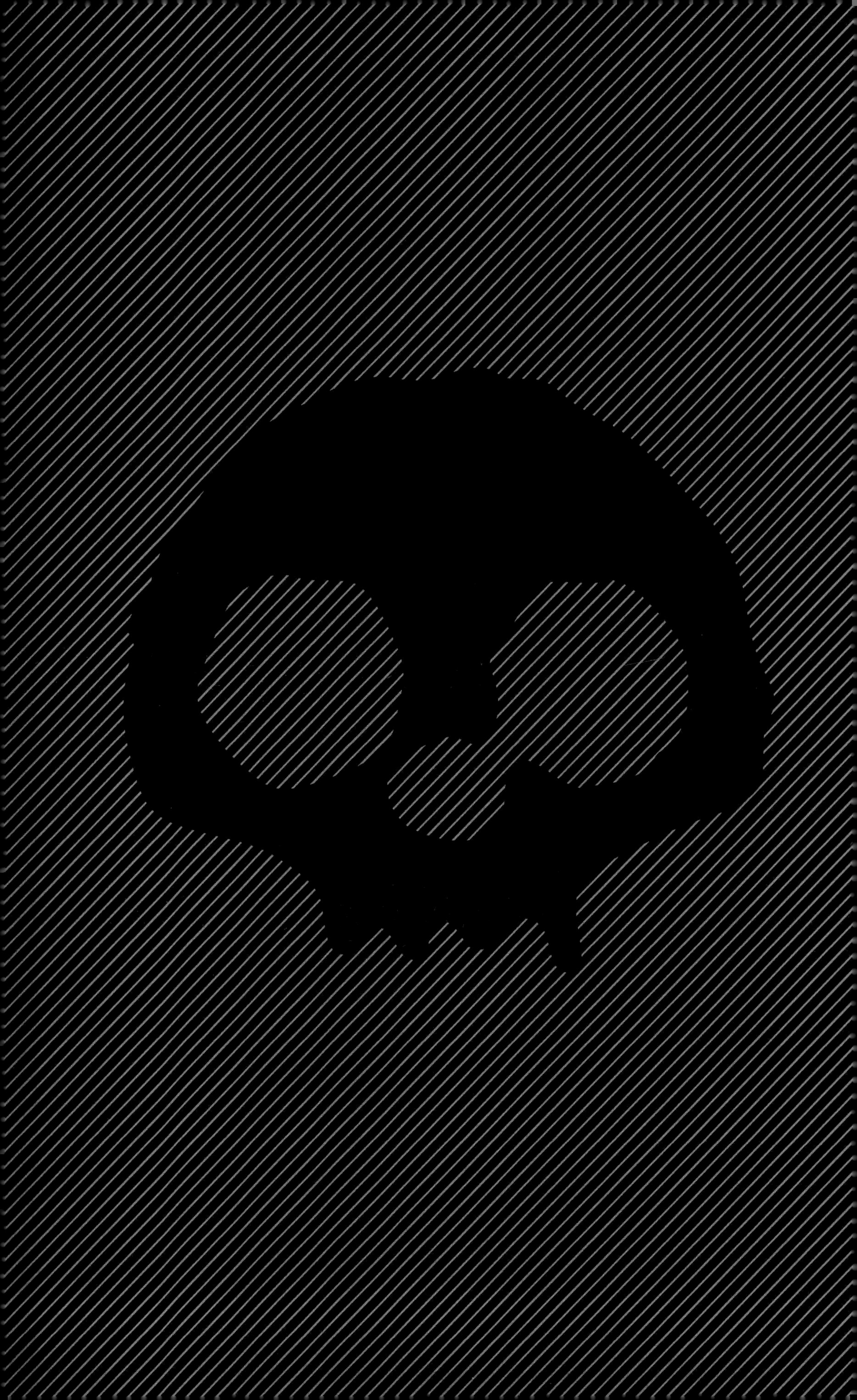

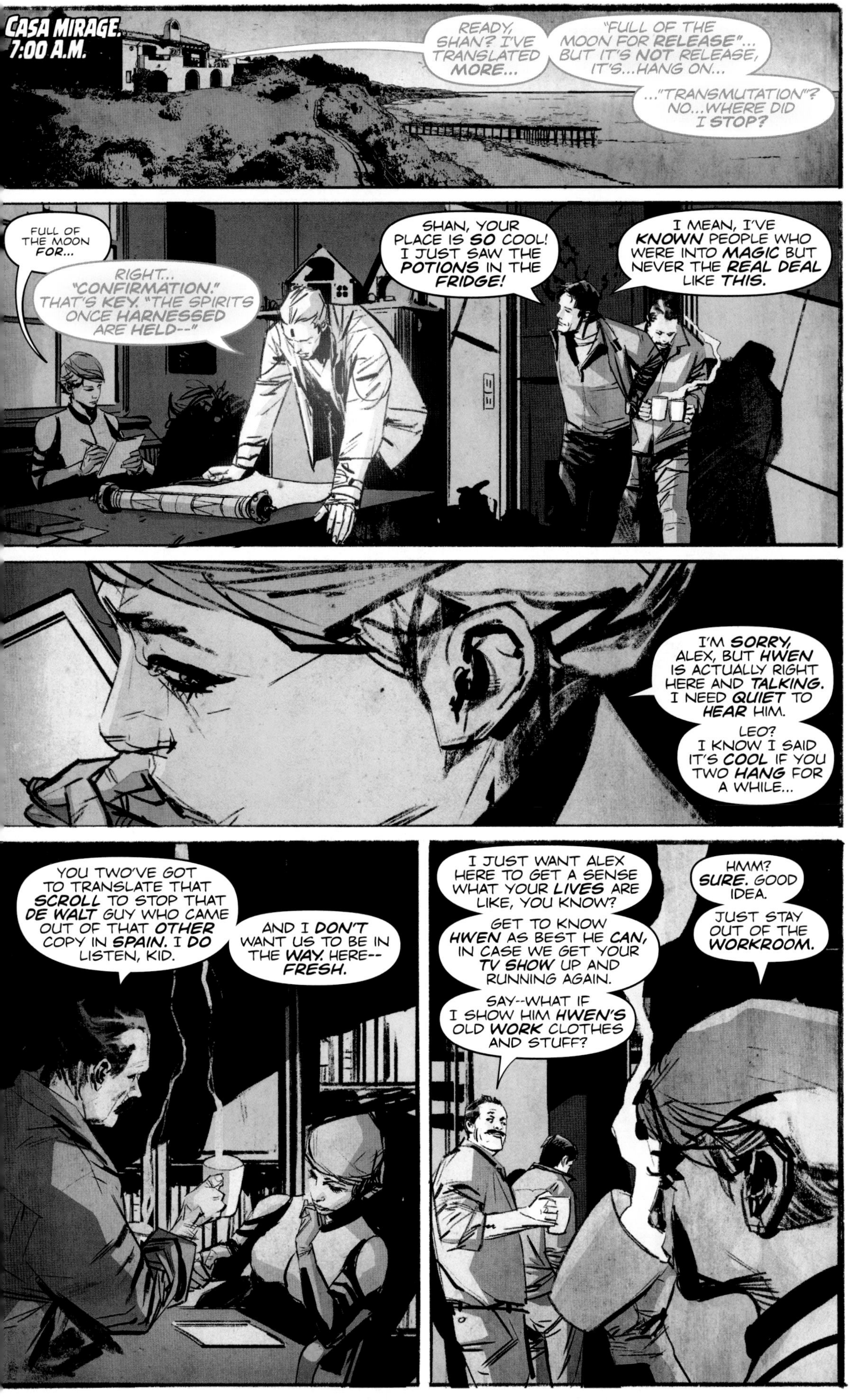
CASA MIRAGE. 7:00 A.M.
READY, SHAN? I'VE TRANSLATED MORE...
"FULL OF THE MOON FOR RELEASE"... BUT IT'S NOT RELEASE, IT'S...HANG ON...
..."TRANSMUTATION"? NO...WHERE DID I STOP?
FULL OF THE MOON FOR...
RIGHT... "CONFIRMATION." THAT'S KEY. "THE SPIRITS ONCE HARNESSED ARE HELD--"
SHAN, YOUR PLACE IS SO COOL! I JUST SAW THE POTIONS IN THE FRIDGE!
I MEAN, I'VE KNOWN PEOPLE WHO WERE INTO MAGIC BUT NEVER THE REAL DEAL LIKE THIS.
I'M SORRY, ALEX, BUT HWEN IS ACTUALLY RIGHT HERE AND TALKING. I NEED QUIET TO HEAR HIM.
LEO? I KNOW I SAID IT'S COOL IF YOU TWO HANG FOR A WHILE...
YOU TWO'VE GOT TO TRANSLATE THAT SCROLL TO STOP THAT DE WALT GUY WHO CAME OUT OF THAT OTHER COPY IN SPAIN. I DO LISTEN, KID.
AND I DON'T WANT US TO BE IN THE WAY. HERE-- FRESH.
I JUST WANT ALEX HERE TO GET A SENSE WHAT YOUR LIVES ARE LIKE, YOU KNOW?
GET TO KNOW HWEN AS BEST HE CAN, IN CASE WE GET YOUR TV SHOW UP AND RUNNING AGAIN.
SAY--WHAT IF I SHOW HIM HWEN'S OLD WORK CLOTHES AND STUFF?
HMM? SURE. GOOD IDEA.
JUST STAY OUT OF THE WORKROOM.

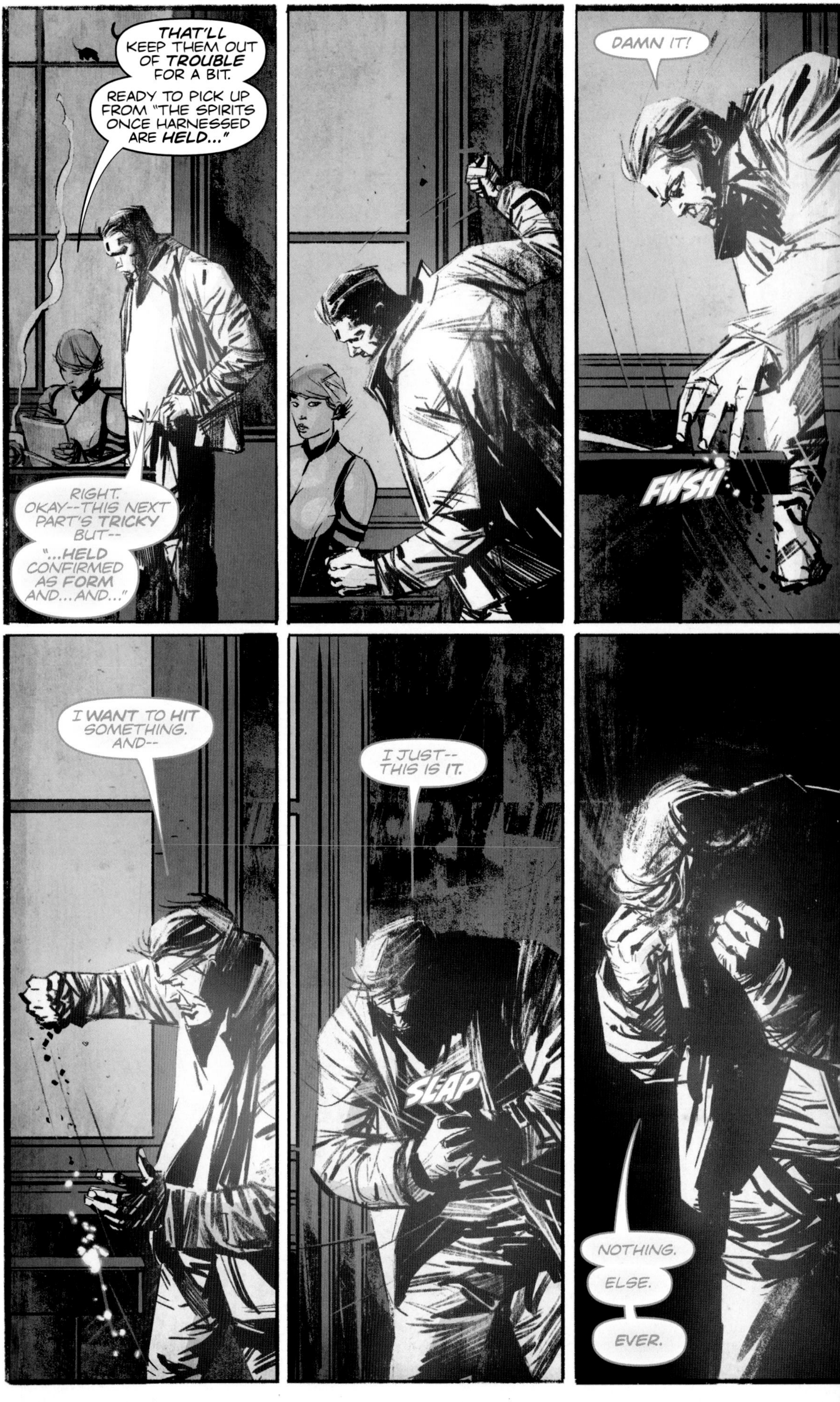
THAT'LL KEEP THEM OUT OF TROUBLE FOR A BIT.
READY TO PICK UP FROM "THE SPIRITS ONCE HARNESSED ARE HELD..."
RIGHT. OKAY--THIS NEXT PART'S TRICKY BUT--
"...HELD CONFIRMED AS FORM AND...AND..."
DAMN IT!
FWSH
I WANT TO HIT SOMETHING. AND--
I JUST-- THIS IS IT.
SLAP
NOTHING.
ELSE.
EVER.

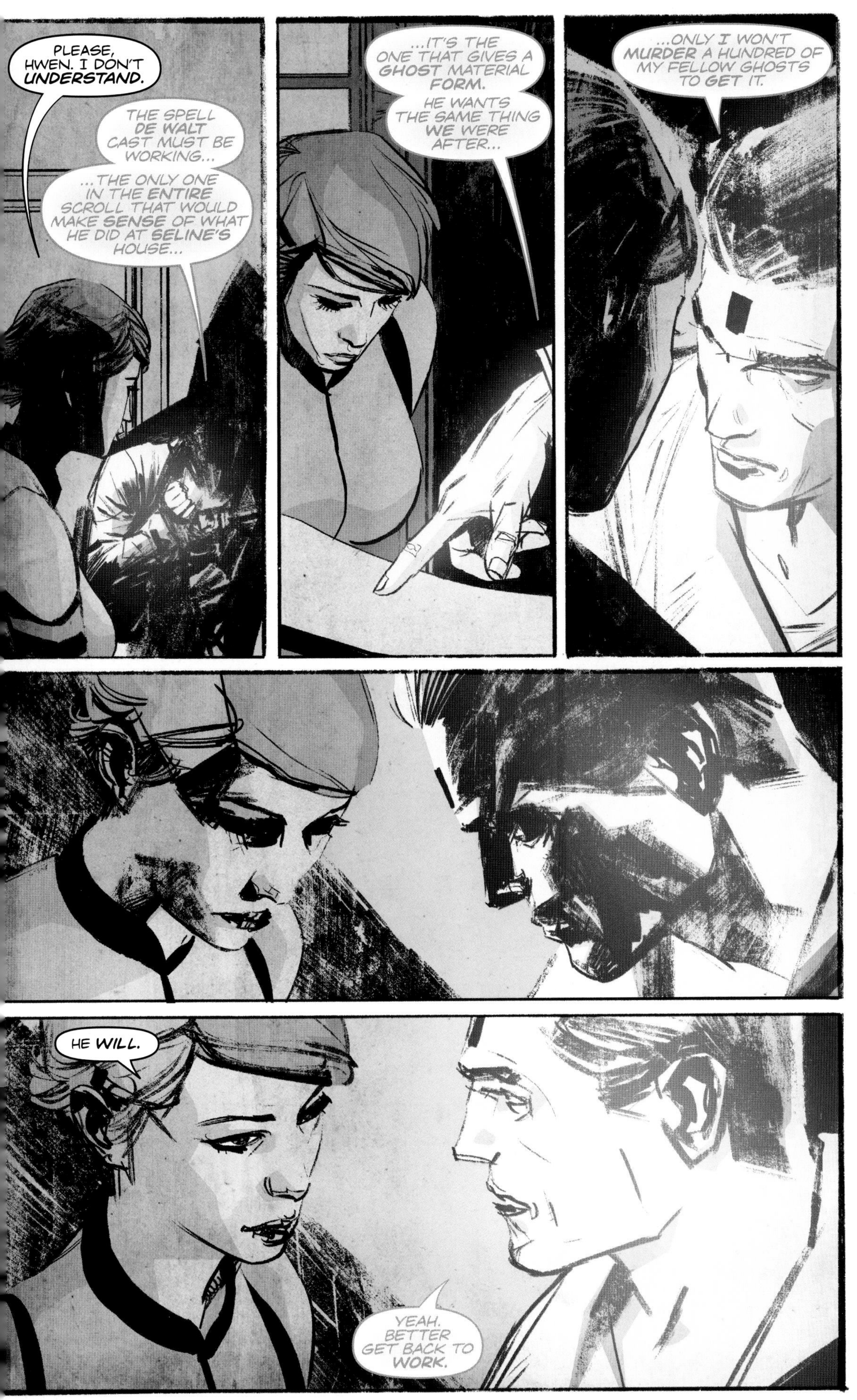
PLEASE, HWEN. I DON'T UNDERSTAND.
THE SPELL DE WALT CAST MUST BE WORKING...
...THE ONLY ONE IN THE ENTIRE SCROLL THAT WOULD MAKE SENSE OF WHAT HE DID AT SELINE'S HOUSE...
...IT'S THE ONE THAT GIVES A GHOST MATERIAL FORM.
HE WANTS THE SAME THING WE WERE AFTER...
...ONLY I WON'T MURDER A HUNDRED OF MY FELLOW GHOSTS TO GET IT.
HE WILL.
YEAH. BETTER GET BACK TO WORK.

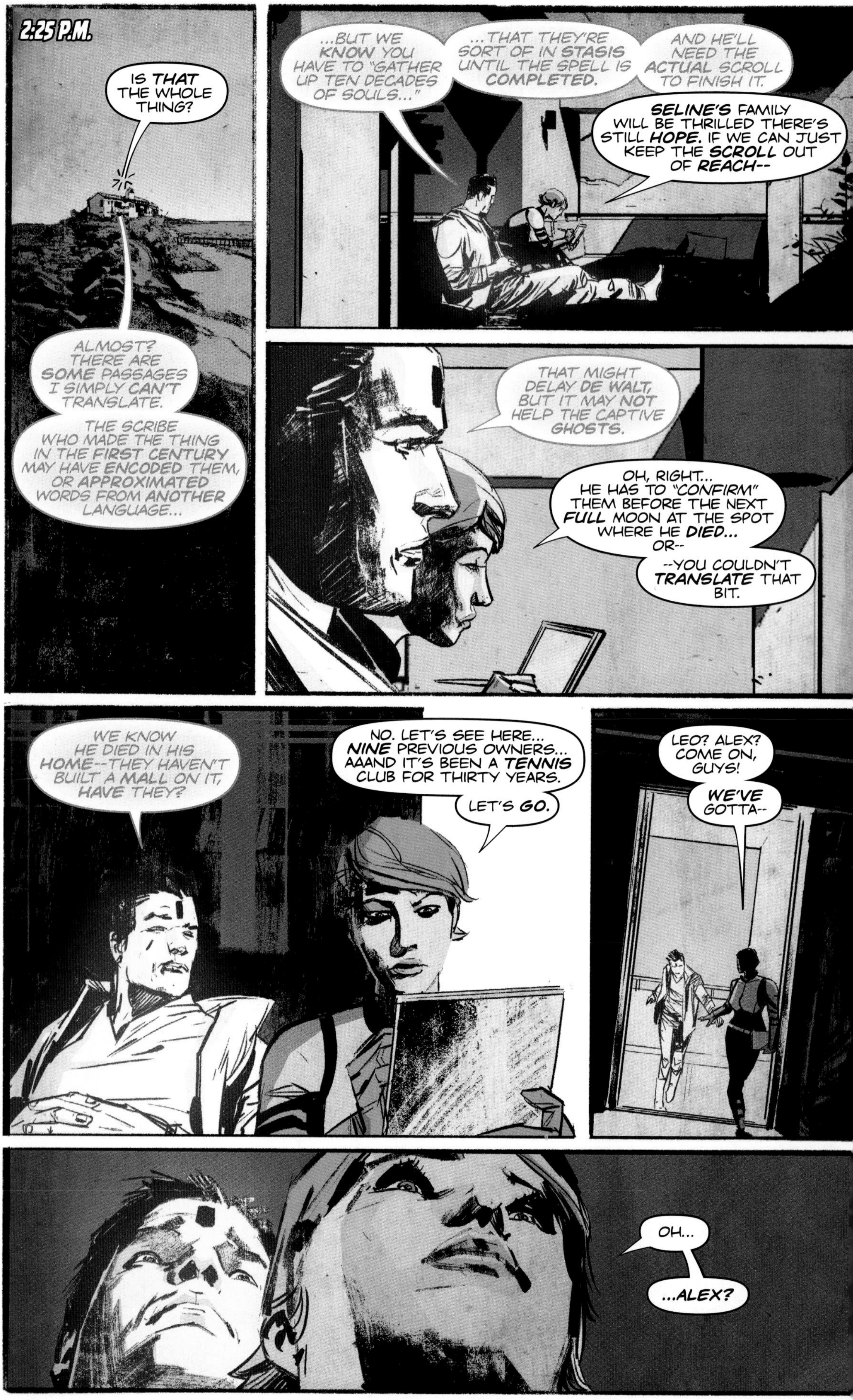
2:25 P.M.
IS THAT THE WHOLE THING?
ALMOST? THERE ARE SOME PASSAGES I SIMPLY CAN'T TRANSLATE.
THE SCRIBE WHO MADE THE THING IN THE FIRST CENTURY MAY HAVE ENCODED THEM, OR APPROXIMATED WORDS FROM ANOTHER LANGUAGE...
...BUT WE KNOW YOU HAVE TO "GATHER UP TEN DECADES OF SOULS..."
...THAT THEY'RE SORT OF IN STASIS UNTIL THE SPELL IS COMPLETED.
AND HE'LL NEED THE ACTUAL SCROLL TO FINISH IT.
SELINE'S FAMILY WILL BE THRILLED THERE'S STILL HOPE. IF WE CAN JUST KEEP THE SCROLL OUT OF REACH--
THAT MIGHT DELAY DE WALT, BUT IT MAY NOT HELP THE CAPTIVE GHOSTS.
OH, RIGHT... HE HAS TO "CONFIRM" THEM BEFORE THE NEXT FULL MOON AT THE SPOT WHERE HE DIED... OR--
--YOU COULDN'T TRANSLATE THAT BIT.
WE KNOW HE DIED IN HIS HOME--THEY HAVEN'T BUILT A MALL ON IT, HAVE THEY?
NO. LET'S SEE HERE... NINE PREVIOUS OWNERS... AAAND IT'S BEEN A TENNIS CLUB FOR THIRTY YEARS.
LET'S GO.
LEO? ALEX? COME ON, GUYS!
WE'VE GOTTA--
OH...
...ALEX?

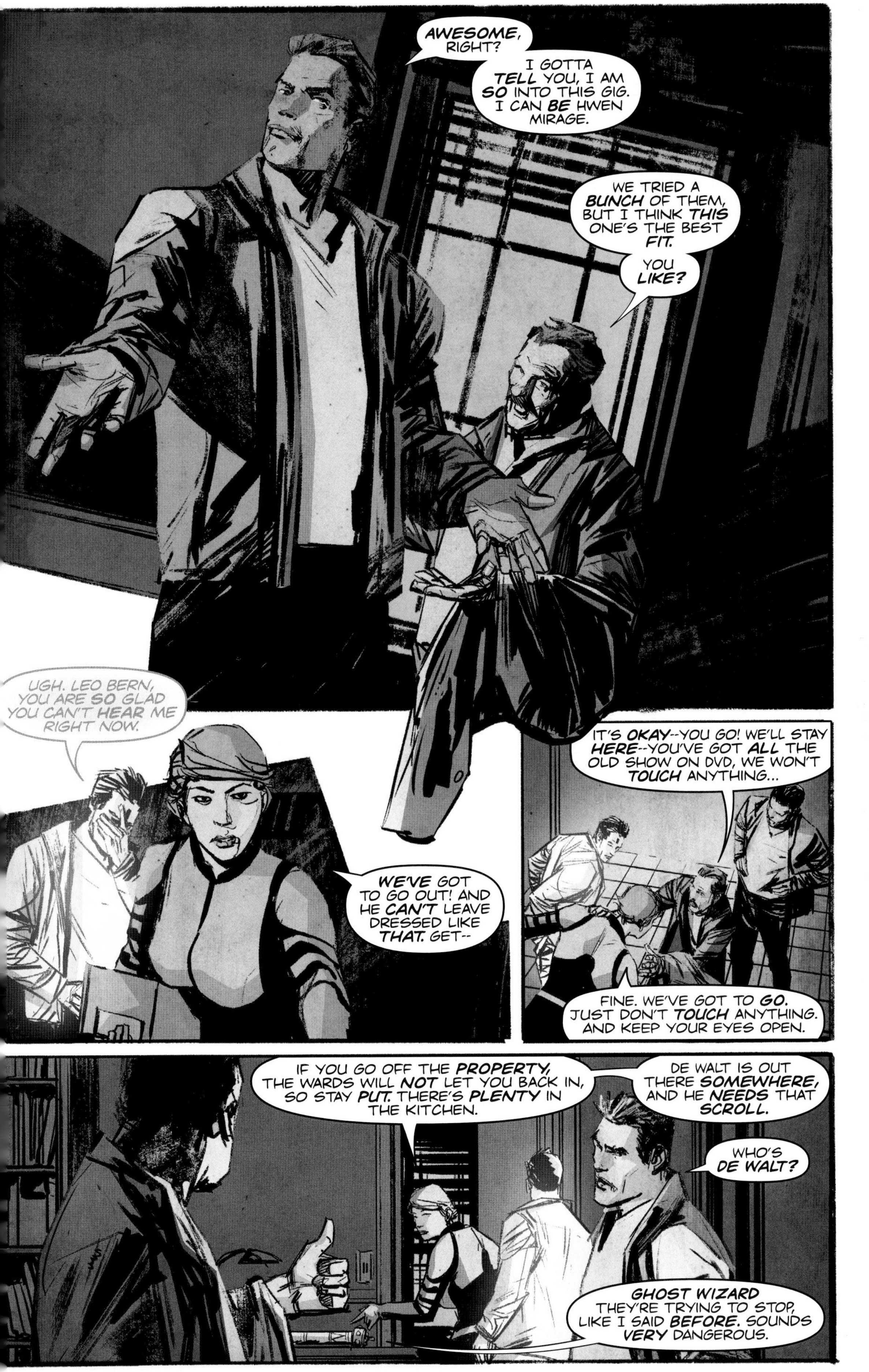

AWESOME, RIGHT?
I GOTTA TELL YOU, I AM SO INTO THIS GIG. I CAN BE HWEN MIRAGE.
WE TRIED A BUNCH OF THEM, BUT I THINK THIS ONE'S THE BEST FIT.
YOU LIKE?
UGH. LEO BERN, YOU ARE SO GLAD YOU CAN'T HEAR ME RIGHT NOW.
WE'VE GOT TO GO OUT! AND HE CAN'T LEAVE DRESSED LIKE THAT. GET--
IT'S OKAY--YOU GO! WE'LL STAY HERE--YOU'VE GOT ALL THE OLD SHOW ON DVD, WE WON'T TOUCH ANYTHING...
FINE. WE'VE GOT TO GO. JUST DON'T TOUCH ANYTHING. AND KEEP YOUR EYES OPEN.
IF YOU GO OFF THE PROPERTY, THE WARDS WILL NOT LET YOU BACK IN, SO STAY PUT. THERE'S PLENTY IN THE KITCHEN.
DE WALT IS OUT THERE SOMEWHERE, AND HE NEEDS THAT SCROLL.
WHO'S DE WALT?
GHOST WIZARD THEY'RE TRYING TO STOP, LIKE I SAID BEFORE. SOUNDS VERY DANGEROUS.

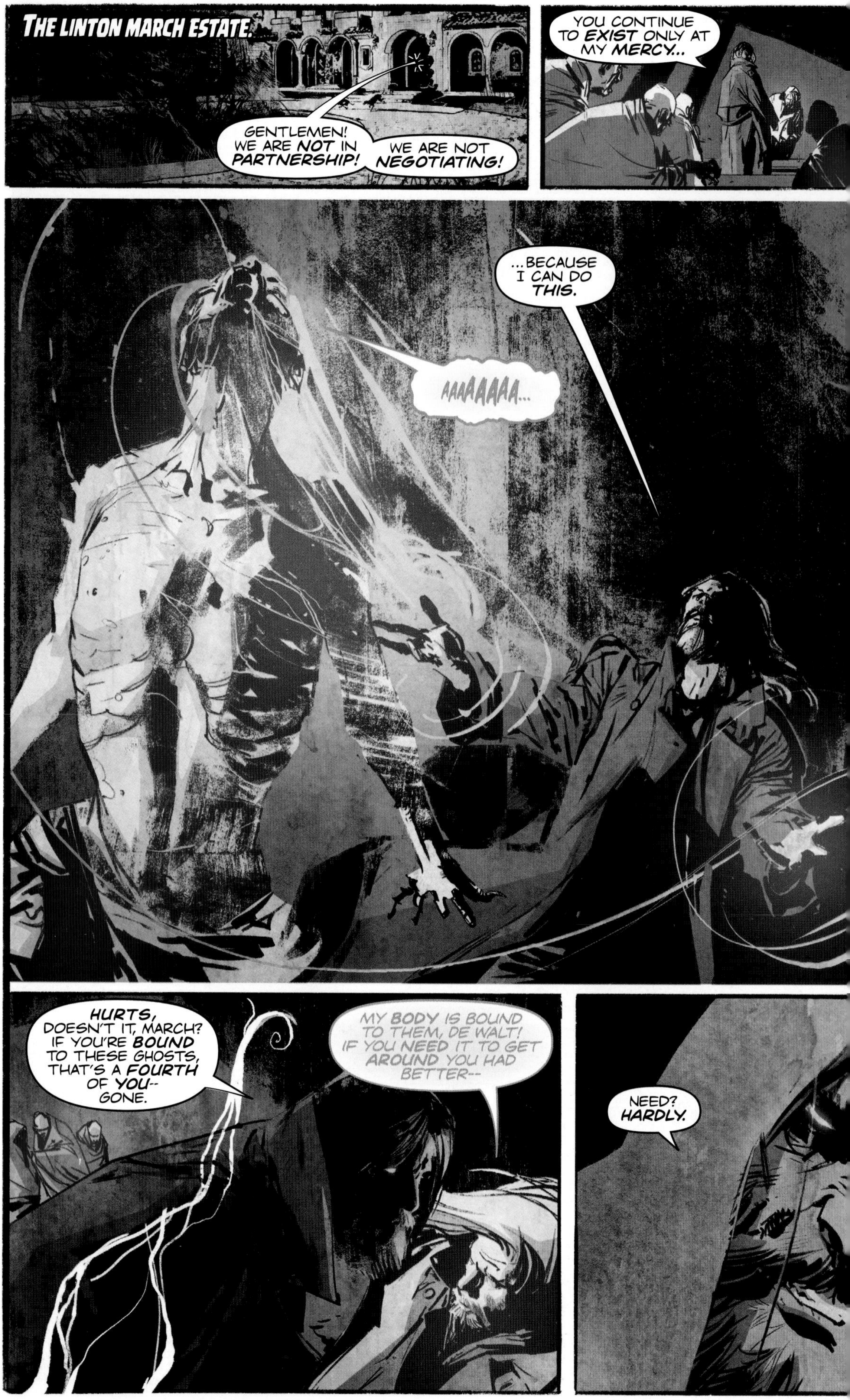
THE LINTON MARCH ESTATE.
GENTLEMEN! WE ARE NOT IN PARTNERSHIP!
WE ARE NOT NEGOTIATING!
YOU CONTINUE TO EXIST ONLY AT MY MERCY...
...BECAUSE I CAN DO THIS.
AAAAAAAA...
HURTS, DOESN'T IT, MARCH? IF YOU'RE BOUND TO THESE GHOSTS, THAT'S A FOURTH OF YOU-- GONE.
MY BODY IS BOUND TO THEM, DE WALT! IF YOU NEED IT TO GET AROUND YOU HAD BETTER--
NEED? HARDLY.

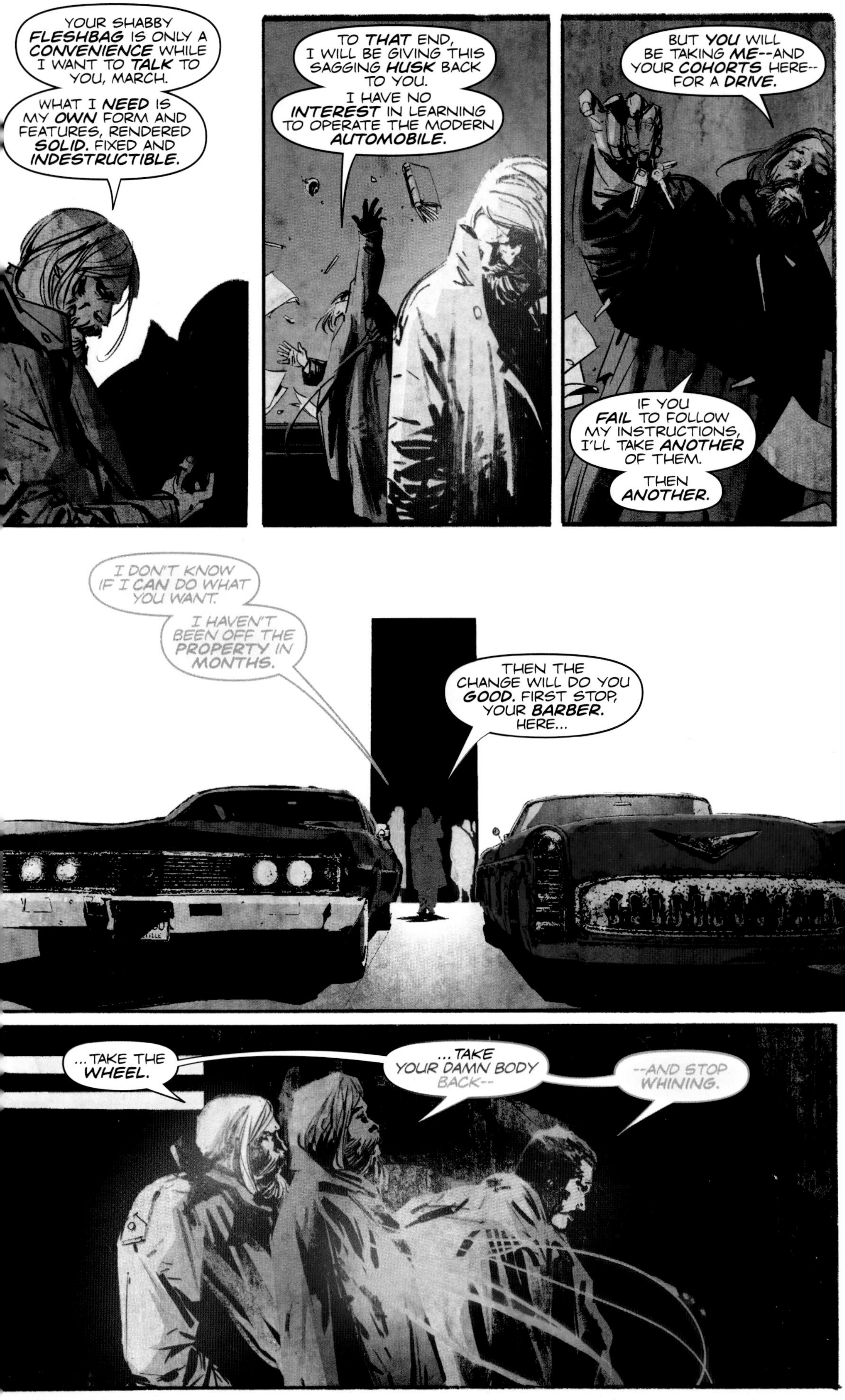
YOUR SHABBY FLESHBAG IS ONLY A CONVENIENCE WHILE I WANT TO TALK TO YOU, MARCH.
WHAT I NEED IS MY OWN FORM AND FEATURES, RENDERED SOLID. FIXED AND INDESTRUCTIBLE.
TO THAT END, I WILL BE GIVING THIS SAGGING HUSK BACK TO YOU.
I HAVE NO INTEREST IN LEARNING TO OPERATE THE MODERN AUTOMOBILE.
BUT YOU WILL BE TAKING ME--AND YOUR COHORTS HERE--FOR A DRIVE.
IF YOU FAIL TO FOLLOW MY INSTRUCTIONS, I'LL TAKE ANOTHER OF THEM.
THEN ANOTHER.
I DON'T KNOW IF I CAN DO WHAT YOU WANT.
I HAVEN'T BEEN OFF THE PROPERTY IN MONTHS.
THEN THE CHANGE WILL DO YOU GOOD. FIRST STOP, YOUR BARBER. HERE...
...TAKE THE WHEEL.
...TAKE YOUR DAMN BODY BACK--
--AND STOP WHINING.

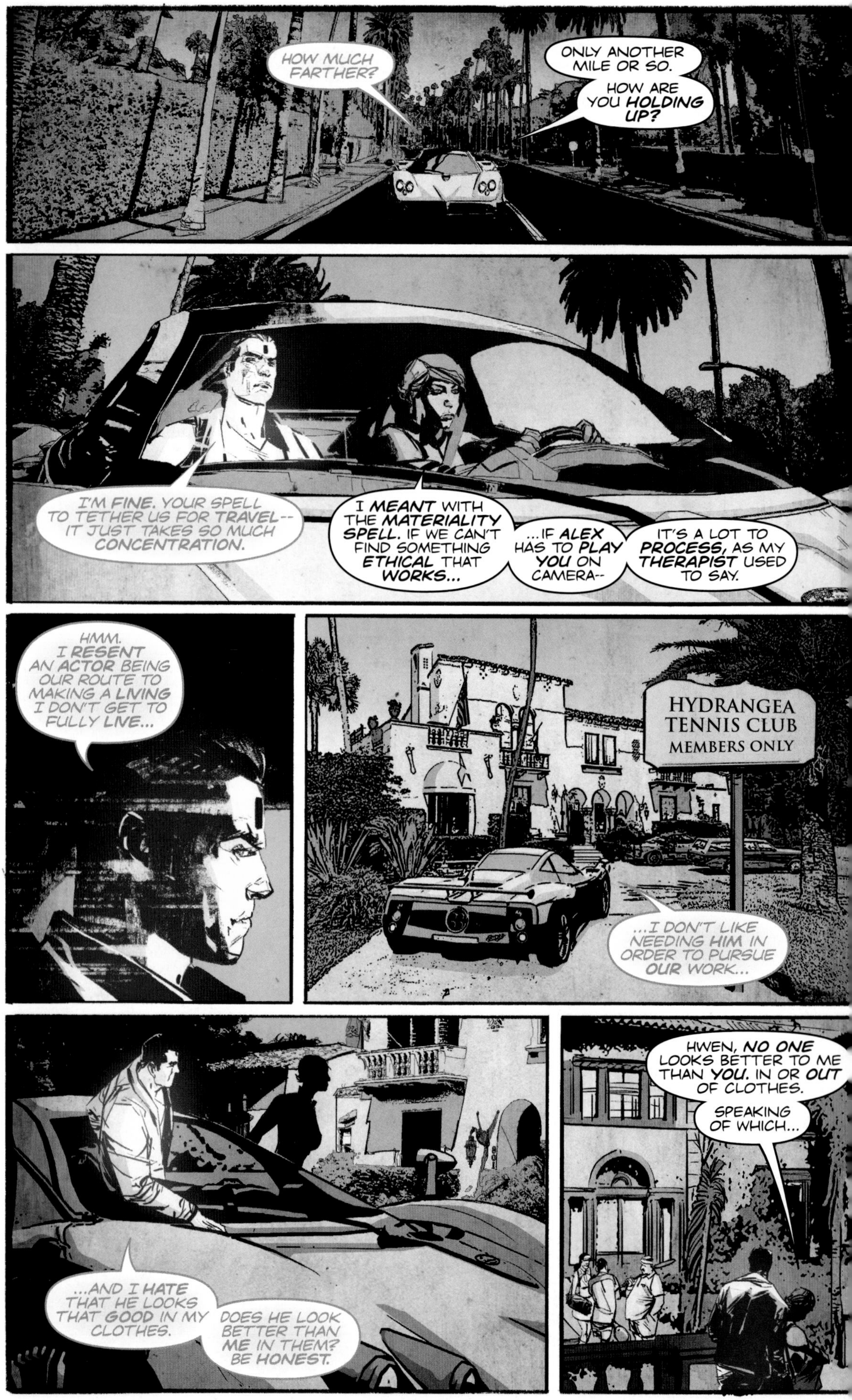
HOW MUCH FARTHER?
ONLY ANOTHER MILE OR SO.
HOW ARE YOU HOLDING UP?
I'M FINE. YOUR SPELL TO TETHER US FOR TRAVEL-- IT JUST TAKES SO MUCH CONCENTRATION.
I MEANT WITH THE MATERIALITY SPELL. IF WE CAN'T FIND SOMETHING ETHICAL THAT WORKS...
...IF ALEX HAS TO PLAY YOU ON CAMERA--
IT'S A LOT TO PROCESS, AS MY THERAPIST USED TO SAY.
HMM. I RESENT AN ACTOR BEING OUR ROUTE TO MAKING A LIVING I DON'T GET TO FULLY LIVE...
HYDRANGEA TENNIS CLUB MEMBERS ONLY
...I DON'T LIKE NEEDING HIM IN ORDER TO PURSUE OUR WORK...
...AND I HATE THAT HE LOOKS THAT GOOD IN MY CLOTHES.
DOES HE LOOK BETTER THAN ME IN THEM? BE HONEST.
HWEN, NO ONE LOOKS BETTER TO ME THAN YOU. IN OR OUT OF CLOTHES.
SPEAKING OF WHICH...

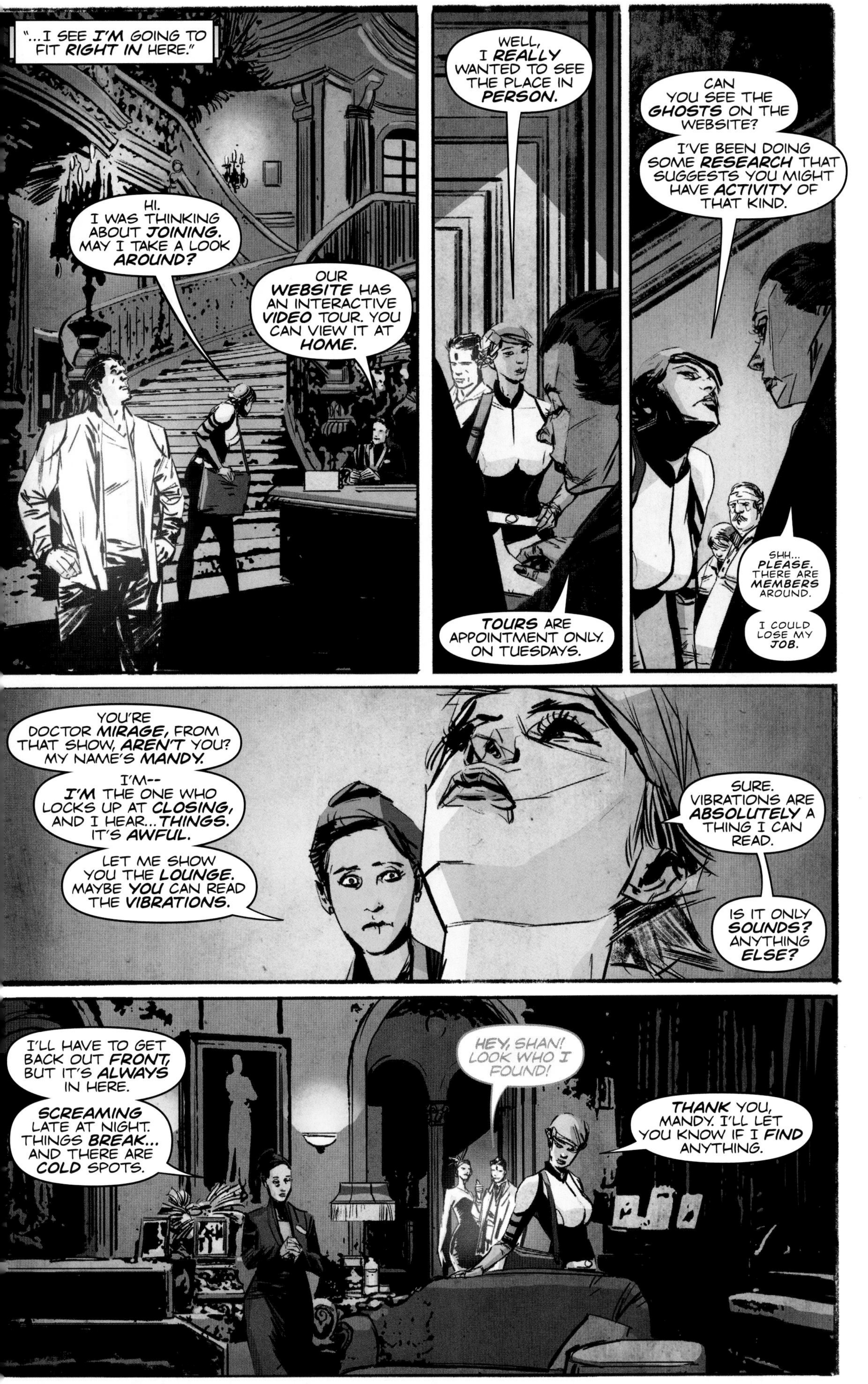

"...I SEE I'M GOING TO FIT RIGHT IN HERE."
HI. I WAS THINKING ABOUT JOINING. MAY I TAKE A LOOK AROUND?
OUR WEBSITE HAS AN INTERACTIVE VIDEO TOUR. YOU CAN VIEW IT AT HOME.
WELL, I REALLY WANTED TO SEE THE PLACE IN PERSON.
TOURS ARE APPOINTMENT ONLY. ON TUESDAYS.
CAN YOU SEE THE GHOSTS ON THE WEBSITE?
I'VE BEEN DOING SOME RESEARCH THAT SUGGESTS YOU MIGHT HAVE ACTIVITY OF THAT KIND.
SHH... PLEASE. THERE ARE MEMBERS AROUND.
I COULD LOSE MY JOB.
YOU'RE DOCTOR MIRAGE, FROM THAT SHOW, AREN'T YOU? MY NAME'S MANDY.
I'M-- I'M THE ONE WHO LOCKS UP AT CLOSING, AND I HEAR...THINGS. IT'S AWFUL.
LET ME SHOW YOU THE LOUNGE. MAYBE YOU CAN READ THE VIBRATIONS.
SURE. VIBRATIONS ARE ABSOLUTELY A THING I CAN READ.
IS IT ONLY SOUNDS? ANYTHING ELSE?
I'LL HAVE TO GET BACK OUT FRONT, BUT IT'S ALWAYS IN HERE.
SCREAMING LATE AT NIGHT. THINGS BREAK... AND THERE ARE COLD SPOTS.
HEY, SHAN! LOOK WHO I FOUND!
THANK YOU, MANDY. I'LL LET YOU KNOW IF I FIND ANYTHING.

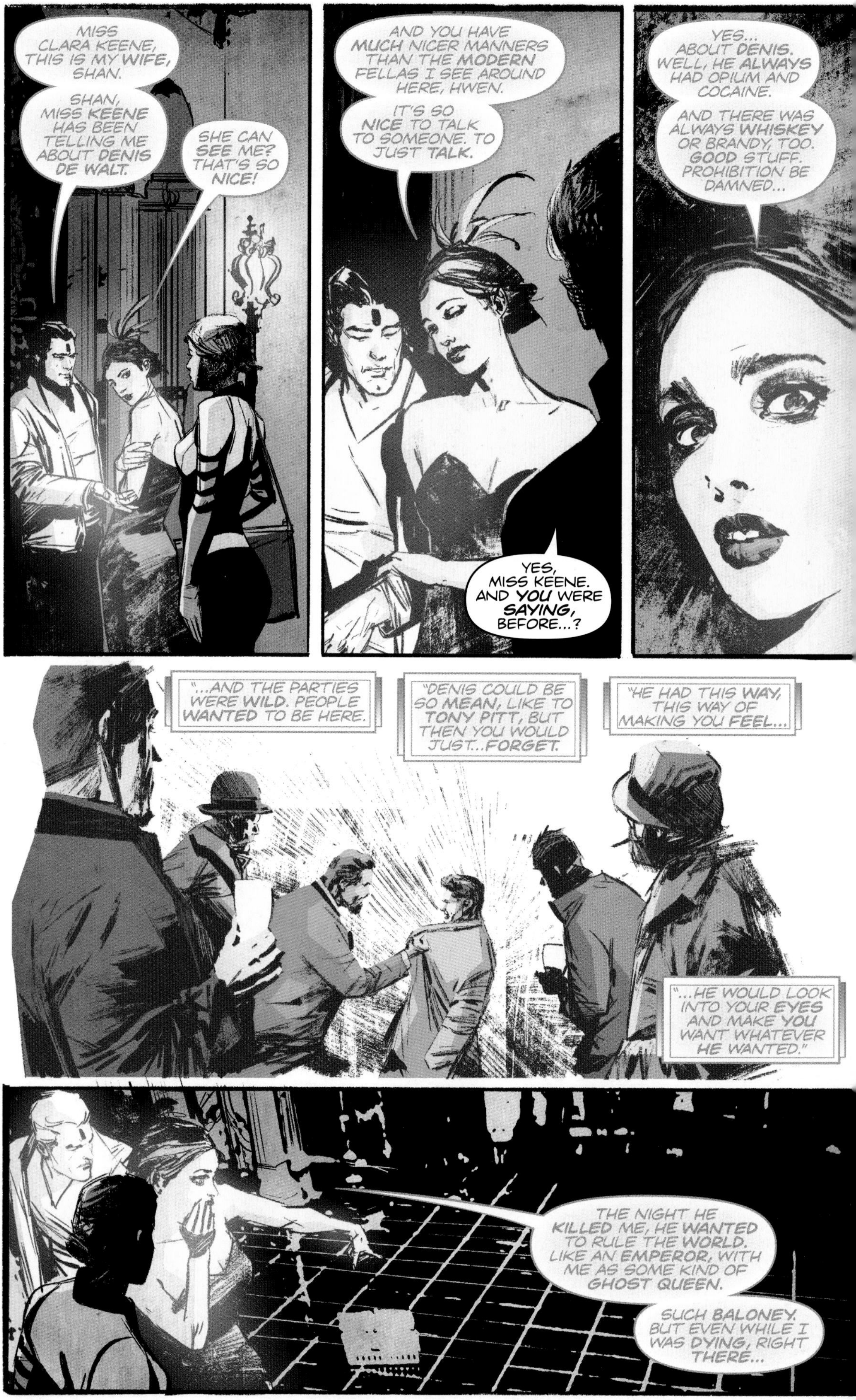
MISS CLARA KEENE, THIS IS MY WIFE, SHAN.
SHAN, MISS KEENE HAS BEEN TELLING ME ABOUT DENIS DE WALT.
SHE CAN SEE ME? THAT'S SO NICE!
AND YOU HAVE MUCH NICER MANNERS THAN THE MODERN FELLAS I SEE AROUND HERE, HWEN.
IT'S SO NICE TO TALK TO SOMEONE. TO JUST TALK.
YES, MISS KEENE. AND YOU WERE SAYING, BEFORE...?
YES... ABOUT DENIS. WELL, HE ALWAYS HAD OPIUM AND COCAINE.
AND THERE WAS ALWAYS WHISKEY OR BRANDY, TOO. GOOD STUFF. PROHIBITION BE DAMNED...
"...AND THE PARTIES WERE WILD. PEOPLE WANTED TO BE HERE.
"DENIS COULD BE SO MEAN, LIKE TO TONY PITT, BUT THEN YOU WOULD JUST...FORGET.
"HE HAD THIS WAY, THIS WAY OF MAKING YOU FEEL...
"...HE WOULD LOOK INTO YOUR EYES AND MAKE YOU WANT WHATEVER HE WANTED."
THE NIGHT HE KILLED ME, HE WANTED TO RULE THE WORLD. LIKE AN EMPEROR, WITH ME AS SOME KIND OF GHOST QUEEN.
SUCH BALONEY. BUT EVEN WHILE I WAS DYING, RIGHT THERE...

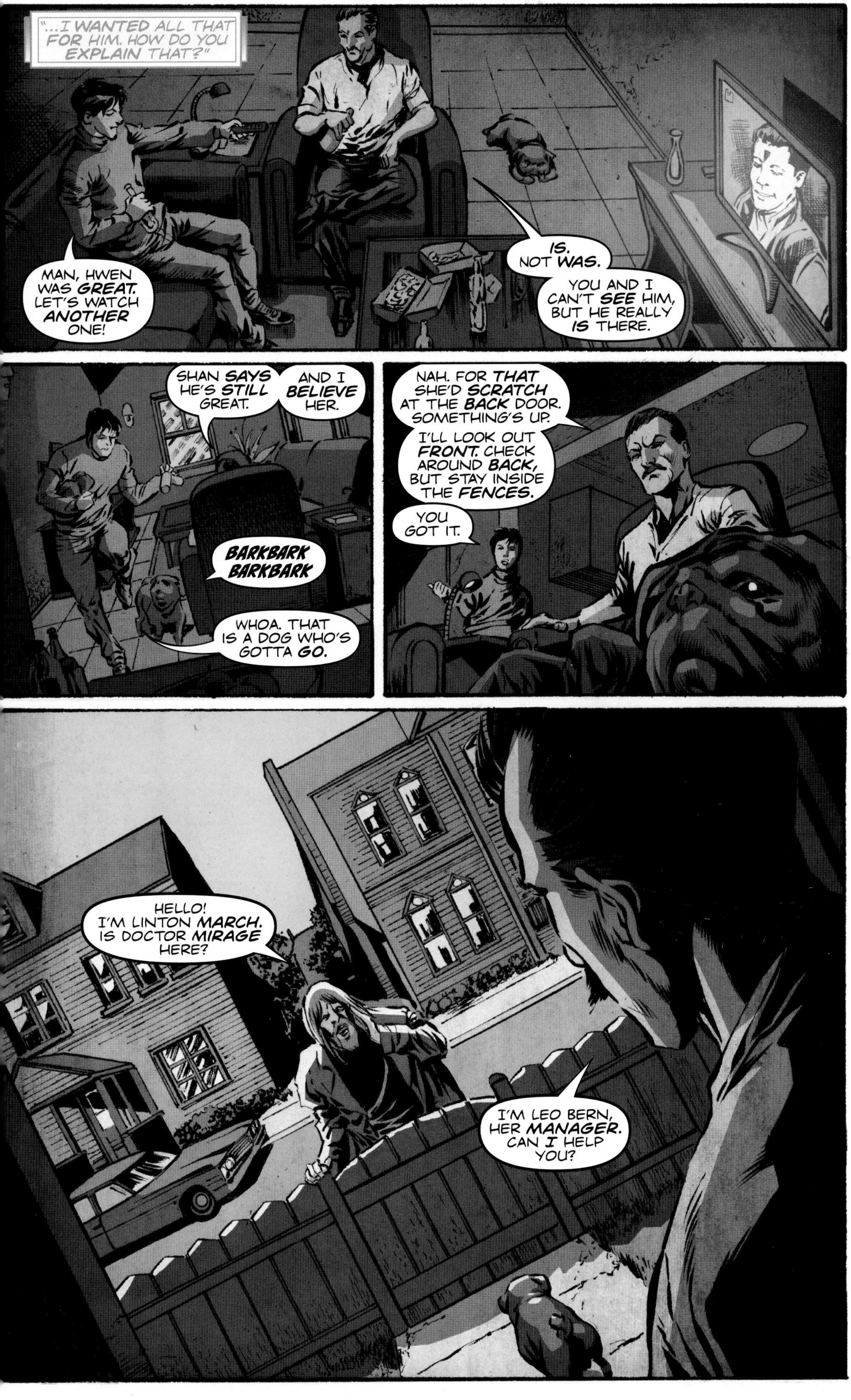
"...I WANTED ALL THAT FOR HIM. HOW DO YOU EXPLAIN THAT?"
MAN, HWEN WAS GREAT. LET'S WATCH ANOTHER ONE!
IS. NOT WAS.
YOU AND I CAN'T SEE HIM, BUT HE REALLY IS THERE.
SHAN SAYS HE'S STILL GREAT.
AND I BELIEVE HER.
BARKBARK BARKBARK
WHOA. THAT IS A DOG WHO'S GOTTA GO.
NAH. FOR THAT SHE'D SCRATCH AT THE BACK DOOR. SOMETHING'S UP.
I'LL LOOK OUT FRONT. CHECK AROUND BACK, BUT STAY INSIDE THE FENCES.
YOU GOT IT.
HELLO! I'M LINTON MARCH. IS DOCTOR MIRAGE HERE?
I'M LEO BERN, HER MANAGER. CAN I HELP YOU?

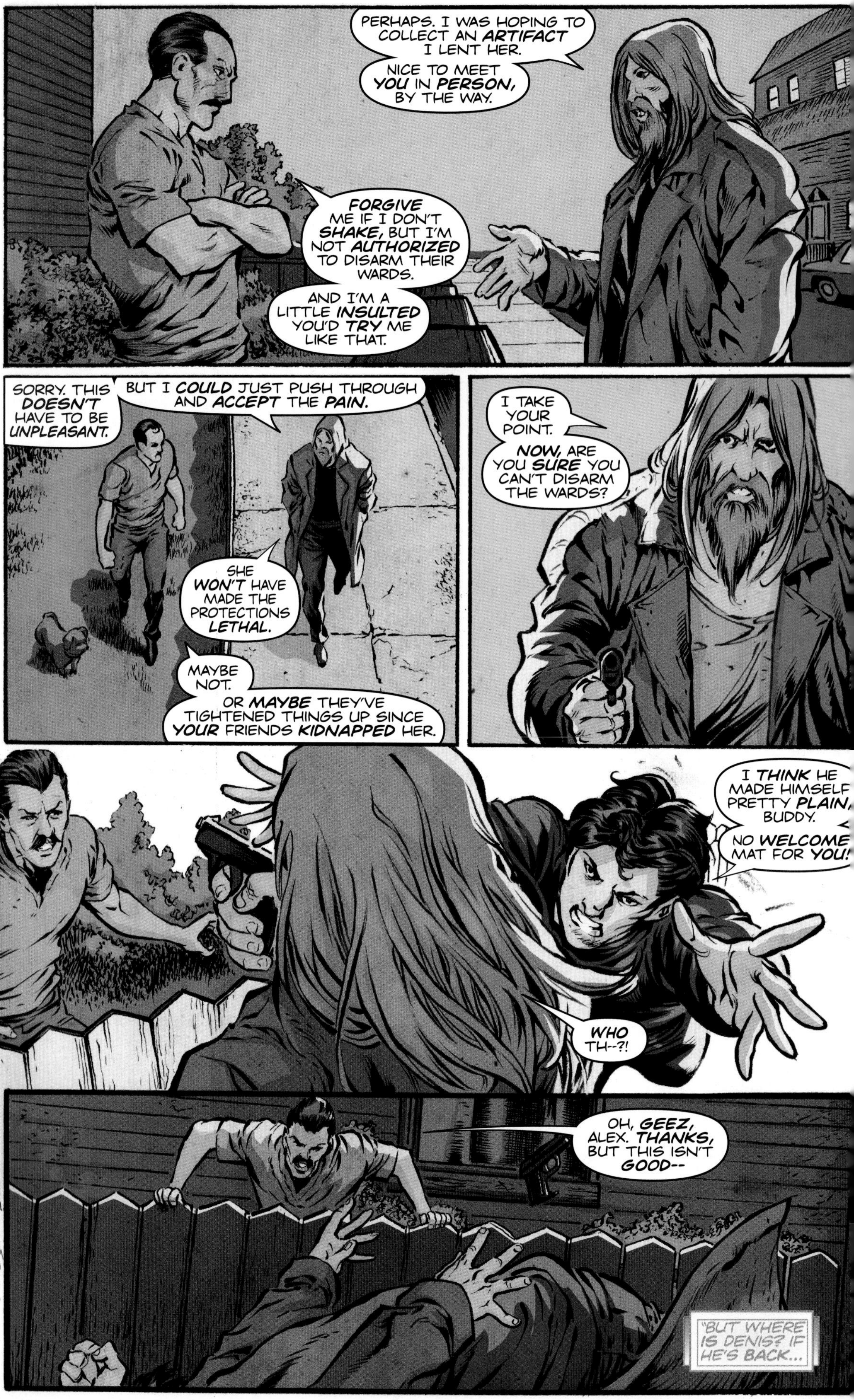
PERHAPS. I WAS HOPING TO COLLECT AN ARTIFACT I LENT HER.
NICE TO MEET YOU IN PERSON, BY THE WAY.
FORGIVE ME IF I DON'T SHAKE, BUT I'M NOT AUTHORIZED TO DISARM THEIR WARDS.
AND I'M A LITTLE INSULTED YOU'D TRY ME LIKE THAT.
SORRY. THIS DOESN'T HAVE TO BE UNPLEASANT.
BUT I COULD JUST PUSH THROUGH AND ACCEPT THE PAIN.
SHE WON'T HAVE MADE THE PROTECTIONS LETHAL.
MAYBE NOT.
OR MAYBE THEY'VE TIGHTENED THINGS UP SINCE YOUR FRIENDS KIDNAPPED HER.
I TAKE YOUR POINT.
NOW, ARE YOU SURE YOU CAN'T DISARM THE WARDS?
I THINK HE MADE HIMSELF PRETTY PLAIN, BUDDY.
NO WELCOME MAT FOR YOU!
WHO TH--?!
OH, GEEZ, ALEX. THANKS, BUT THIS ISN'T GOOD--
"BUT WHERE IS DENIS? IF HE'S BACK...

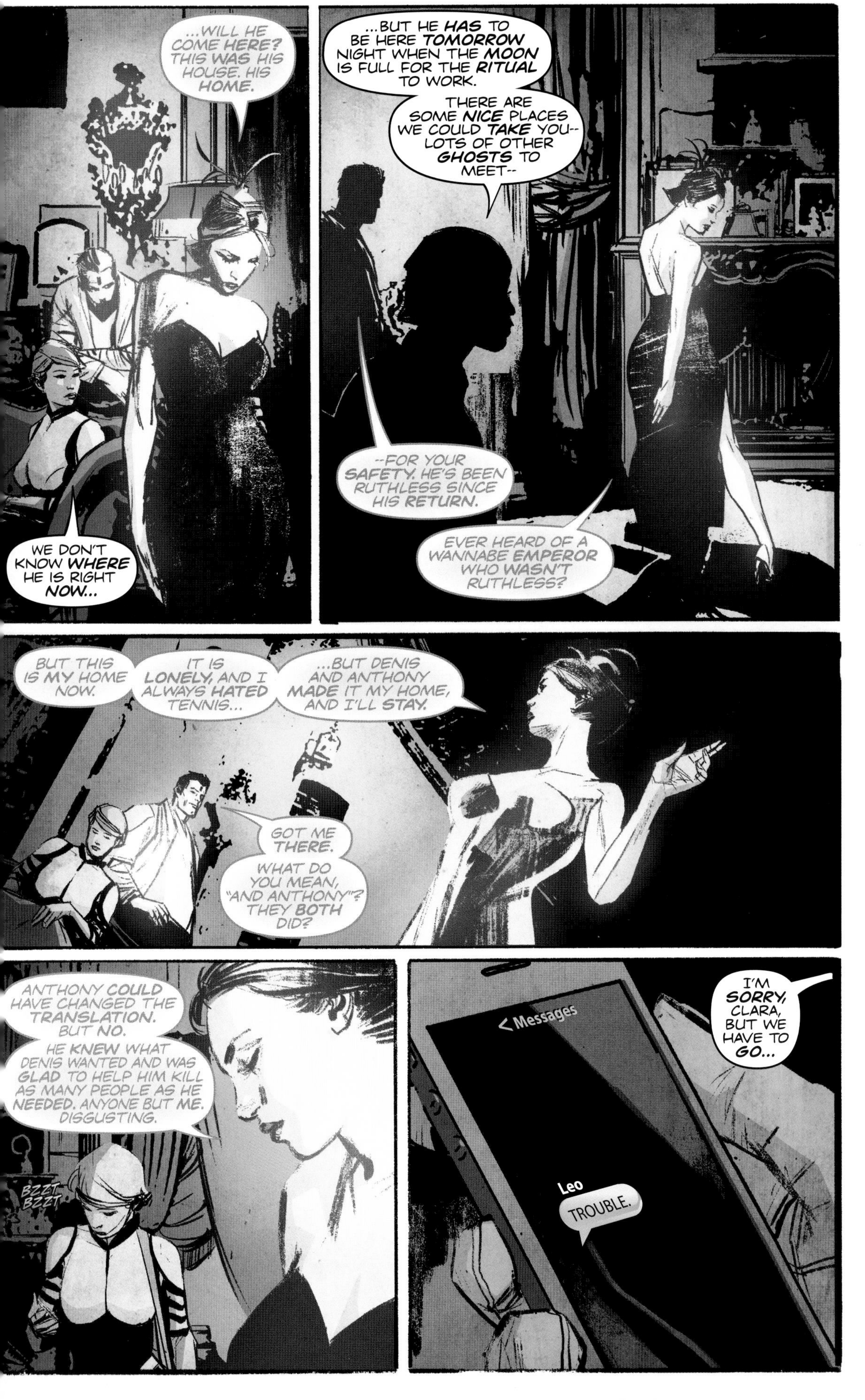
...WILL HE COME HERE? THIS WAS HIS HOUSE. HIS HOME.
WE DON'T KNOW WHERE HE IS RIGHT NOW...
...BUT HE HAS TO BE HERE TOMORROW NIGHT WHEN THE MOON IS FULL FOR THE RITUAL TO WORK.
THERE ARE SOME NICE PLACES WE COULD TAKE YOU-- LOTS OF OTHER GHOSTS TO MEET--
--FOR YOUR SAFETY. HE'S BEEN RUTHLESS SINCE HIS RETURN.
EVER HEARD OF A WANNABE EMPEROR WHO WASN'T RUTHLESS?
BUT THIS IS MY HOME NOW.
IT IS LONELY, AND I ALWAYS HATED TENNIS...
...BUT DENIS AND ANTHONY MADE IT MY HOME, AND I'LL STAY.
GOT ME THERE.
WHAT DO YOU MEAN, "AND ANTHONY"? THEY BOTH DID?
ANTHONY COULD HAVE CHANGED THE TRANSLATION. BUT NO.
HE KNEW WHAT DENIS WANTED AND WAS GLAD TO HELP HIM KILL AS MANY PEOPLE AS HE NEEDED. ANYONE BUT ME. DISGUSTING.
BZZT BZZT
< Messages
Leo
TROUBLE.
I'M SORRY, CLARA, BUT WE HAVE TO GO...

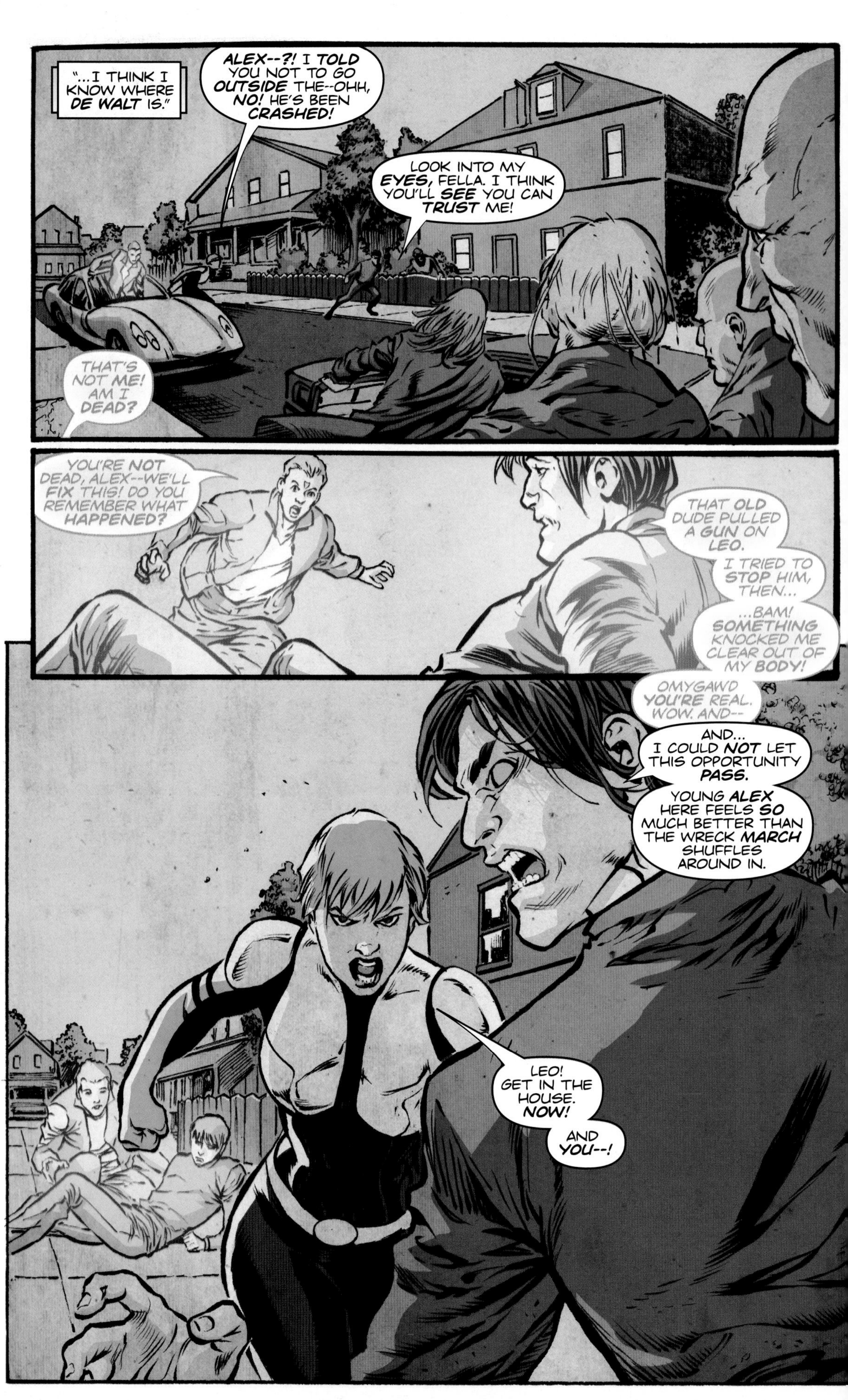
"...I THINK I KNOW WHERE DE WALT IS."
ALEX--?! I TOLD YOU NOT TO GO OUTSIDE THE--OHH, NO! HE'S BEEN CRASHED!
LOOK INTO MY EYES, FELLA. I THINK YOU'LL SEE YOU CAN TRUST ME!
THAT'S NOT ME! AM I DEAD?
YOU'RE NOT DEAD, ALEX--WE'LL FIX THIS! DO YOU REMEMBER WHAT HAPPENED?
THAT OLD DUDE PULLED A GUN ON LEO.
I TRIED TO STOP HIM, THEN...
...BAM! SOMETHING KNOCKED ME CLEAR OUT OF MY BODY!
OMYGAWD YOU'RE REAL. WOW. AND--
AND... I COULD NOT LET THIS OPPORTUNITY PASS.
YOUNG ALEX HERE FEELS SO MUCH BETTER THAN THE WRECK MARCH SHUFFLES AROUND IN.
LEO! GET IN THE HOUSE. NOW!
AND YOU--!

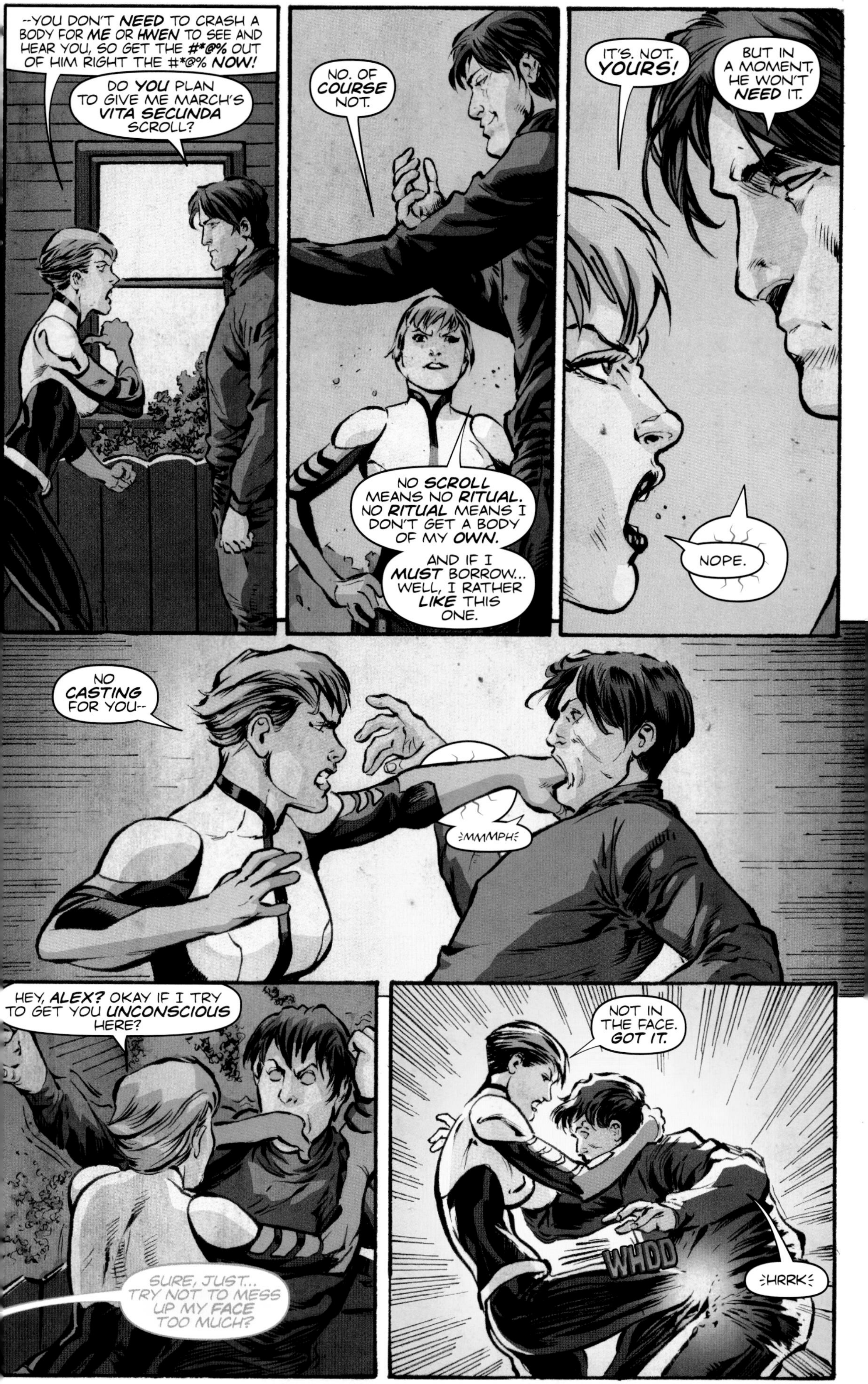
--YOU DON'T NEED TO CRASH A BODY FOR ME OR HWEN TO SEE AND HEAR YOU, SO GET THE #*@% OUT OF HIM RIGHT THE #*@% NOW!
DO YOU PLAN TO GIVE ME MARCH'S VITA SECUNDA SCROLL?
NO. OF COURSE NOT.
NO SCROLL MEANS NO RITUAL. NO RITUAL MEANS I DON'T GET A BODY OF MY OWN.
AND IF I MUST BORROW... WELL, I RATHER LIKE THIS ONE.
IT'S. NOT. YOURS!
BUT IN A MOMENT, HE WON'T NEED IT.
NOPE.
NO CASTING FOR YOU--
MMMPH
HEY, ALEX? OKAY IF I TRY TO GET YOU UNCONSCIOUS HERE?
SURE, JUST... TRY NOT TO MESS UP MY FACE TOO MUCH?
NOT IN THE FACE. GOT IT.
WHDD
HRRK

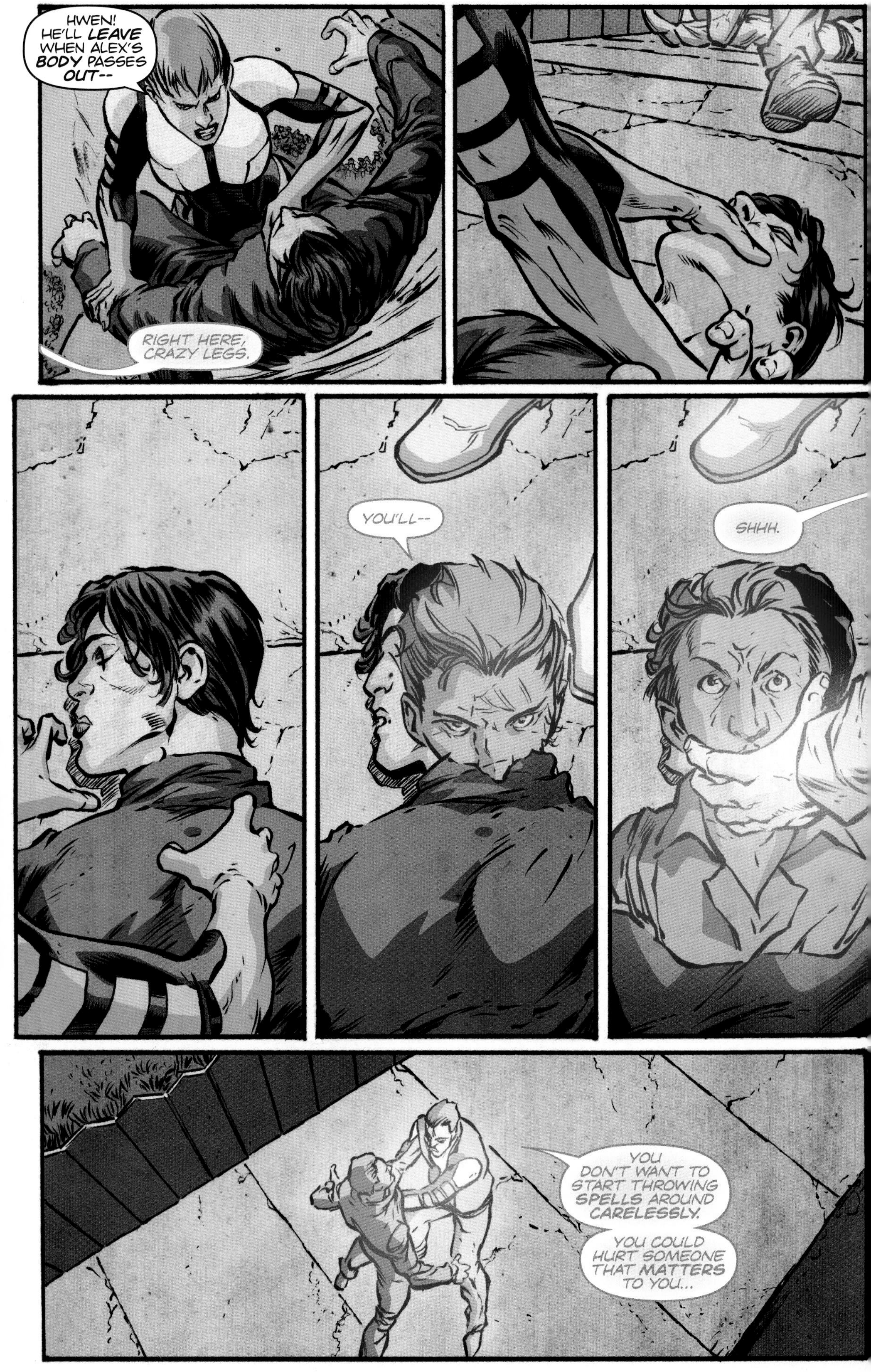
HWEN! HE'LL LEAVE WHEN ALEX'S BODY PASSES OUT--
RIGHT HERE, CRAZY LEGS.
YOU'LL--
SHHH.
YOU DON'T WANT TO START THROWING SPELLS AROUND CARELESSLY.
YOU COULD HURT SOMEONE THAT MATTERS TO YOU...

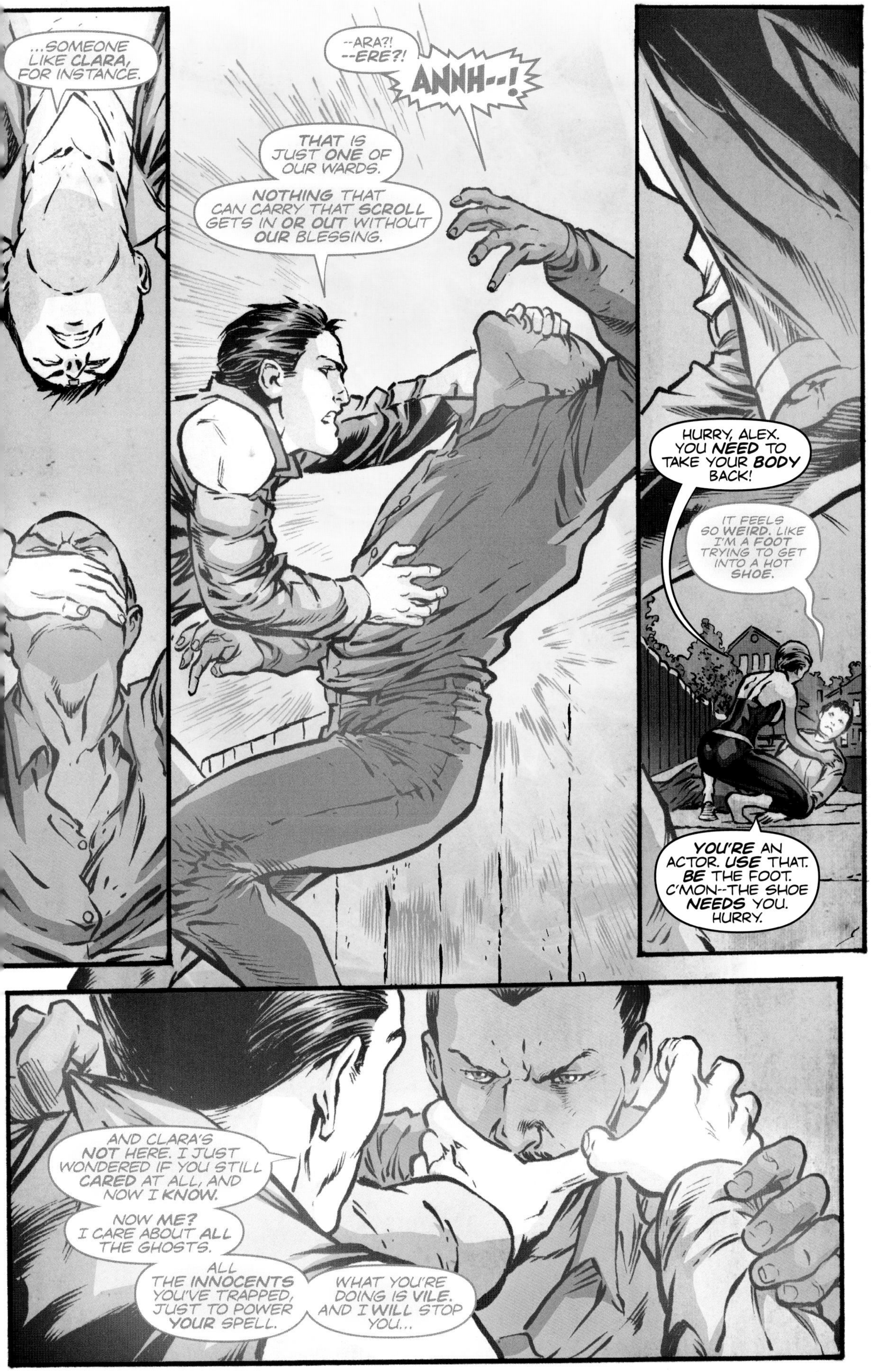
...SOMEONE LIKE CLARA, FOR INSTANCE.
--ARA?! --ERE?!
ANNH--!
THAT IS JUST ONE OF OUR WARDS.
NOTHING THAT CAN CARRY THAT SCROLL GETS IN OR OUT WITHOUT OUR BLESSING.
HURRY, ALEX. YOU NEED TO TAKE YOUR BODY BACK!
IT FEELS SO WEIRD. LIKE I'M A FOOT TRYING TO GET INTO A HOT SHOE.
YOU'RE AN ACTOR. USE THAT. BE THE FOOT. C'MON--THE SHOE NEEDS YOU. HURRY.
AND CLARA'S NOT HERE. I JUST WONDERED IF YOU STILL CARED AT ALL, AND NOW I KNOW.
NOW ME? I CARE ABOUT ALL THE GHOSTS.
ALL THE INNOCENTS YOU'VE TRAPPED, JUST TO POWER YOUR SPELL.
WHAT YOU'RE DOING IS VILE. AND I WILL STOP YOU...

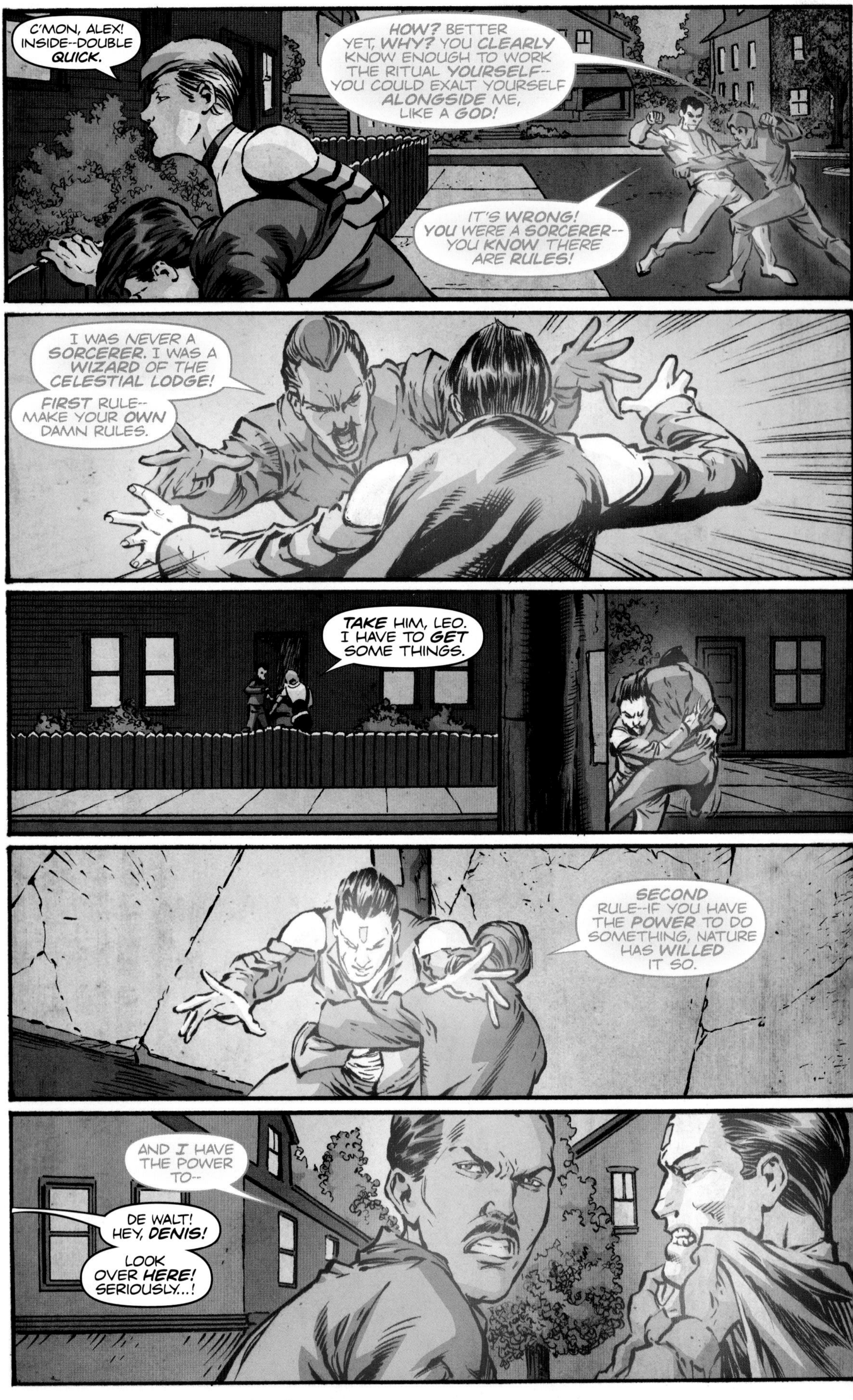
C'MON, ALEX! INSIDE--DOUBLE QUICK.
HOW? BETTER YET, WHY? YOU CLEARLY KNOW ENOUGH TO WORK THE RITUAL YOURSELF-- YOU COULD EXALT YOURSELF ALONGSIDE ME, LIKE A GOD!
IT'S WRONG! YOU WERE A SORCERER-- YOU KNOW THERE ARE RULES!
I WAS NEVER A SORCERER. I WAS A WIZARD OF THE CELESTIAL LODGE!
FIRST RULE-- MAKE YOUR OWN DAMN RULES.
TAKE HIM, LEO. I HAVE TO GET SOME THINGS.
SECOND RULE--IF YOU HAVE THE POWER TO DO SOMETHING, NATURE HAS WILLED IT SO.
AND I HAVE THE POWER TO--
DE WALT! HEY, DENIS!
LOOK OVER HERE! SERIOUSLY...!

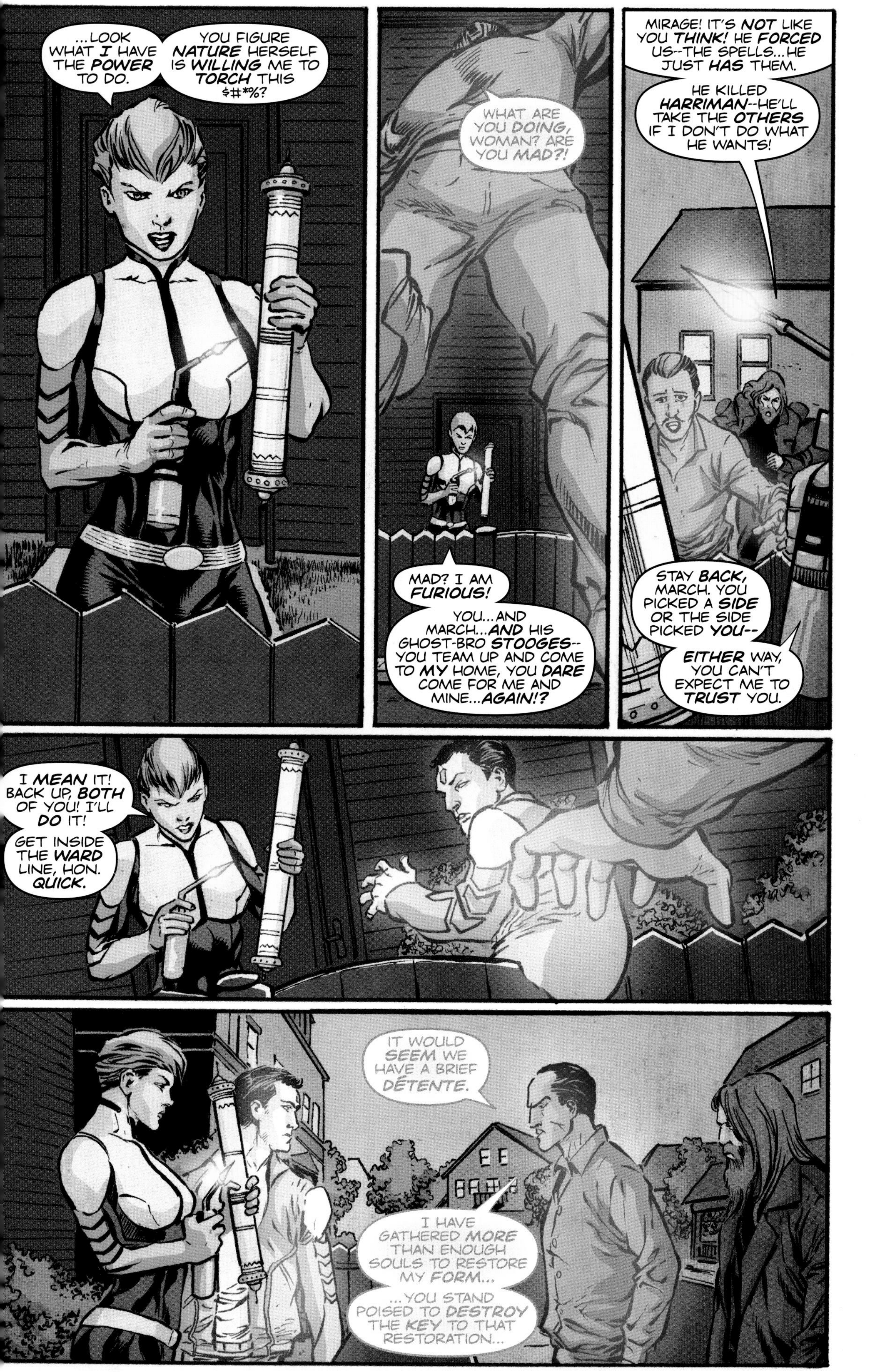
...LOOK WHAT I HAVE THE POWER TO DO.
YOU FIGURE NATURE HERSELF IS WILLING ME TO TORCH THIS $#*%?
WHAT ARE YOU DOING, WOMAN? ARE YOU MAD?!
MAD? I AM FURIOUS!
YOU...AND MARCH...AND HIS GHOST-BRO STOOGES--YOU TEAM UP AND COME TO MY HOME, YOU DARE COME FOR ME AND MINE...AGAIN!?
MIRAGE! IT'S NOT LIKE YOU THINK! HE FORCED US--THE SPELLS...HE JUST HAS THEM.
HE KILLED HARRIMAN--HE'LL TAKE THE OTHERS IF I DON'T DO WHAT HE WANTS!
STAY BACK, MARCH. YOU PICKED A SIDE OR THE SIDE PICKED YOU--
EITHER WAY, YOU CAN'T EXPECT ME TO TRUST YOU.
I MEAN IT! BACK UP, BOTH OF YOU! I'LL DO IT!
GET INSIDE THE WARD LINE, HON. QUICK.
IT WOULD SEEM WE HAVE A BRIEF DÉTENTE.
I HAVE GATHERED MORE THAN ENOUGH SOULS TO RESTORE MY FORM...
...YOU STAND POISED TO DESTROY THE KEY TO THAT RESTORATION...

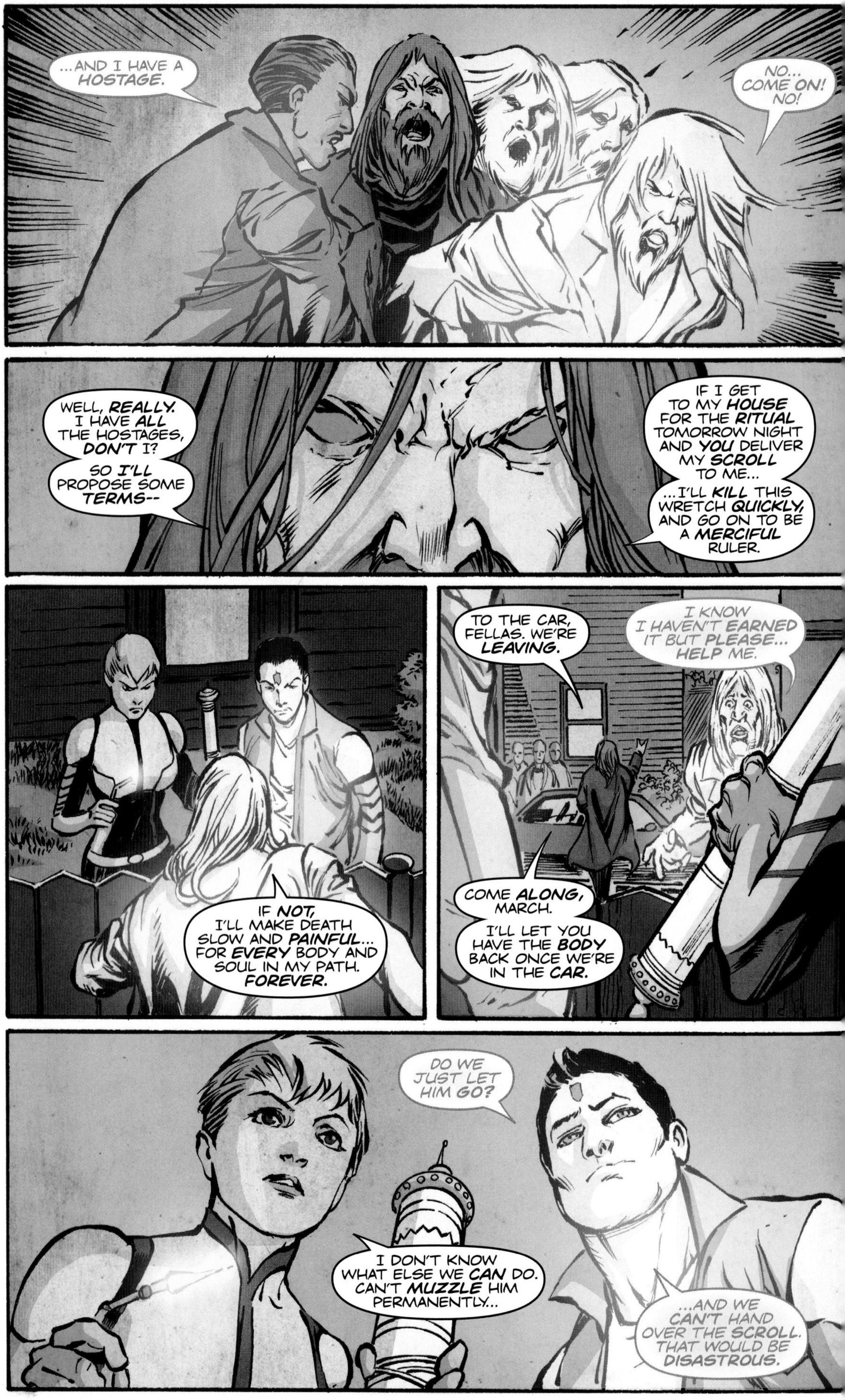
...AND I HAVE A HOSTAGE.
NO... COME ON! NO!
WELL, REALLY. I HAVE ALL THE HOSTAGES, DON'T I?
SO I'LL PROPOSE SOME TERMS--
IF I GET TO MY HOUSE FOR THE RITUAL TOMORROW NIGHT AND YOU DELIVER MY SCROLL TO ME...
...I'LL KILL THIS WRETCH QUICKLY, AND GO ON TO BE A MERCIFUL RULER.
IF NOT, I'LL MAKE DEATH SLOW AND PAINFUL... FOR EVERY BODY AND SOUL IN MY PATH. FOREVER.
TO THE CAR, FELLAS. WE'RE LEAVING.
I KNOW I HAVEN'T EARNED IT BUT PLEASE... HELP ME.
COME ALONG, MARCH.
I'LL LET YOU HAVE THE BODY BACK ONCE WE'RE IN THE CAR.
DO WE JUST LET HIM GO?
I DON'T KNOW WHAT ELSE WE CAN DO. CAN'T MUZZLE HIM PERMANENTLY...
...AND WE CAN'T HAND OVER THE SCROLL. THAT WOULD BE DISASTROUS.

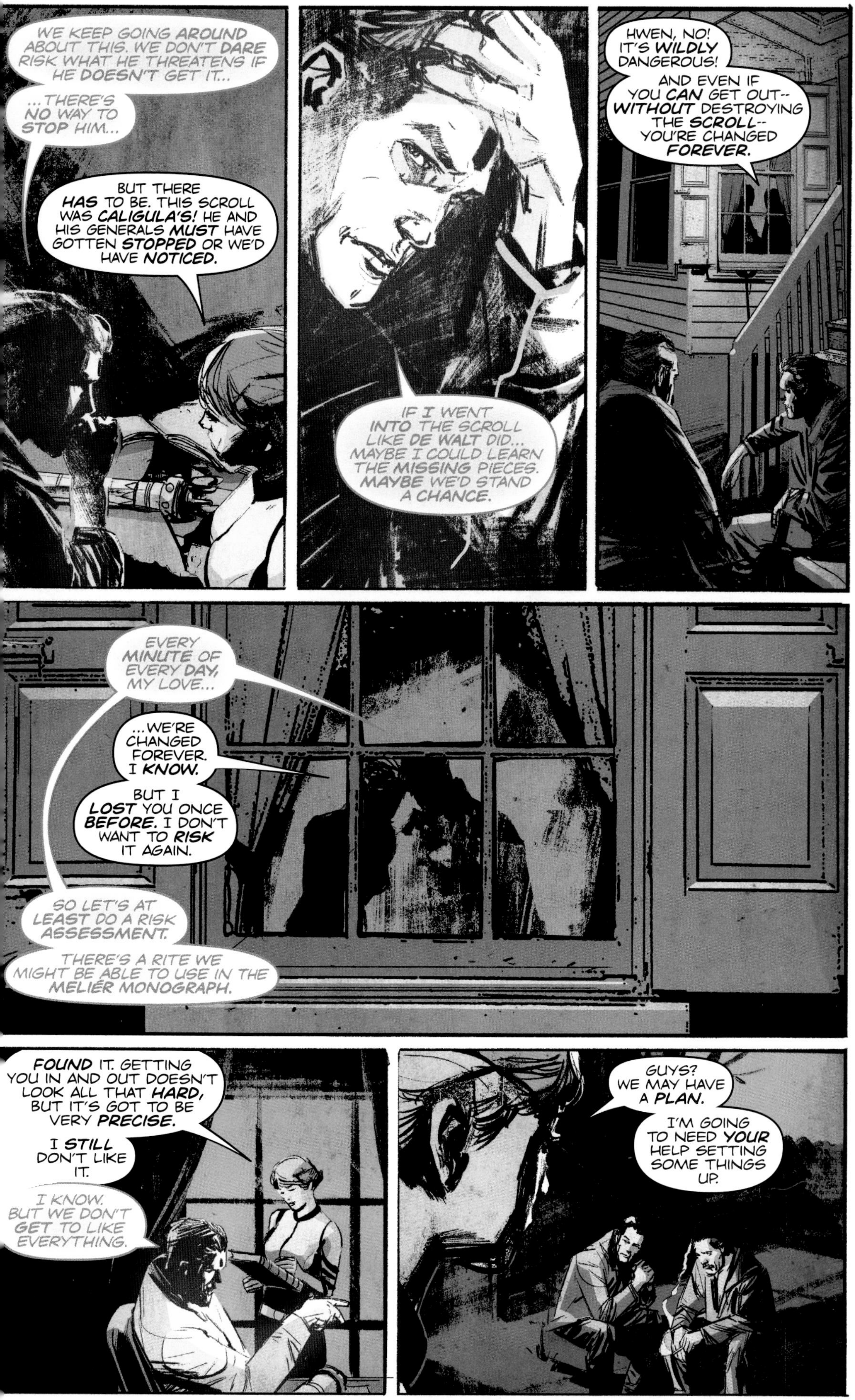
WE KEEP GOING AROUND ABOUT THIS. WE DON'T DARE RISK WHAT HE THREATENS IF HE DOESN'T GET IT...
...THERE'S NO WAY TO STOP HIM...
BUT THERE HAS TO BE. THIS SCROLL WAS CALIGULA'S! HE AND HIS GENERALS MUST HAVE GOTTEN STOPPED OR WE'D HAVE NOTICED.
IF I WENT INTO THE SCROLL LIKE DE WALT DID... MAYBE I COULD LEARN THE MISSING PIECES. MAYBE WE'D STAND A CHANCE.
HWEN, NO! IT'S WILDLY DANGEROUS!
AND EVEN IF YOU CAN GET OUT-- WITHOUT DESTROYING THE SCROLL-- YOU'RE CHANGED FOREVER.
EVERY MINUTE OF EVERY DAY, MY LOVE...
...WE'RE CHANGED FOREVER. I KNOW.
BUT I LOST YOU ONCE BEFORE. I DON'T WANT TO RISK IT AGAIN.
SO LET'S AT LEAST DO A RISK ASSESSMENT.
THERE'S A RITE WE MIGHT BE ABLE TO USE IN THE MELIÉR MONOGRAPH.
FOUND IT. GETTING YOU IN AND OUT DOESN'T LOOK ALL THAT HARD, BUT IT'S GOT TO BE VERY PRECISE.
I STILL DON'T LIKE IT.
I KNOW. BUT WE DON'T GET TO LIKE EVERYTHING.
GUYS? WE MAY HAVE A PLAN.
I'M GOING TO NEED YOUR HELP SETTING SOME THINGS UP.

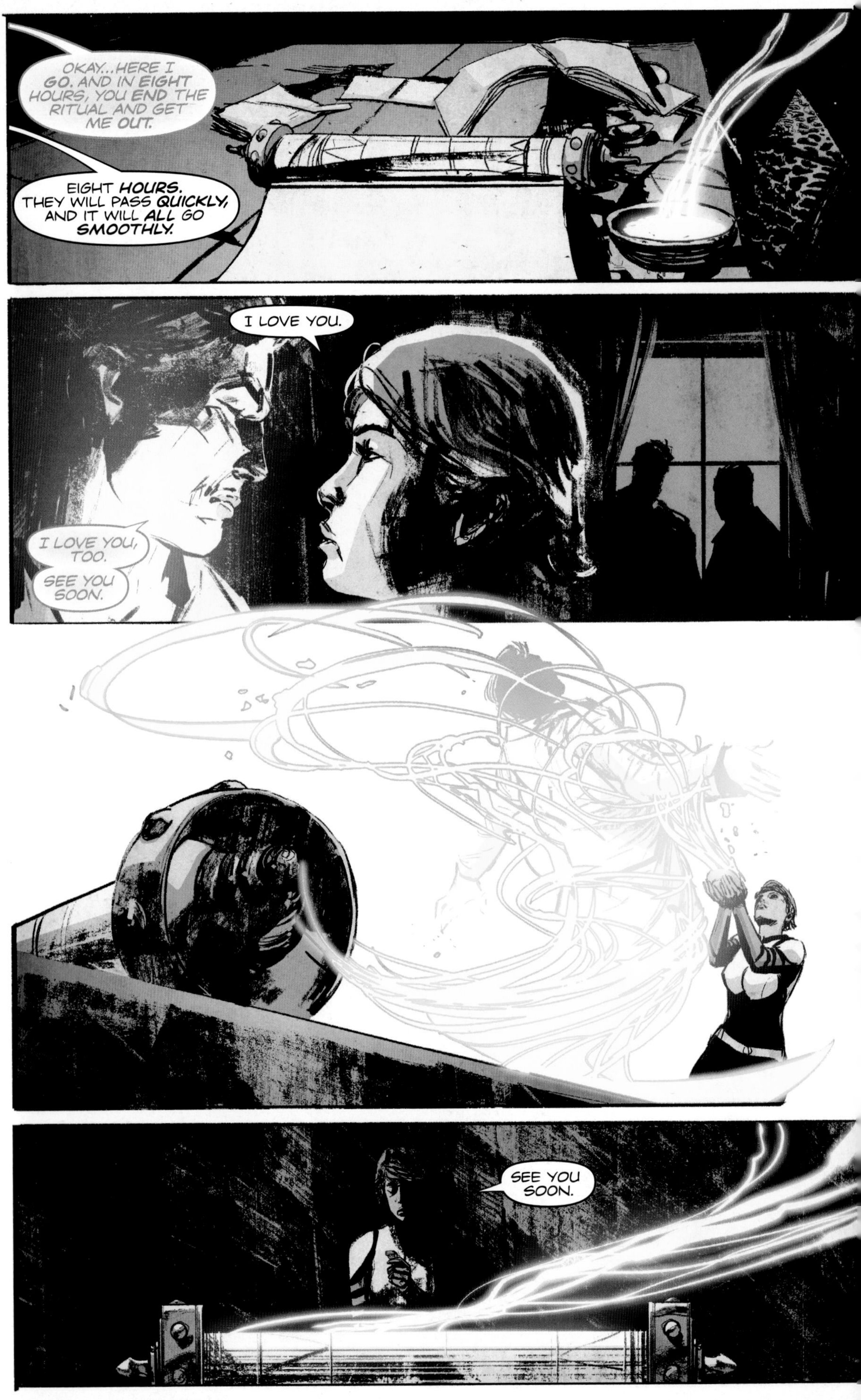
OKAY...HERE I GO. AND IN EIGHT HOURS, YOU END THE RITUAL AND GET ME OUT.
EIGHT HOURS. THEY WILL PASS QUICKLY, AND IT WILL ALL GO SMOOTHLY.
I LOVE YOU.
I LOVE YOU, TOO.
SEE YOU SOON.
SEE YOU SOON.

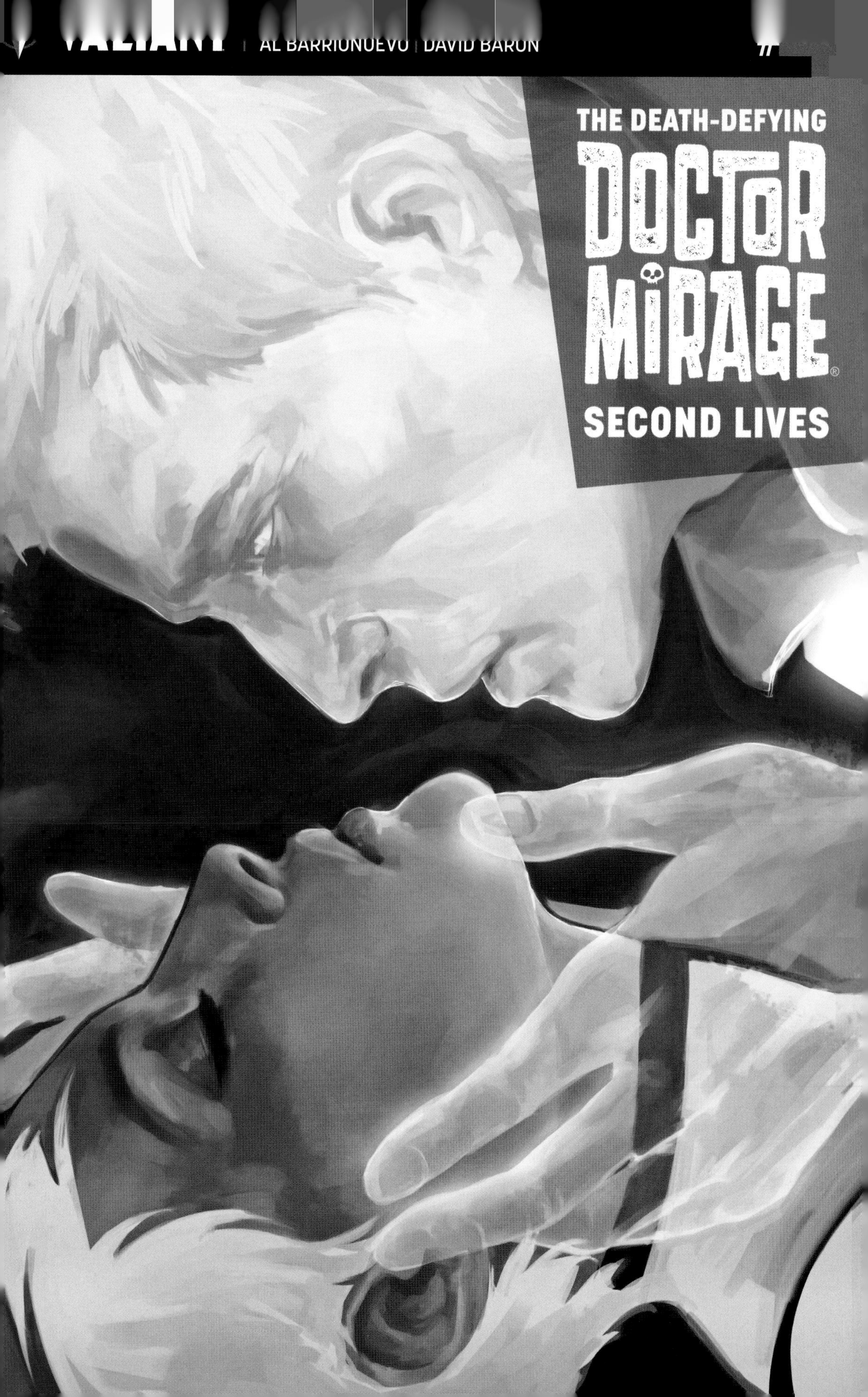
VALIANT
AL BARRIONUEVO | DAVID BARON
THE DEATH-DEFYING
DOCTOR MIRAGE®
SECOND LIVES

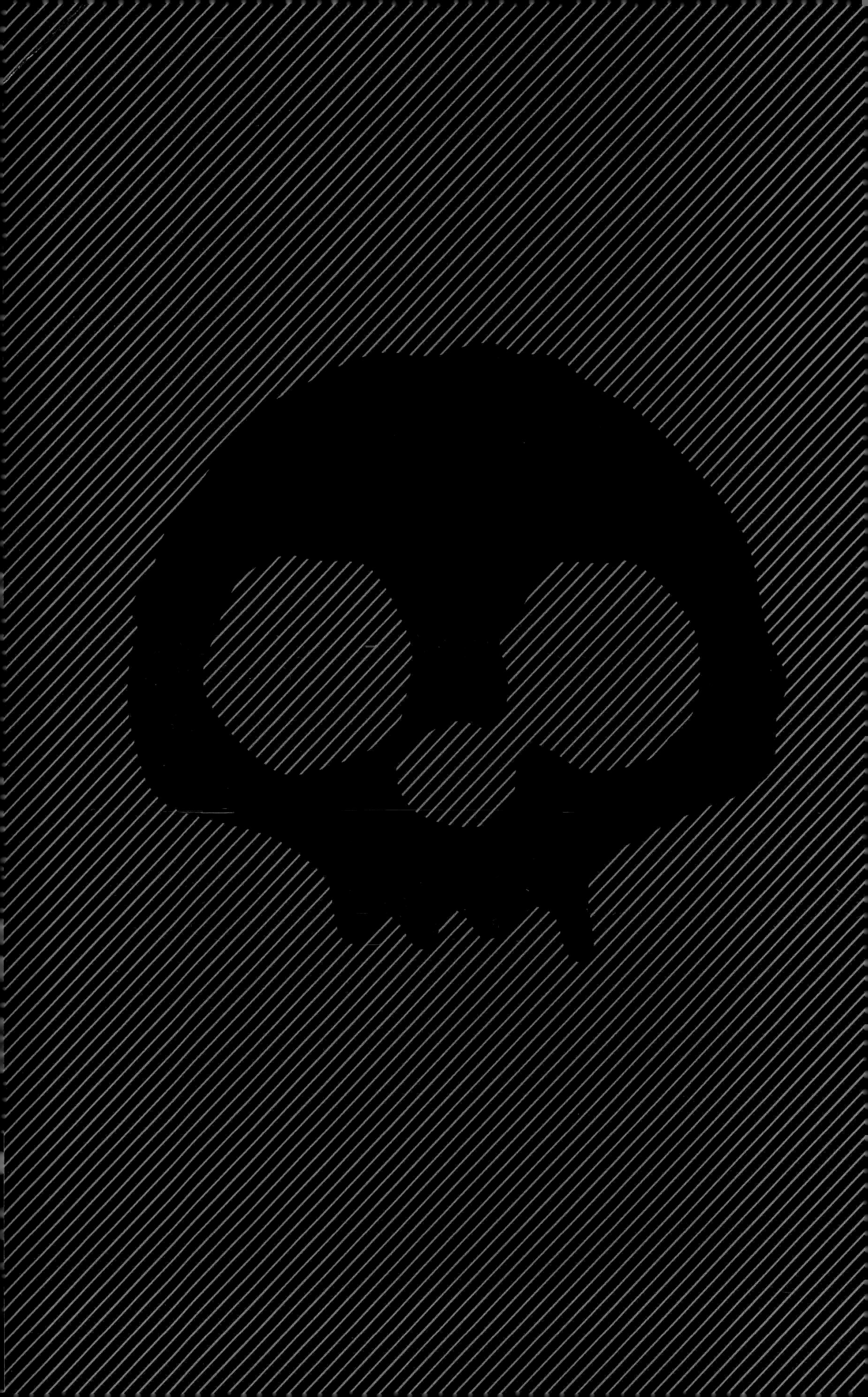

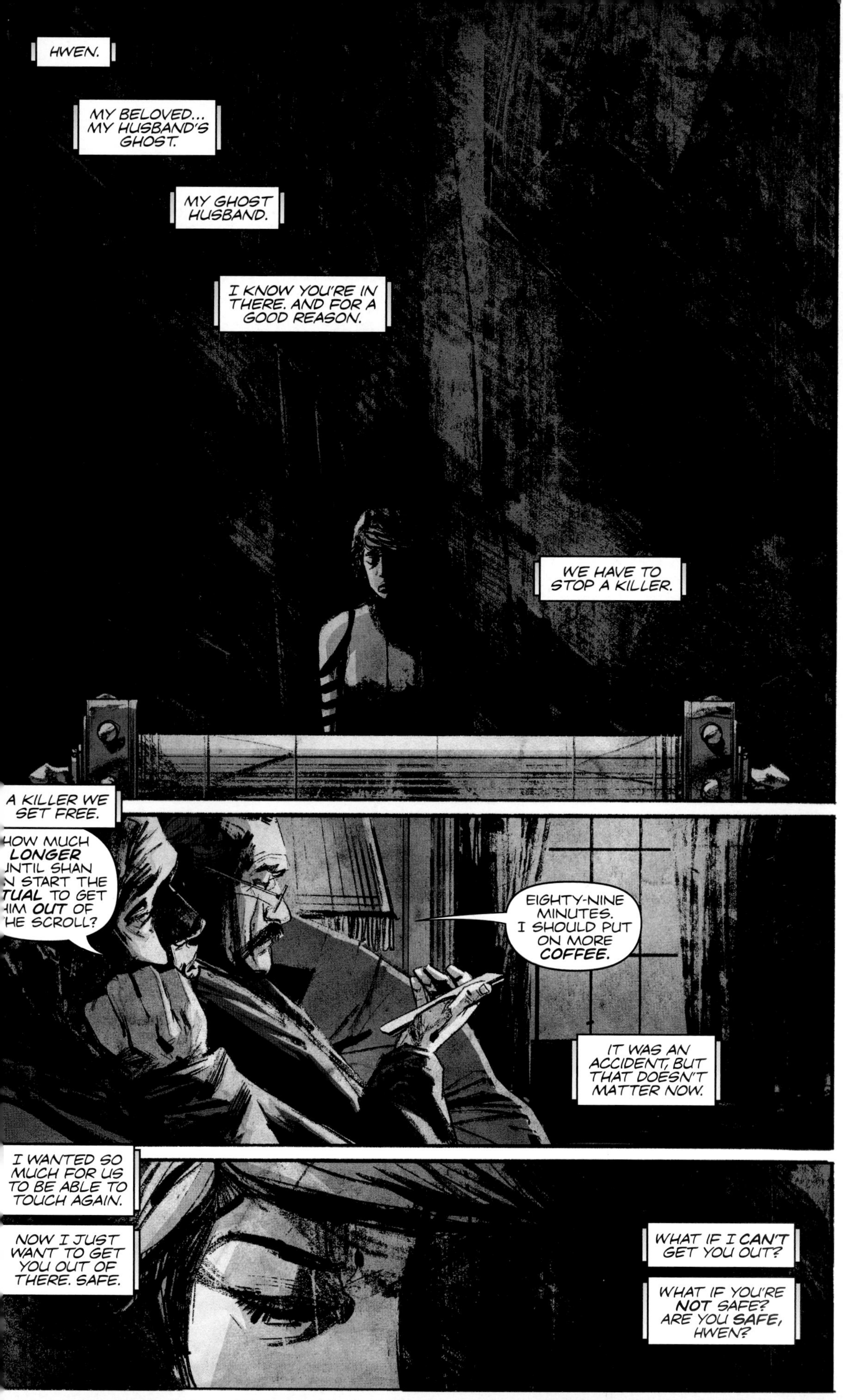
HWEN.
MY BELOVED... MY HUSBAND'S GHOST.
MY GHOST HUSBAND.
I KNOW YOU'RE IN THERE. AND FOR A GOOD REASON.
WE HAVE TO STOP A KILLER.
A KILLER WE SET FREE.
HOW MUCH LONGER UNTIL SHAN CAN START THE RITUAL TO GET HIM OUT OF THE SCROLL?
EIGHTY-NINE MINUTES. I SHOULD PUT ON MORE COFFEE.
IT WAS AN ACCIDENT, BUT THAT DOESN'T MATTER NOW.
I WANTED SO MUCH FOR US TO BE ABLE TO TOUCH AGAIN.
NOW I JUST WANT TO GET YOU OUT OF THERE. SAFE.
WHAT IF I CAN'T GET YOU OUT?
WHAT IF YOU'RE NOT SAFE? ARE YOU SAFE, HWEN?

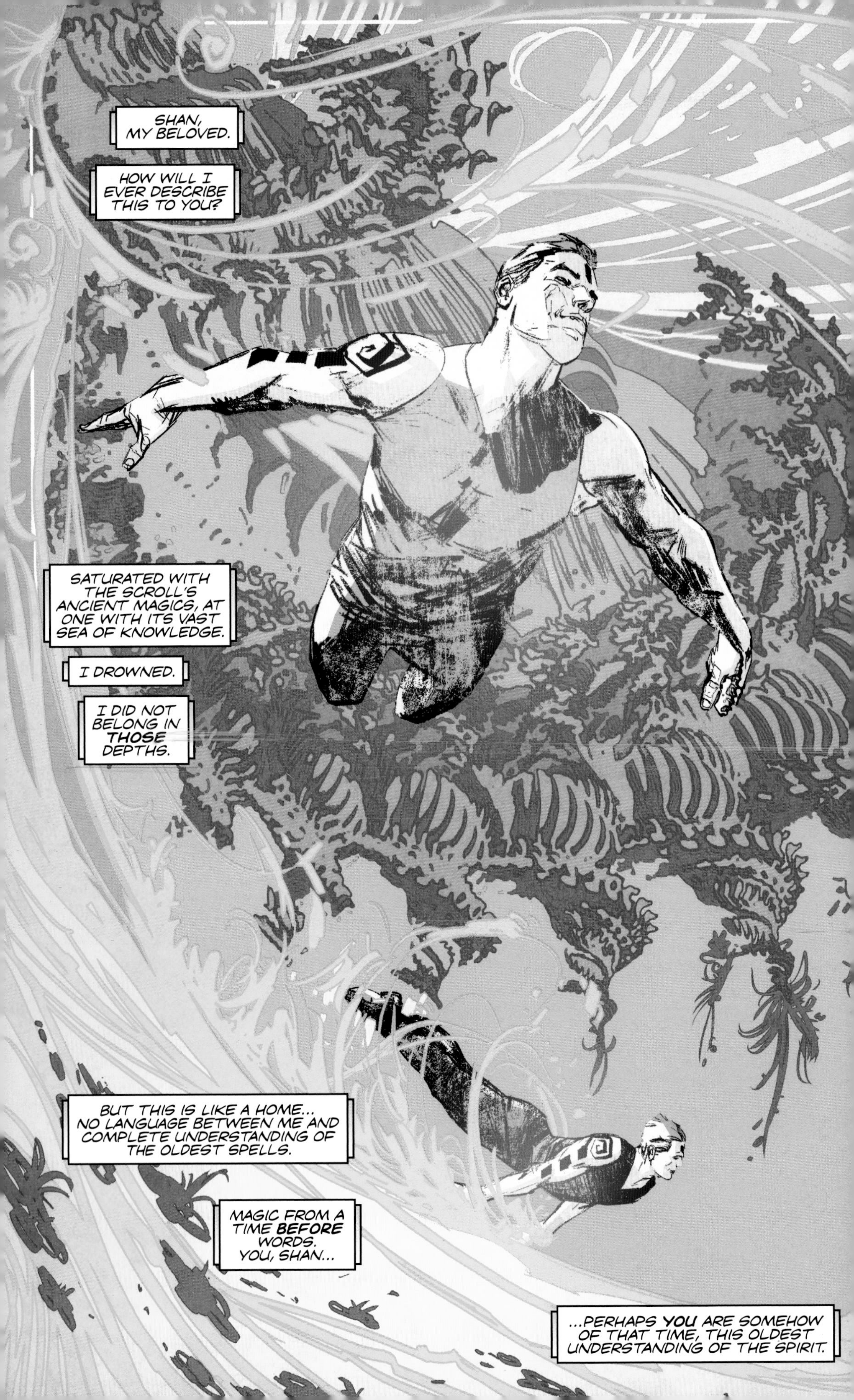
SHAN, MY BELOVED.
HOW WILL I EVER DESCRIBE THIS TO YOU?
SATURATED WITH THE SCROLL'S ANCIENT MAGICS, AT ONE WITH ITS VAST SEA OF KNOWLEDGE.
I DROWNED.
I DID NOT BELONG IN **THOSE** DEPTHS.
BUT THIS IS LIKE A HOME... NO LANGUAGE BETWEEN ME AND COMPLETE UNDERSTANDING OF THE OLDEST SPELLS.
MAGIC FROM A TIME **BEFORE** WORDS. YOU, SHAN...
...PERHAPS **YOU** ARE SOMEHOW OF THAT TIME, THIS OLDEST UNDERSTANDING OF THE SPIRIT.

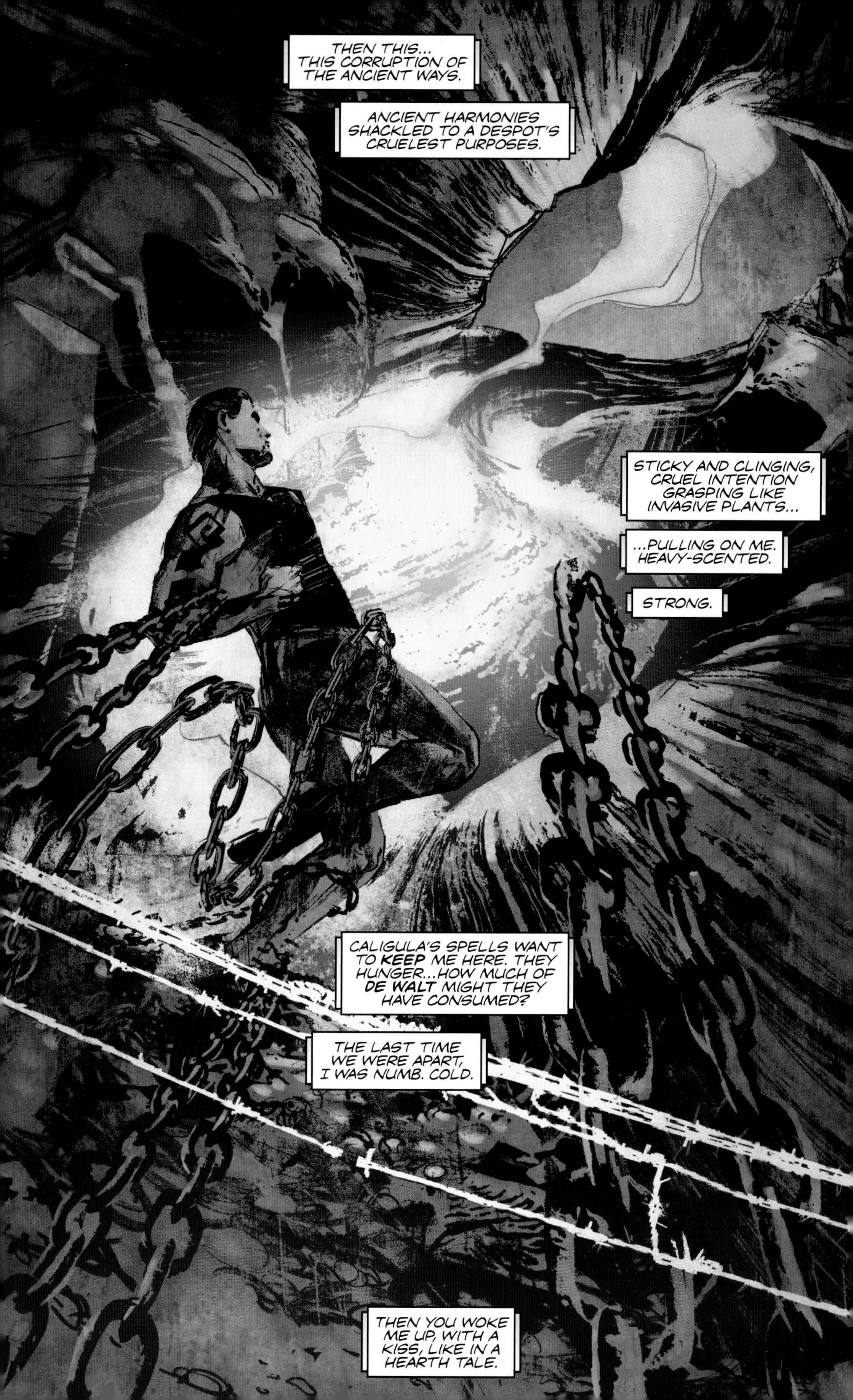
THEN THIS... THIS CORRUPTION OF THE ANCIENT WAYS.
ANCIENT HARMONIES SHACKLED TO A DESPOT'S CRUELEST PURPOSES.
STICKY AND CLINGING, CRUEL INTENTION GRASPING LIKE INVASIVE PLANTS...
...PULLING ON ME. HEAVY-SCENTED.
STRONG.
CALIGULA'S SPELLS WANT TO **KEEP** ME HERE. THEY HUNGER...HOW MUCH OF **DE WALT** MIGHT THEY HAVE CONSUMED?
THE LAST TIME WE WERE APART, I WAS NUMB. COLD.
THEN YOU WOKE ME UP, WITH A KISS, LIKE IN A HEARTH TALE.

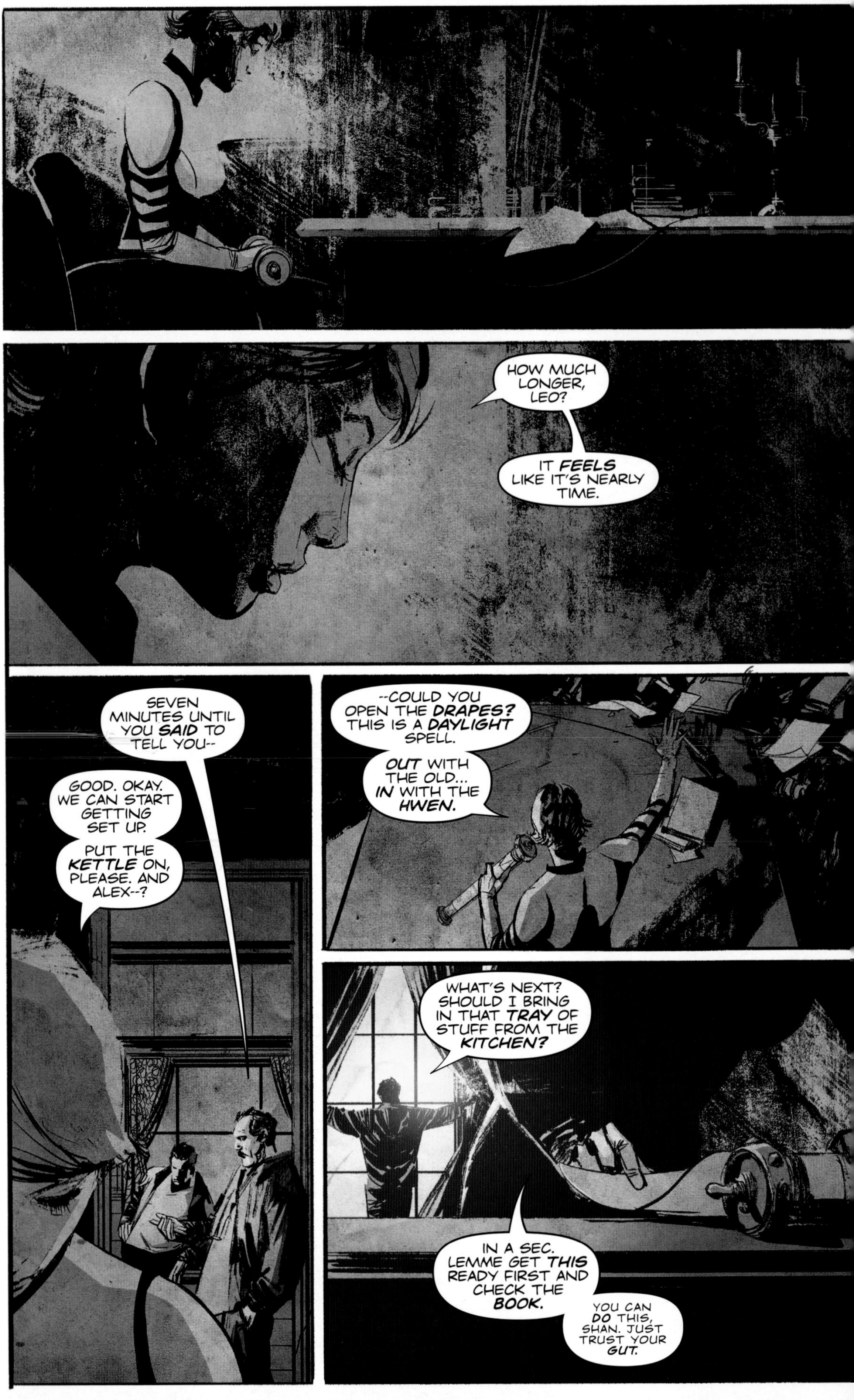
HOW MUCH LONGER, LEO?
IT FEELS LIKE IT'S NEARLY TIME.
SEVEN MINUTES UNTIL YOU SAID TO TELL YOU--
GOOD. OKAY. WE CAN START GETTING SET UP.
PUT THE KETTLE ON, PLEASE. AND ALEX--?
--COULD YOU OPEN THE DRAPES? THIS IS A DAYLIGHT SPELL.
OUT WITH THE OLD... IN WITH THE HWEN.
WHAT'S NEXT? SHOULD I BRING IN THAT TRAY OF STUFF FROM THE KITCHEN?
IN A SEC. LEMME GET THIS READY FIRST AND CHECK THE BOOK.
YOU CAN DO THIS, SHAN. JUST TRUST YOUR GUT.

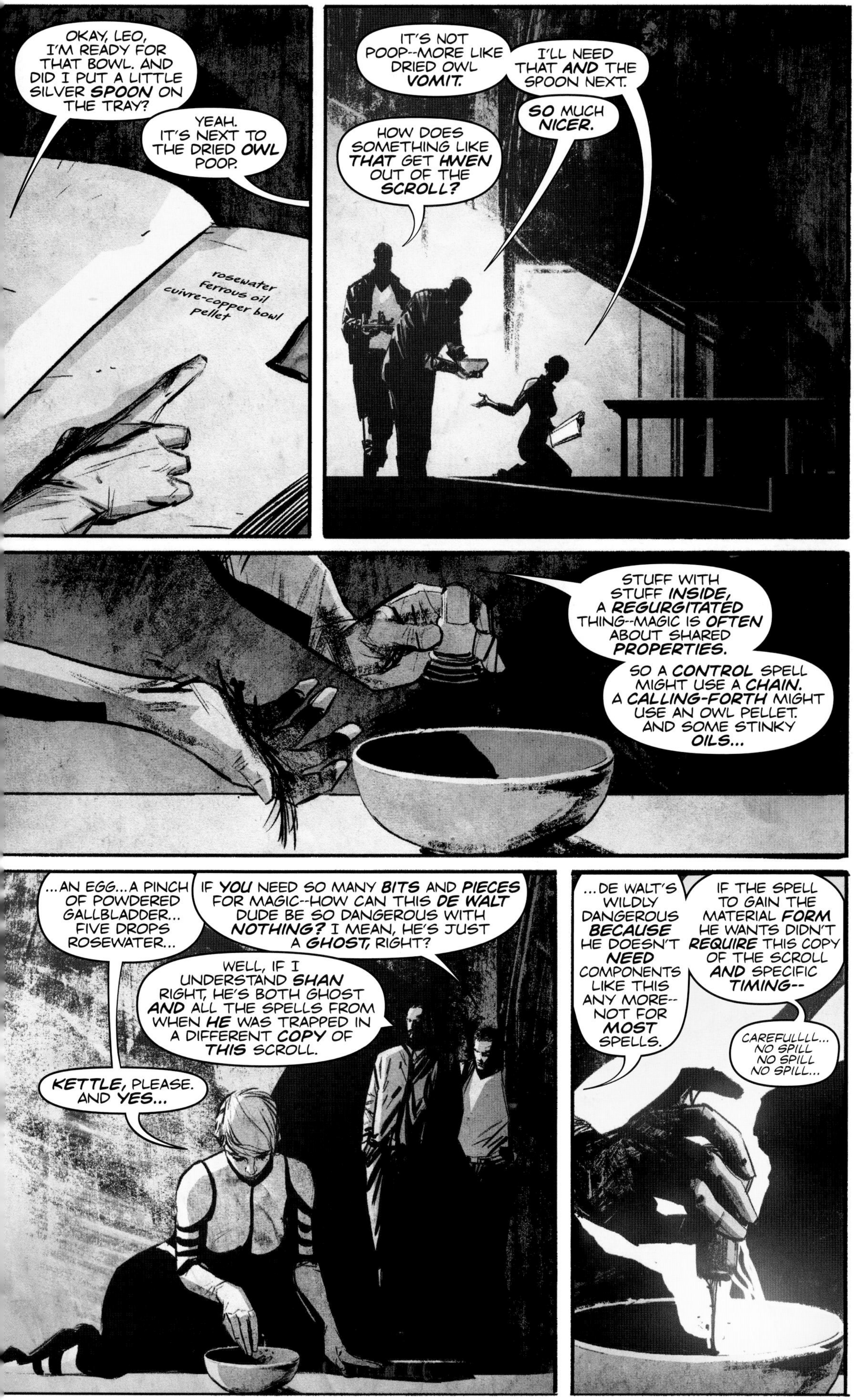
OKAY, LEO, I'M READY FOR THAT BOWL. AND DID I PUT A LITTLE SILVER SPOON ON THE TRAY?
YEAH. IT'S NEXT TO THE DRIED OWL POOP.
rosewater
ferrous oil
cuivre-copper bowl
pellet
IT'S NOT POOP--MORE LIKE DRIED OWL VOMIT.
I'LL NEED THAT AND THE SPOON NEXT.
HOW DOES SOMETHING LIKE THAT GET HWEN OUT OF THE SCROLL?
SO MUCH NICER.
STUFF WITH STUFF INSIDE, A REGURGITATED THING--MAGIC IS OFTEN ABOUT SHARED PROPERTIES.
SO A CONTROL SPELL MIGHT USE A CHAIN. A CALLING-FORTH MIGHT USE AN OWL PELLET. AND SOME STINKY OILS...
...AN EGG...A PINCH OF POWDERED GALLBLADDER... FIVE DROPS ROSEWATER...
IF YOU NEED SO MANY BITS AND PIECES FOR MAGIC--HOW CAN THIS DE WALT DUDE BE SO DANGEROUS WITH NOTHING? I MEAN, HE'S JUST A GHOST, RIGHT?
WELL, IF I UNDERSTAND SHAN RIGHT, HE'S BOTH GHOST AND ALL THE SPELLS FROM WHEN HE WAS TRAPPED IN A DIFFERENT COPY OF THIS SCROLL.
KETTLE, PLEASE. AND YES...
...DE WALT'S WILDLY DANGEROUS BECAUSE HE DOESN'T NEED COMPONENTS LIKE THIS ANY MORE-- NOT FOR MOST SPELLS.
IF THE SPELL TO GAIN THE MATERIAL FORM HE WANTS DIDN'T REQUIRE THIS COPY OF THE SCROLL AND SPECIFIC TIMING--
CAREFULLLL... NO SPILL NO SPILL NO SPILL...

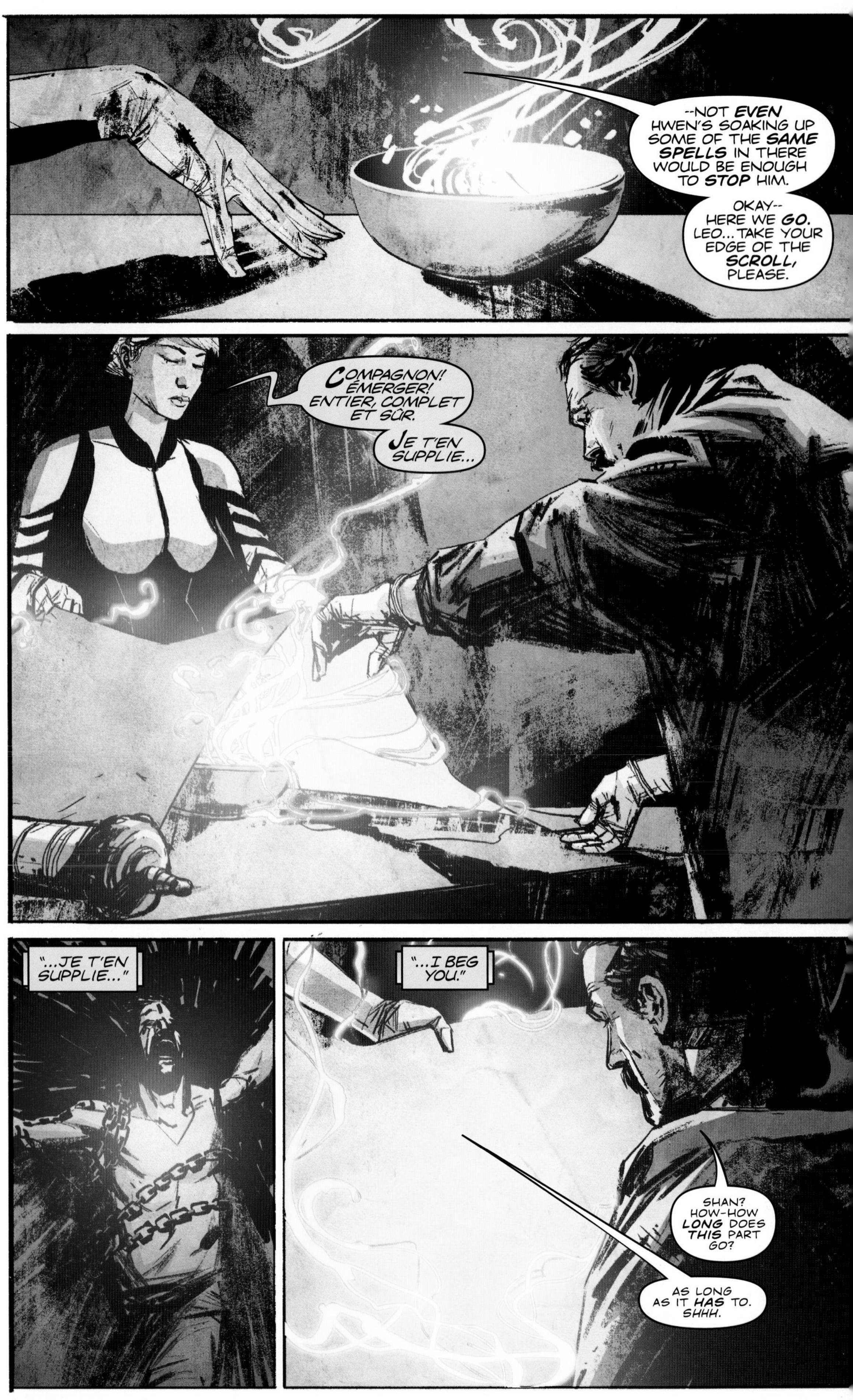
--NOT EVEN HWEN'S SOAKING UP SOME OF THE SAME SPELLS IN THERE WOULD BE ENOUGH TO STOP HIM.
OKAY-- HERE WE GO. LEO... TAKE YOUR EDGE OF THE SCROLL, PLEASE.
COMPAGNON! ÉMERGER! ENTIER, COMPLET ET SÛR.
JE T'EN SUPPLIE...
"...JE T'EN SUPPLIE..."
"...I BEG YOU."
SHAN? HOW-HOW LONG DOES THIS PART GO?
AS LONG AS IT HAS TO. SHHH.

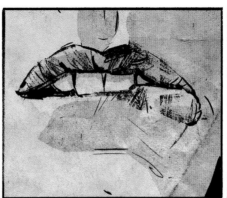

AAAARGH!

SHAN! SHAN YOU *DID* IT! I *KNEW* YOU COULD!

OH, *WOW!*

WOW *WHAT?* I-IS SOMETHING *HAPPENING?* IS IT *WORKING?*

IS IT *WORKING?* IS HWEN *BACK?*

HE *IS!* HE'S RIGHT *HERE--!* ARE YOU *OKAY,* BABE?

I'M *FINE,* BUT IT ALMOST TURNED *VERY BAD.* I--

I DON'T EVEN *CARE* THAT YOU CAN'T FEEL ME--IF YOU *COULD,* I'D PROBABLY BE *HUGGING* YOU TOO TIGHTLY!

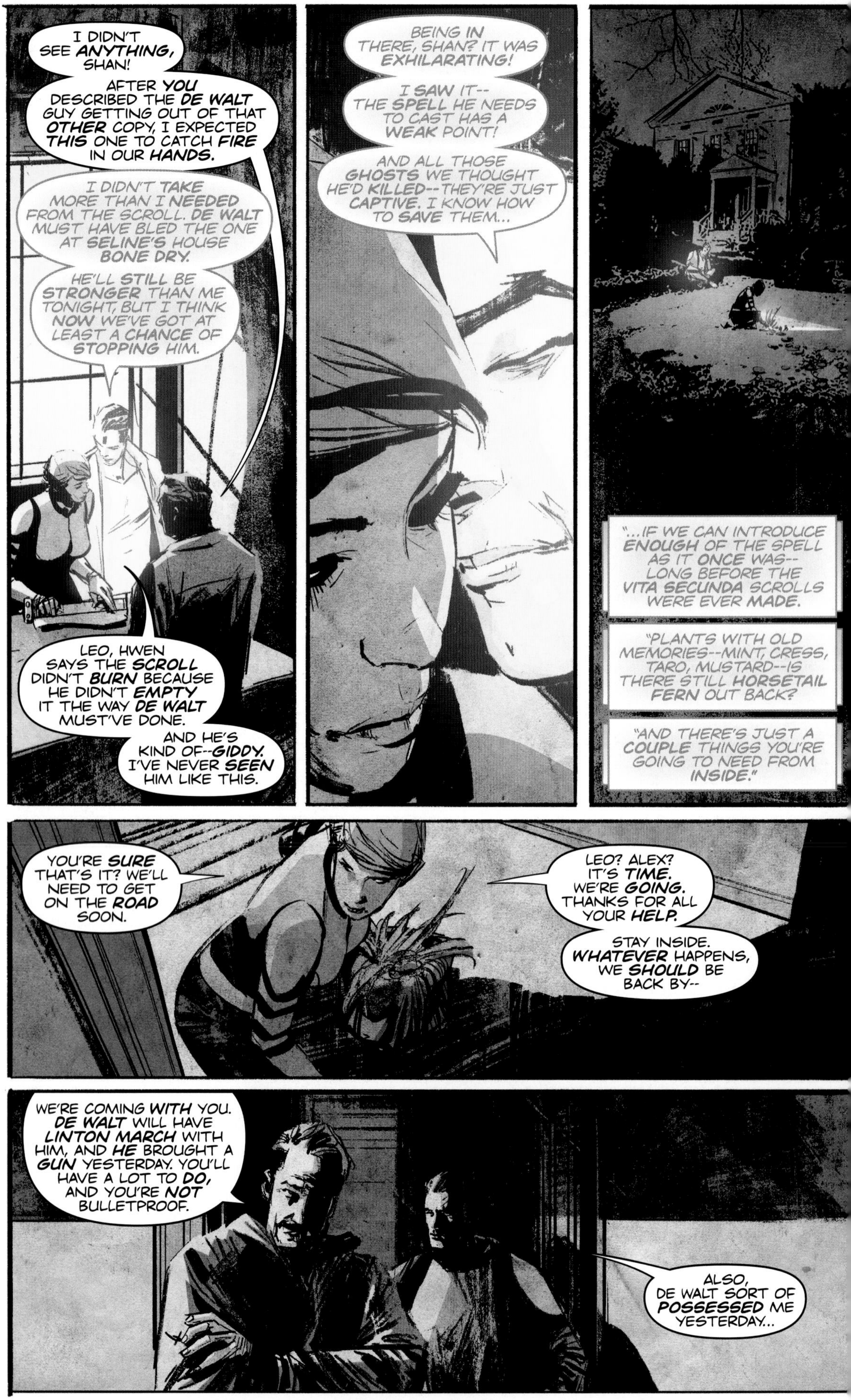
I DIDN'T SEE ANYTHING, SHAN!
AFTER YOU DESCRIBED THE DE WALT GUY GETTING OUT OF THAT OTHER COPY, I EXPECTED THIS ONE TO CATCH FIRE IN OUR HANDS.
I DIDN'T TAKE MORE THAN I NEEDED FROM THE SCROLL. DE WALT MUST HAVE BLED THE ONE AT SELINE'S HOUSE BONE DRY.
HE'LL STILL BE STRONGER THAN ME TONIGHT, BUT I THINK NOW WE'VE GOT AT LEAST A CHANCE OF STOPPING HIM.
LEO, HWEN SAYS THE SCROLL DIDN'T BURN BECAUSE HE DIDN'T EMPTY IT THE WAY DE WALT MUST'VE DONE.
AND HE'S KIND OF--GIDDY. I'VE NEVER SEEN HIM LIKE THIS.
BEING IN THERE, SHAN? IT WAS EXHILARATING!
I SAW IT-- THE SPELL HE NEEDS TO CAST HAS A WEAK POINT!
AND ALL THOSE GHOSTS WE THOUGHT HE'D KILLED--THEY'RE JUST CAPTIVE. I KNOW HOW TO SAVE THEM...
"...IF WE CAN INTRODUCE ENOUGH OF THE SPELL AS IT ONCE WAS-- LONG BEFORE THE VITA SECUNDA SCROLLS WERE EVER MADE.
"PLANTS WITH OLD MEMORIES--MINT, CRESS, TARO, MUSTARD--IS THERE STILL HORSETAIL FERN OUT BACK?
"AND THERE'S JUST A COUPLE THINGS YOU'RE GOING TO NEED FROM INSIDE."
YOU'RE SURE THAT'S IT? WE'LL NEED TO GET ON THE ROAD SOON.
LEO? ALEX? IT'S TIME. WE'RE GOING. THANKS FOR ALL YOUR HELP.
STAY INSIDE. WHATEVER HAPPENS, WE SHOULD BE BACK BY--
WE'RE COMING WITH YOU. DE WALT WILL HAVE LINTON MARCH WITH HIM, AND HE BROUGHT A GUN YESTERDAY. YOU'LL HAVE A LOT TO DO, AND YOU'RE NOT BULLETPROOF.
ALSO, DE WALT SORT OF POSSESSED ME YESTERDAY...

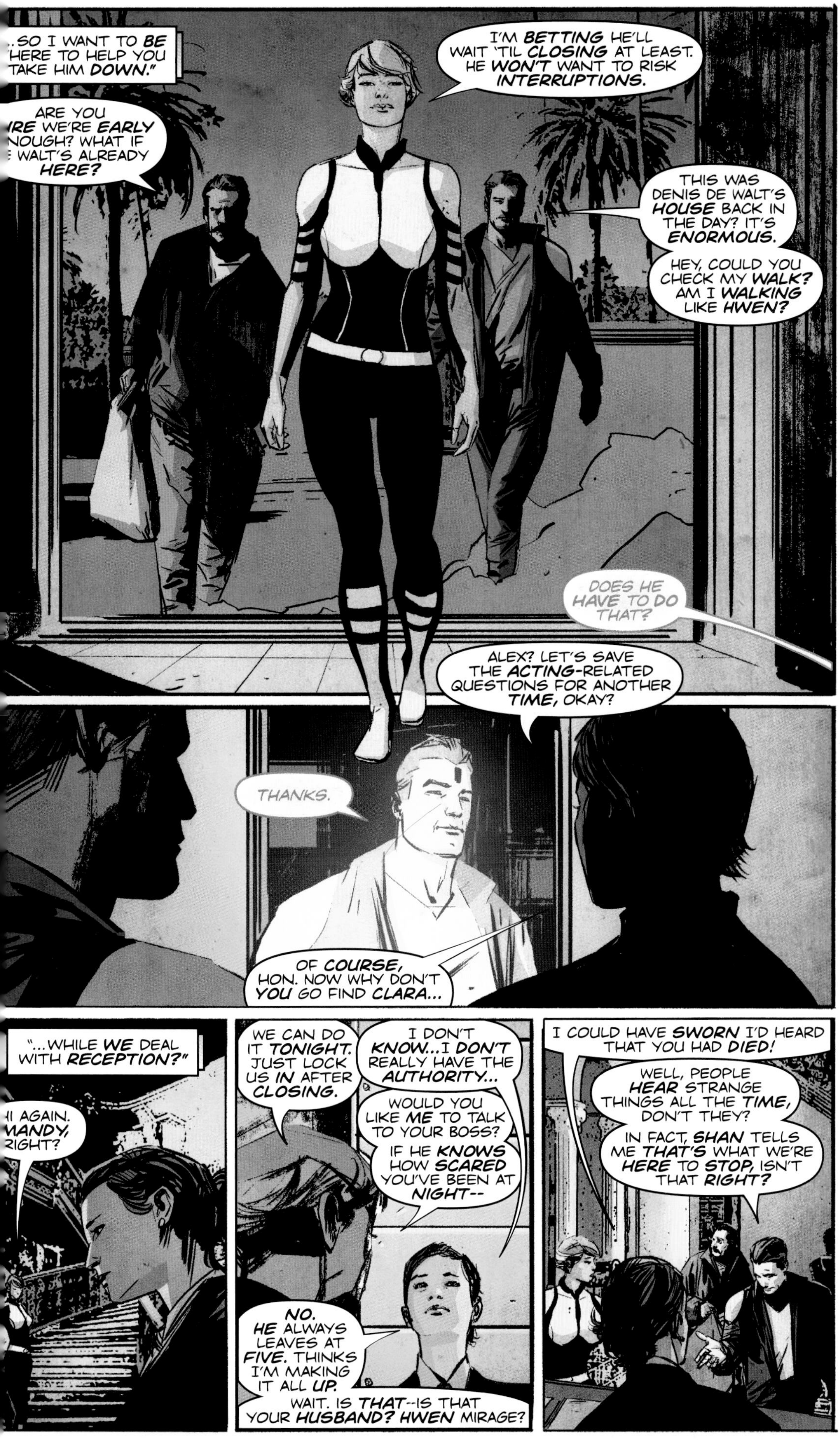
..SO I WANT TO BE HERE TO HELP YOU TAKE HIM DOWN."
I'M BETTING HE'LL WAIT 'TIL CLOSING AT LEAST. HE WON'T WANT TO RISK INTERRUPTIONS.
ARE YOU RE WE'RE EARLY NOUGH? WHAT IF WALT'S ALREADY HERE?
THIS WAS DENIS DE WALT'S HOUSE BACK IN THE DAY? IT'S ENORMOUS.
HEY, COULD YOU CHECK MY WALK? AM I WALKING LIKE HWEN?
DOES HE HAVE TO DO THAT?
ALEX? LET'S SAVE THE ACTING-RELATED QUESTIONS FOR ANOTHER TIME, OKAY?
THANKS.
OF COURSE, HON. NOW WHY DON'T YOU GO FIND CLARA...
"...WHILE WE DEAL WITH RECEPTION?"
HI AGAIN. MANDY, RIGHT?
WE CAN DO IT TONIGHT. JUST LOCK US IN AFTER CLOSING.
I DON'T KNOW...I DON'T REALLY HAVE THE AUTHORITY...
WOULD YOU LIKE ME TO TALK TO YOUR BOSS?
IF HE KNOWS HOW SCARED YOU'VE BEEN AT NIGHT--
NO. HE ALWAYS LEAVES AT FIVE. THINKS I'M MAKING IT ALL UP.
WAIT. IS THAT--IS THAT YOUR HUSBAND? HWEN MIRAGE?
I COULD HAVE SWORN I'D HEARD THAT YOU HAD DIED!
WELL, PEOPLE HEAR STRANGE THINGS ALL THE TIME, DON'T THEY?
IN FACT, SHAN TELLS ME THAT'S WHAT WE'RE HERE TO STOP, ISN'T THAT RIGHT?

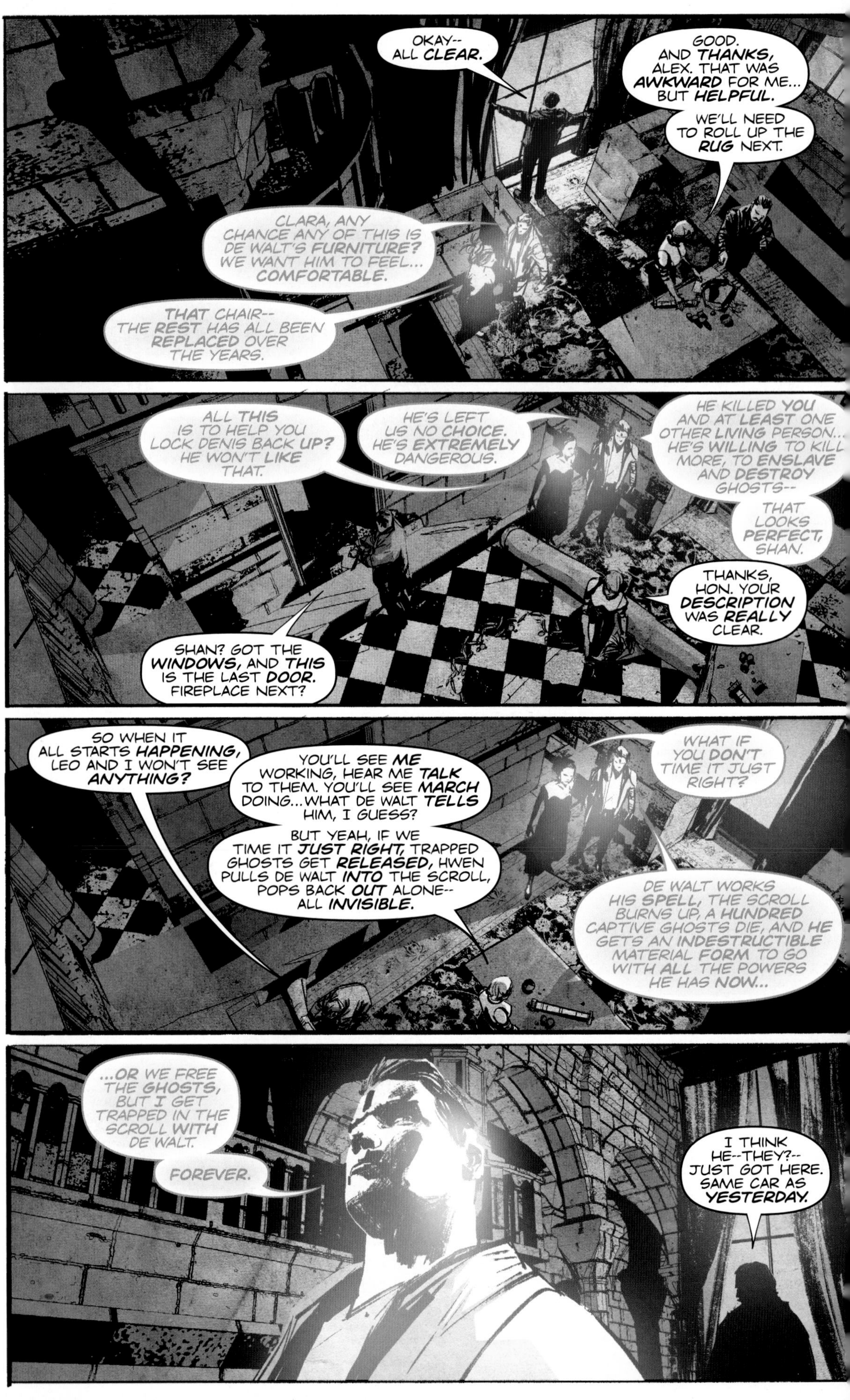
OKAY-- ALL CLEAR.
GOOD. AND THANKS, ALEX. THAT WAS AWKWARD FOR ME... BUT HELPFUL.
WE'LL NEED TO ROLL UP THE RUG NEXT.
CLARA, ANY CHANCE ANY OF THIS IS DE WALT'S FURNITURE? WE WANT HIM TO FEEL... COMFORTABLE.
THAT CHAIR-- THE REST HAS ALL BEEN REPLACED OVER THE YEARS.
ALL THIS IS TO HELP YOU LOCK DENIS BACK UP? HE WON'T LIKE THAT.
HE'S LEFT US NO CHOICE. HE'S EXTREMELY DANGEROUS.
HE KILLED YOU AND AT LEAST ONE OTHER LIVING PERSON... HE'S WILLING TO KILL MORE, TO ENSLAVE AND DESTROY GHOSTS--
THAT LOOKS PERFECT, SHAN.
THANKS, HON. YOUR DESCRIPTION WAS REALLY CLEAR.
SHAN? GOT THE WINDOWS, AND THIS IS THE LAST DOOR. FIREPLACE NEXT?
SO WHEN IT ALL STARTS HAPPENING, LEO AND I WON'T SEE ANYTHING?
YOU'LL SEE ME WORKING, HEAR ME TALK TO THEM. YOU'LL SEE MARCH DOING...WHAT DE WALT TELLS HIM, I GUESS?
BUT YEAH, IF WE TIME IT JUST RIGHT, TRAPPED GHOSTS GET RELEASED, HWEN PULLS DE WALT INTO THE SCROLL, POPS BACK OUT ALONE-- ALL INVISIBLE.
WHAT IF YOU DON'T TIME IT JUST RIGHT?
DE WALT WORKS HIS SPELL, THE SCROLL BURNS UP, A HUNDRED CAPTIVE GHOSTS DIE, AND HE GETS AN INDESTRUCTIBLE MATERIAL FORM TO GO WITH ALL THE POWERS HE HAS NOW...
...OR WE FREE THE GHOSTS, BUT I GET TRAPPED IN THE SCROLL WITH DE WALT.
FOREVER.
I THINK HE--THEY?-- JUST GOT HERE. SAME CAR AS YESTERDAY.

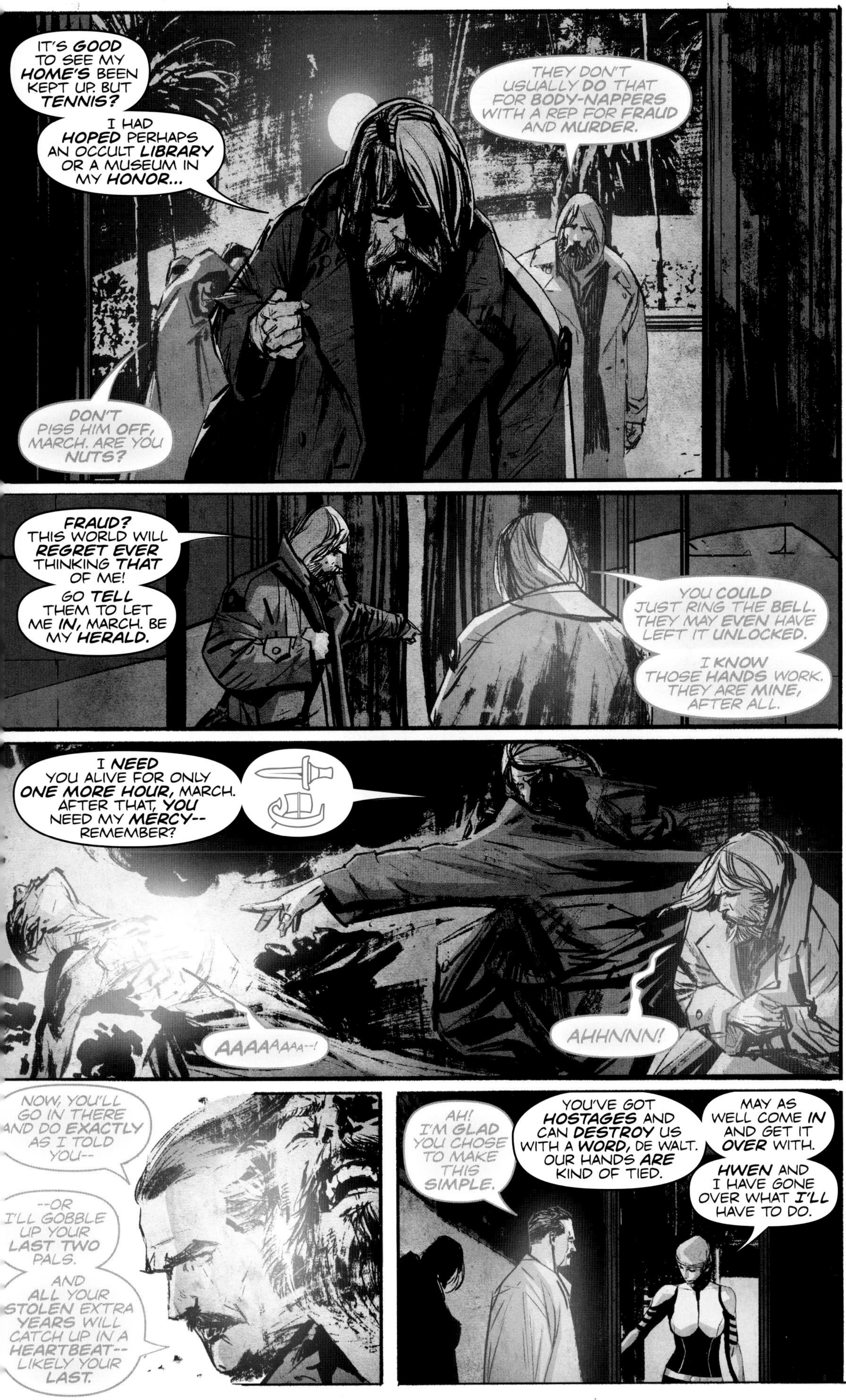

IT'S GOOD TO SEE MY HOME'S BEEN KEPT UP. BUT TENNIS?
I HAD HOPED PERHAPS AN OCCULT LIBRARY OR A MUSEUM IN MY HONOR...
THEY DON'T USUALLY DO THAT FOR BODY-NAPPERS WITH A REP FOR FRAUD AND MURDER.
DON'T PISS HIM OFF, MARCH. ARE YOU NUTS?
FRAUD? THIS WORLD WILL REGRET EVER THINKING THAT OF ME!
GO TELL THEM TO LET ME IN, MARCH. BE MY HERALD.
YOU COULD JUST RING THE BELL. THEY MAY EVEN HAVE LEFT IT UNLOCKED.
I KNOW THOSE HANDS WORK. THEY ARE MINE, AFTER ALL.
I NEED YOU ALIVE FOR ONLY ONE MORE HOUR, MARCH. AFTER THAT, YOU NEED MY MERCY-- REMEMBER?
AAAAAAA--!
AHHNNN!
NOW, YOU'LL GO IN THERE AND DO EXACTLY AS I TOLD YOU--
--OR I'LL GOBBLE UP YOUR LAST TWO PALS.
AND ALL YOUR STOLEN EXTRA YEARS WILL CATCH UP IN A HEARTBEAT-- LIKELY YOUR LAST.
AH! I'M GLAD YOU CHOSE TO MAKE THIS SIMPLE.
YOU'VE GOT HOSTAGES AND CAN DESTROY US WITH A WORD, DE WALT. OUR HANDS ARE KIND OF TIED.
MAY AS WELL COME IN AND GET IT OVER WITH.
HWEN AND I HAVE GONE OVER WHAT I'LL HAVE TO DO.

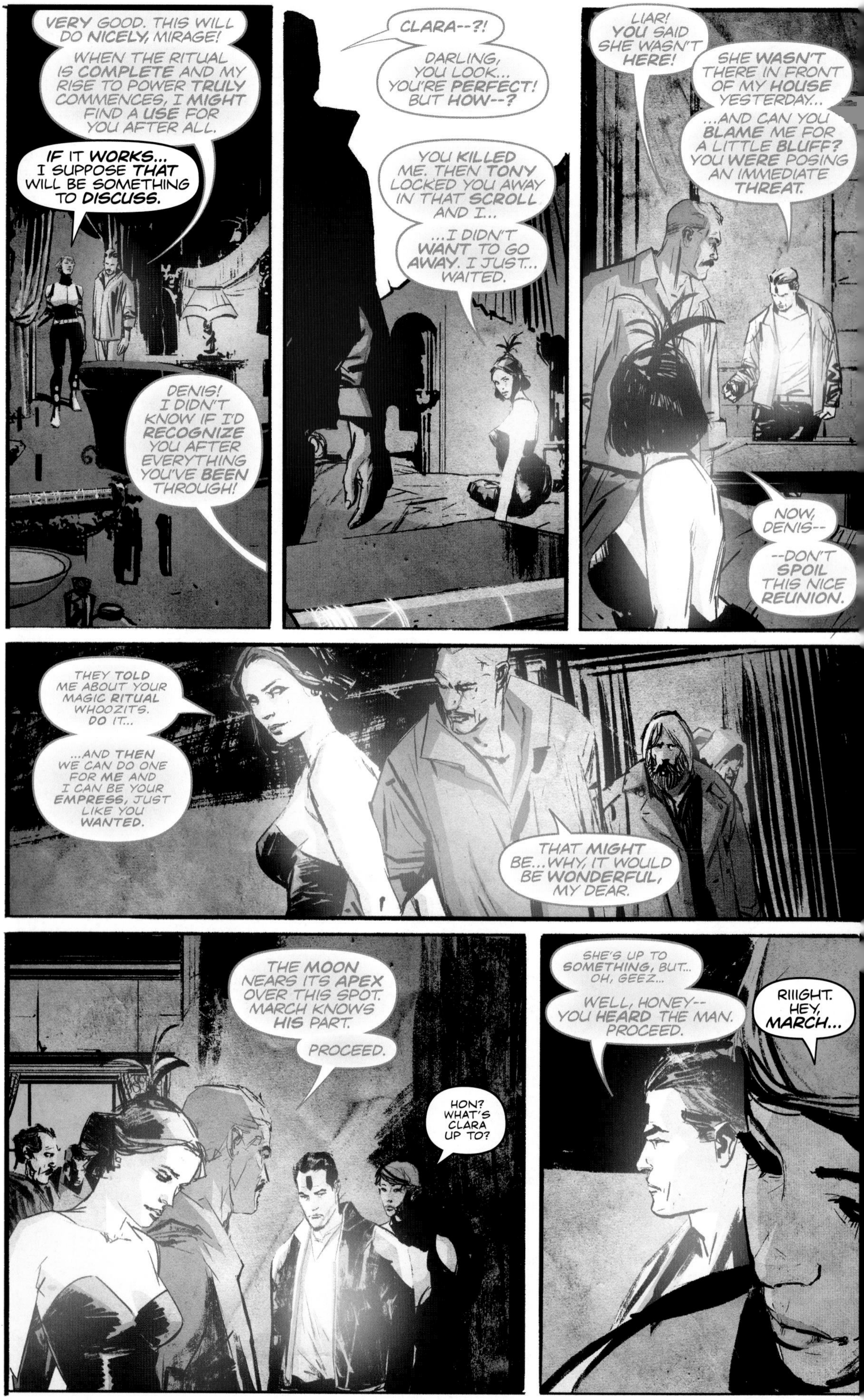
VERY GOOD. THIS WILL DO NICELY, MIRAGE!
WHEN THE RITUAL IS COMPLETE AND MY RISE TO POWER TRULY COMMENCES, I MIGHT FIND A USE FOR YOU AFTER ALL.
IF IT WORKS... I SUPPOSE THAT WILL BE SOMETHING TO DISCUSS.
DENIS! I DIDN'T KNOW IF I'D RECOGNIZE YOU AFTER EVERYTHING YOU'VE BEEN THROUGH!
CLARA--?!
DARLING, YOU LOOK... YOU'RE PERFECT! BUT HOW--?
YOU KILLED ME. THEN TONY LOCKED YOU AWAY IN THAT SCROLL AND I...
...I DIDN'T WANT TO GO AWAY. I JUST... WAITED.
LIAR! YOU SAID SHE WASN'T HERE!
SHE WASN'T THERE IN FRONT OF MY HOUSE YESTERDAY...
...AND CAN YOU BLAME ME FOR A LITTLE BLUFF? YOU WERE POSING AN IMMEDIATE THREAT.
NOW, DENIS--
--DON'T SPOIL THIS NICE REUNION.
THEY TOLD ME ABOUT YOUR MAGIC RITUAL WHOOZITS. DO IT...
...AND THEN WE CAN DO ONE FOR ME AND I CAN BE YOUR EMPRESS, JUST LIKE YOU WANTED.
THAT MIGHT BE...WHY, IT WOULD BE WONDERFUL, MY DEAR.
THE MOON NEARS ITS APEX OVER THIS SPOT. MARCH KNOWS HIS PART.
PROCEED.
HON? WHAT'S CLARA UP TO?
SHE'S UP TO SOMETHING, BUT... OH, GEEZ...
WELL, HONEY-- YOU HEARD THE MAN. PROCEED.
RIIIGHT. HEY, MARCH...

...DE WALT SAYS THERE ARE *THINGS* HE'S TOLD *YOU* TO DO?

IT *LOOKS* LIKE YOU'VE DONE *MOST* OF IT-- I GUESS I WON'T *NEED* A LOT OF WHAT HE HAD ME *BRING.*

COME, DEAR, THEY'LL BE BUSY FOR A FEW MINUTES--

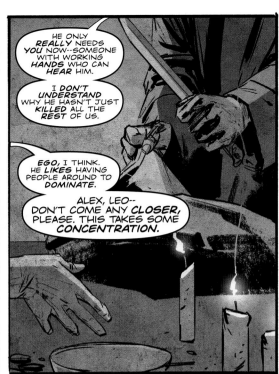

HE ONLY *REALLY* NEEDS *YOU* NOW--SOMEONE WITH WORKING *HANDS* WHO CAN *HEAR* HIM.

I *DON'T* UNDERSTAND WHY HE HASN'T JUST *KILLED* ALL THE *REST* OF US.

EGO, I THINK. HE *LIKES* HAVING PEOPLE AROUND TO *DOMINATE.*

ALEX, LEO-- DON'T COME ANY *CLOSER,* PLEASE. THIS TAKES SOME *CONCENTRATION.*

YOU LOOK WORSE THAN *EVER,* MARCH. DID HE TAKE *ANOTHER* OF YOUR *GHOSTS?*

JUST AS WE *ARRIVED.* I...IT TAKES HIM *NO TIME* AT ALL.

THERE'S *NO* WAY TO DEFY HIM THAT *I* CAN SEE. CAN'T YOU AND HWEN DO *ANYTHING?*

WE'RE *ABOUT* TO FIND OUT.

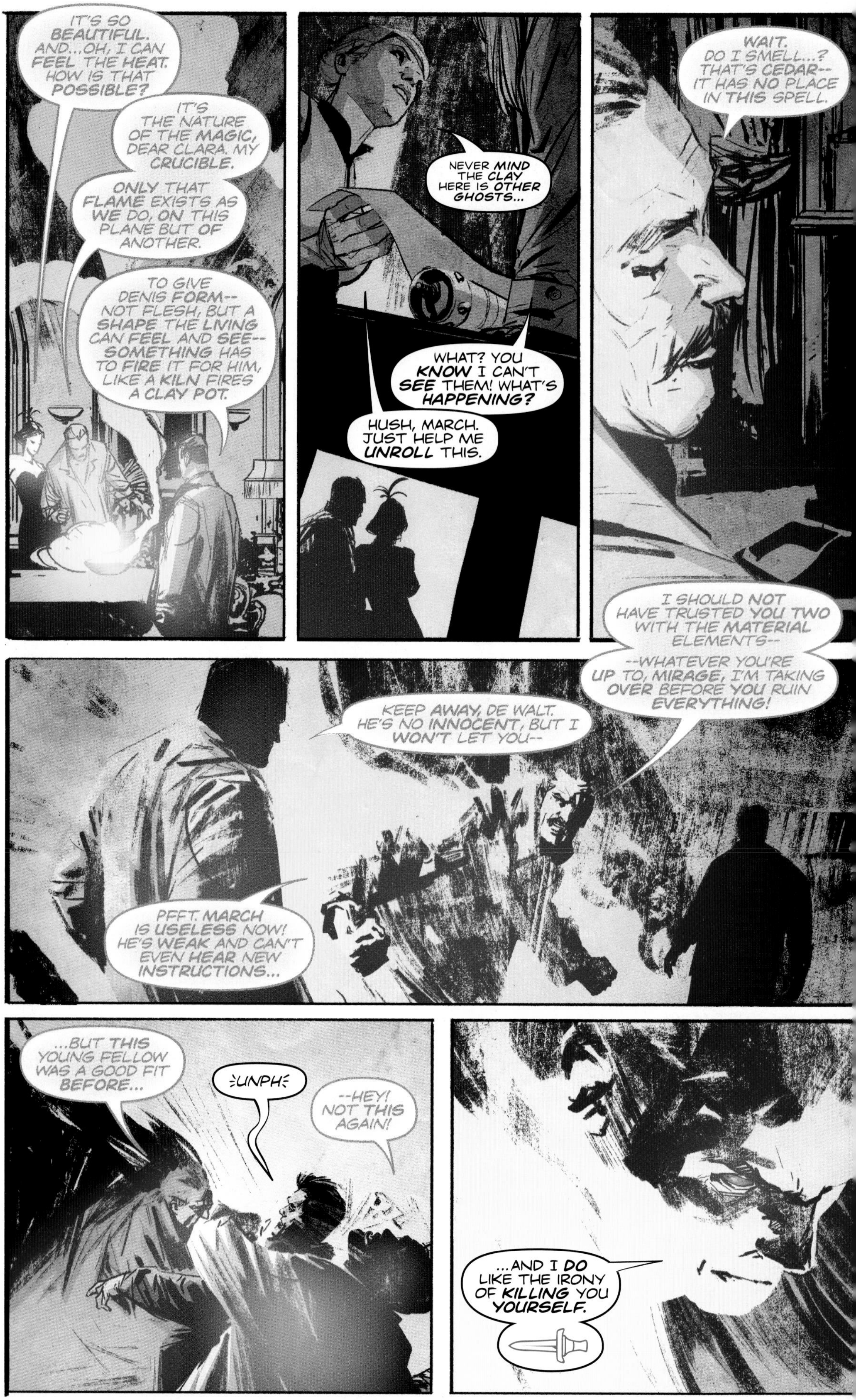
IT'S SO BEAUTIFUL. AND...OH, I CAN FEEL THE HEAT. HOW IS THAT POSSIBLE?
IT'S THE NATURE OF THE MAGIC, DEAR CLARA. MY CRUCIBLE.
ONLY THAT FLAME EXISTS AS WE DO, ON THIS PLANE BUT OF ANOTHER.
TO GIVE DENIS FORM-- NOT FLESH, BUT A SHAPE THE LIVING CAN FEEL AND SEE-- SOMETHING HAS TO FIRE IT FOR HIM, LIKE A KILN FIRES A CLAY POT.
NEVER MIND THE CLAY HERE IS OTHER GHOSTS...
WHAT? YOU KNOW I CAN'T SEE THEM! WHAT'S HAPPENING?
HUSH, MARCH. JUST HELP ME UNROLL THIS.
WAIT. DO I SMELL...? THAT'S CEDAR-- IT HAS NO PLACE IN THIS SPELL.
I SHOULD NOT HAVE TRUSTED YOU TWO WITH THE MATERIAL ELEMENTS--
--WHATEVER YOU'RE UP TO, MIRAGE, I'M TAKING OVER BEFORE YOU RUIN EVERYTHING!
KEEP AWAY, DE WALT. HE'S NO INNOCENT, BUT I WON'T LET YOU--
PFFT. MARCH IS USELESS NOW! HE'S WEAK AND CAN'T EVEN HEAR NEW INSTRUCTIONS...
...BUT THIS YOUNG FELLOW WAS A GOOD FIT BEFORE...
UNPH
--HEY! NOT THIS AGAIN!
...AND I DO LIKE THE IRONY OF KILLING YOU YOURSELF.

YOU DARE EVOKE THE ROOT MAGIC OF THE VITA SECUNDA?! AGAINST ME?!

THE SCROLL, MARCH! NOW! IT MUST BE CONSUMED BY THE FIRE! HE'S LEARNED THE OLD SPELLS SOMEHOW AND MEANS TO DISRUPT THE RITE!

DO AS I INSTRUCTED, OR YOU KNOW WHAT I'LL DO TO YOU!

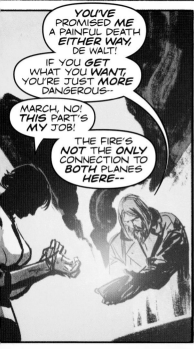

YOU'VE PROMISED ME A PAINFUL DEATH EITHER WAY, DE WALT!

IF YOU GET WHAT YOU WANT, YOU'RE JUST MORE DANGEROUS--

MARCH, NO! THIS PART'S MY JOB!

THE FIRE'S NOT THE ONLY CONNECTION TO BOTH PLANES HERE--

AAANGH!

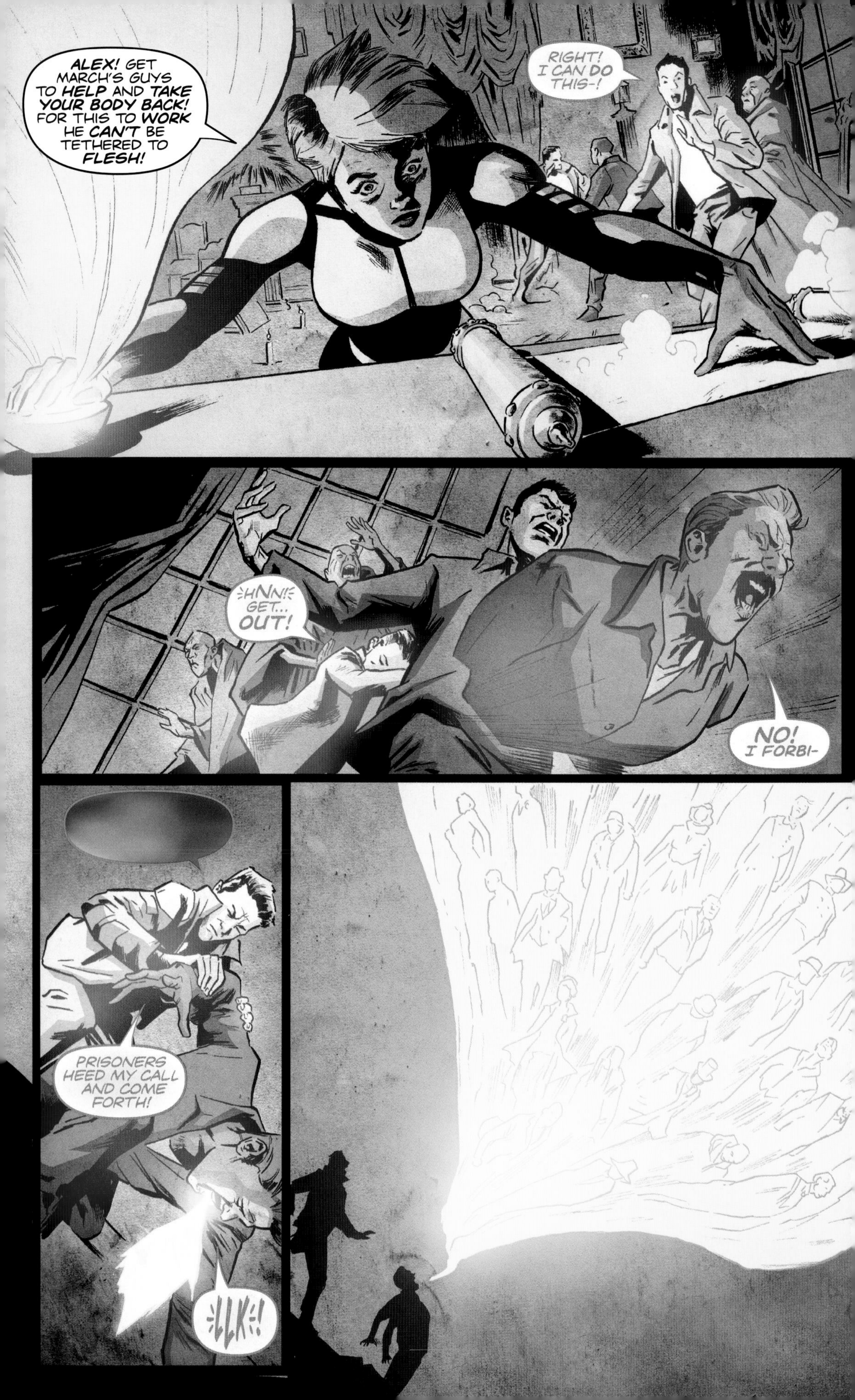
ALEX! GET MARCH'S GUYS TO HELP AND TAKE YOUR BODY BACK! FOR THIS TO WORK HE CAN'T BE TETHERED TO FLESH!
RIGHT! I CAN DO THIS-!
HNN! GET... OUT!
NO! I FORBI-
PRISONERS HEED MY CALL AND COME FORTH!
LLK-!

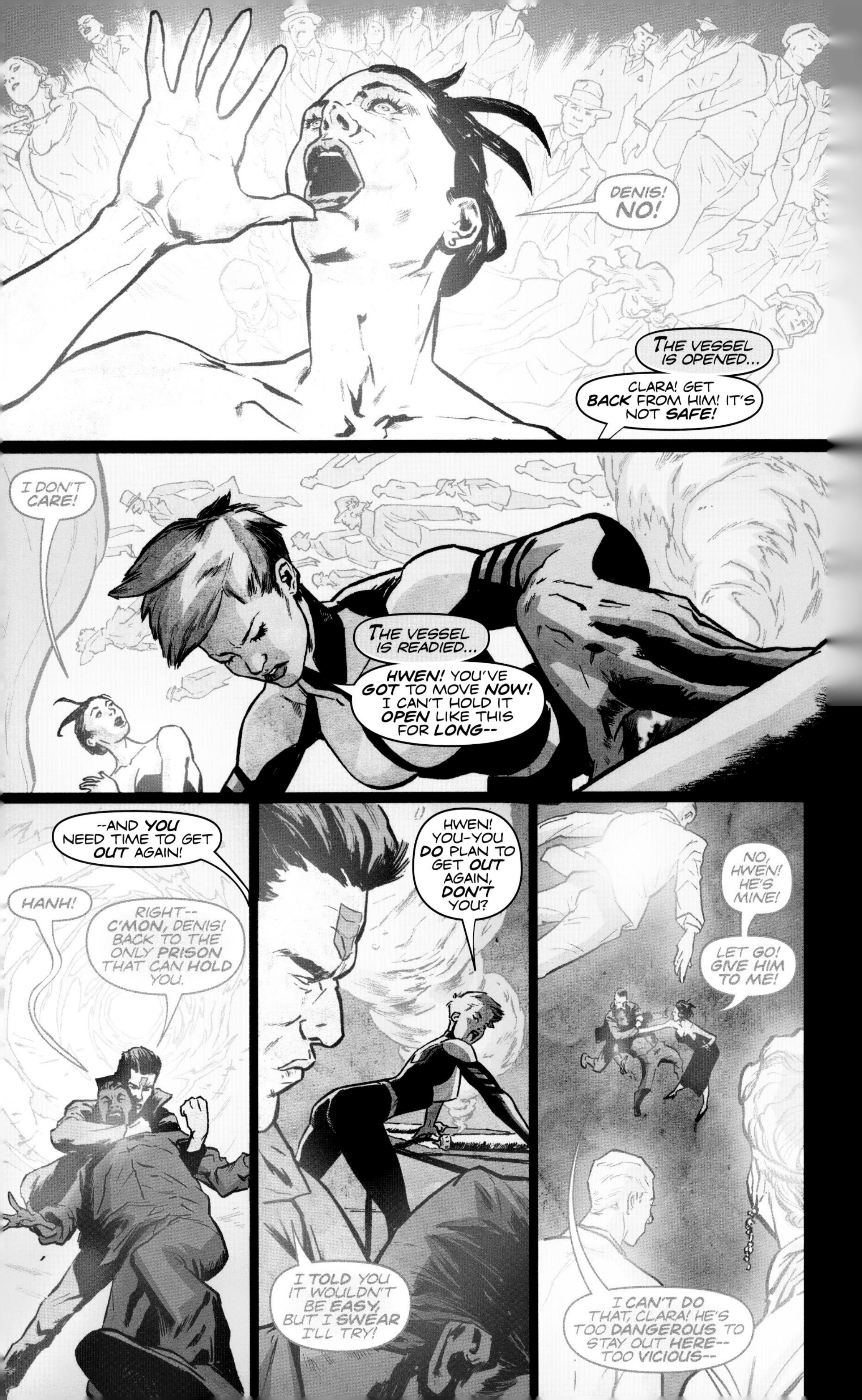
DENIS! NO!
THE VESSEL IS OPENED...
CLARA! GET BACK FROM HIM! IT'S NOT SAFE!
I DON'T CARE!
THE VESSEL IS READIED...
HWEN! YOU'VE GOT TO MOVE NOW! I CAN'T HOLD IT OPEN LIKE THIS FOR LONG--
--AND YOU NEED TIME TO GET OUT AGAIN!
HANH!
RIGHT-- C'MON, DENIS! BACK TO THE ONLY PRISON THAT CAN HOLD YOU.
HWEN! YOU-YOU DO PLAN TO GET OUT AGAIN, DON'T YOU?
I TOLD YOU IT WOULDN'T BE EASY, BUT I SWEAR I'LL TRY!
NO, HWEN! HE'S MINE!
LET GO! GIVE HIM TO ME!
I CAN'T DO THAT, CLARA! HE'S TOO DANGEROUS TO STAY OUT HERE-- TOO VICIOUS--

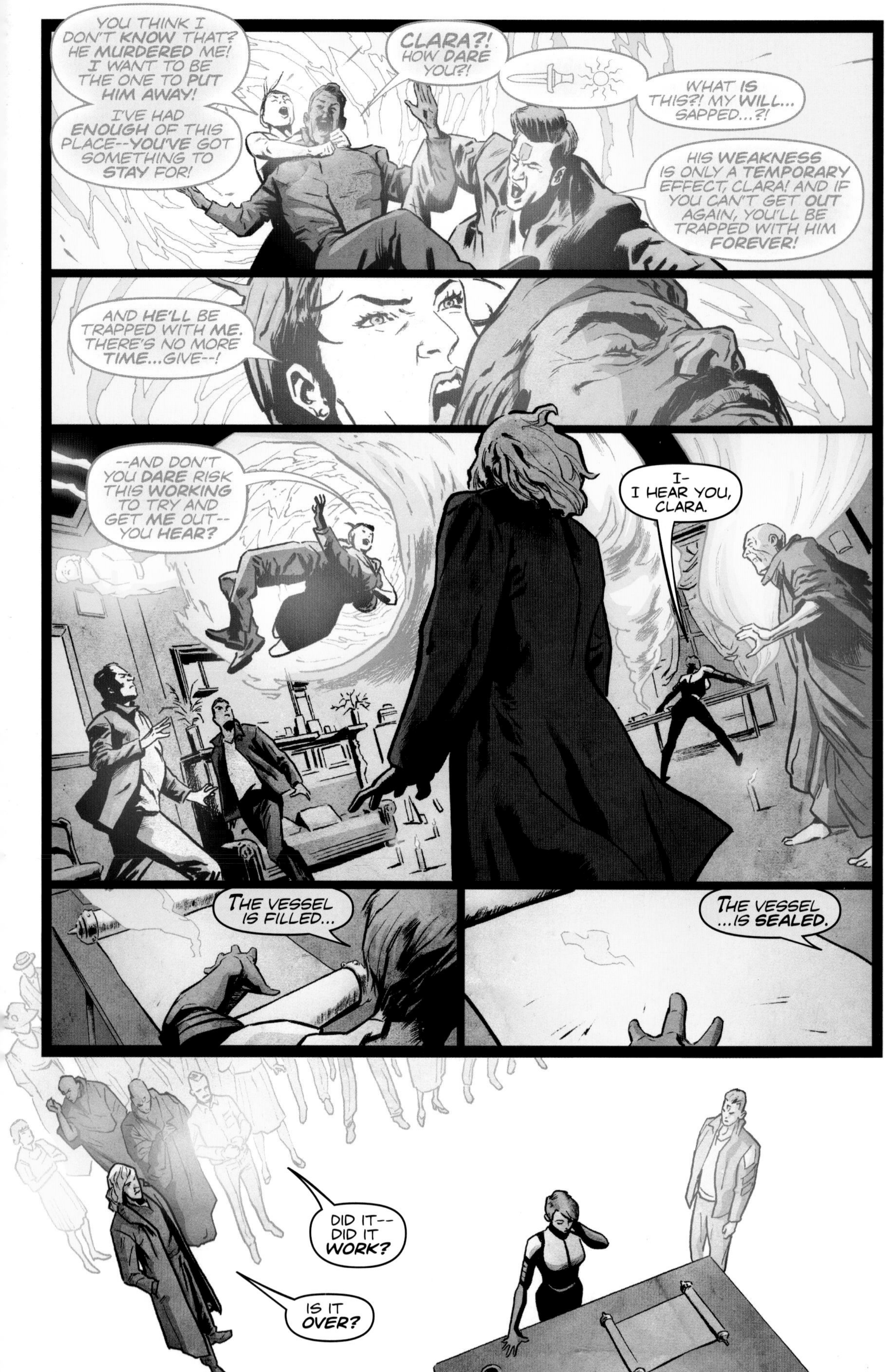
YOU THINK I DON'T KNOW THAT? HE MURDERED ME! I WANT TO BE THE ONE TO PUT HIM AWAY!
I'VE HAD ENOUGH OF THIS PLACE--YOU'VE GOT SOMETHING TO STAY FOR!
CLARA?! HOW DARE YOU?!
WHAT IS THIS?! MY WILL... SAPPED...?!
HIS WEAKNESS IS ONLY A TEMPORARY EFFECT, CLARA! AND IF YOU CAN'T GET OUT AGAIN, YOU'LL BE TRAPPED WITH HIM FOREVER!
AND HE'LL BE TRAPPED WITH ME. THERE'S NO MORE TIME...GIVE--!
--AND DON'T YOU DARE RISK THIS WORKING TO TRY AND GET ME OUT--YOU HEAR?
I- I HEAR YOU, CLARA.
THE VESSEL IS FILLED...
THE VESSEL ...IS SEALED.
DID IT-- DID IT WORK?
IS IT OVER?

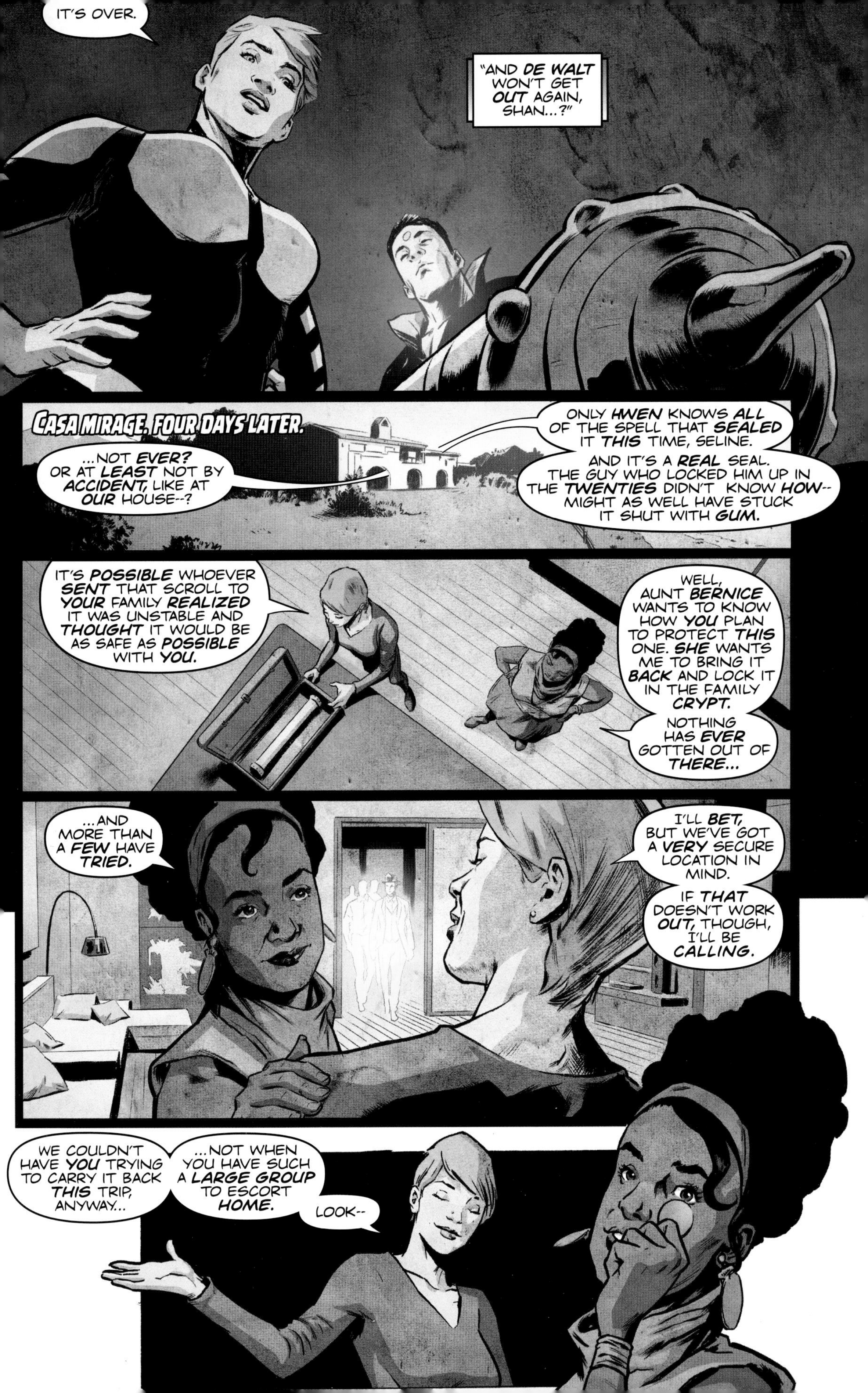
IT'S OVER.
"AND DE WALT WON'T GET OUT AGAIN, SHAN...?"
CASA MIRAGE. FOUR DAYS LATER.
...NOT EVER? OR AT LEAST NOT BY ACCIDENT, LIKE AT OUR HOUSE--?
ONLY HWEN KNOWS ALL OF THE SPELL THAT SEALED IT THIS TIME, SELINE.
AND IT'S A REAL SEAL. THE GUY WHO LOCKED HIM UP IN THE TWENTIES DIDN'T KNOW HOW--MIGHT AS WELL HAVE STUCK IT SHUT WITH GUM.
IT'S POSSIBLE WHOEVER SENT THAT SCROLL TO YOUR FAMILY REALIZED IT WAS UNSTABLE AND THOUGHT IT WOULD BE AS SAFE AS POSSIBLE WITH YOU.
WELL, AUNT BERNICE WANTS TO KNOW HOW YOU PLAN TO PROTECT THIS ONE. SHE WANTS ME TO BRING IT BACK AND LOCK IT IN THE FAMILY CRYPT.
NOTHING HAS EVER GOTTEN OUT OF THERE...
...AND MORE THAN A FEW HAVE TRIED.
I'LL BET, BUT WE'VE GOT A VERY SECURE LOCATION IN MIND.
IF THAT DOESN'T WORK OUT, THOUGH, I'LL BE CALLING.
WE COULDN'T HAVE YOU TRYING TO CARRY IT BACK THIS TRIP, ANYWAY...
...NOT WHEN YOU HAVE SUCH A LARGE GROUP TO ESCORT HOME.
LOOK--

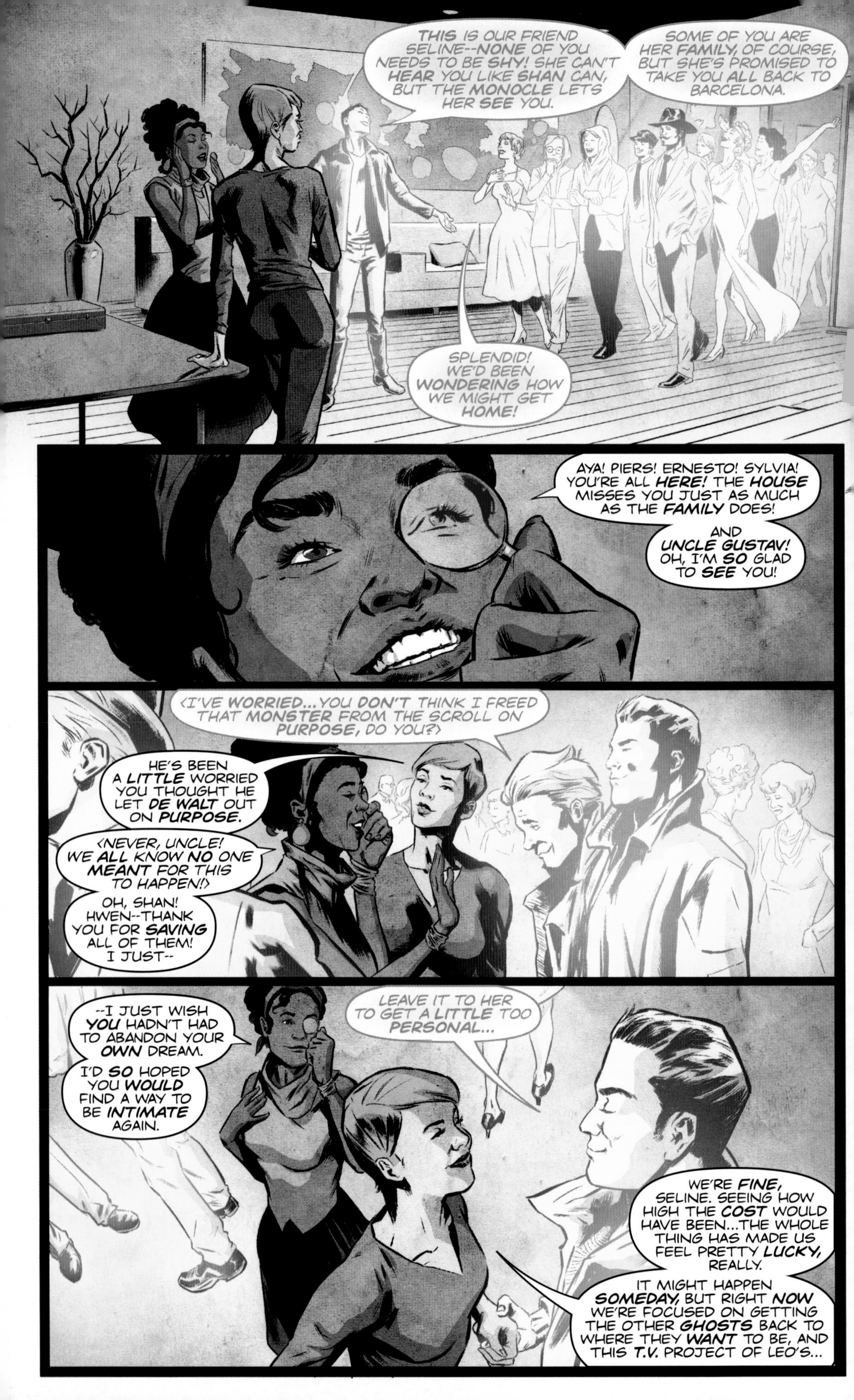
THIS IS OUR FRIEND SELINE--NONE OF YOU NEEDS TO BE SHY! SHE CAN'T HEAR YOU LIKE SHAN CAN, BUT THE MONOCLE LETS HER SEE YOU.
SOME OF YOU ARE HER FAMILY, OF COURSE, BUT SHE'S PROMISED TO TAKE YOU ALL BACK TO BARCELONA.
SPLENDID! WE'D BEEN WONDERING HOW WE MIGHT GET HOME!
AYA! PIERS! ERNESTO! SYLVIA! YOU'RE ALL HERE! THE HOUSE MISSES YOU JUST AS MUCH AS THE FAMILY DOES!
AND UNCLE GUSTAV! OH, I'M SO GLAD TO SEE YOU!
<I'VE WORRIED...YOU DON'T THINK I FREED THAT MONSTER FROM THE SCROLL ON PURPOSE, DO YOU?>
HE'S BEEN A LITTLE WORRIED YOU THOUGHT HE LET DE WALT OUT ON PURPOSE.
<NEVER, UNCLE! WE ALL KNOW NO ONE MEANT FOR THIS TO HAPPEN!>
OH, SHAN! HWEN--THANK YOU FOR SAVING ALL OF THEM! I JUST--
--I JUST WISH YOU HADN'T HAD TO ABANDON YOUR OWN DREAM.
I'D SO HOPED YOU WOULD FIND A WAY TO BE INTIMATE AGAIN.
LEAVE IT TO HER TO GET A LITTLE TOO PERSONAL...
WE'RE FINE, SELINE. SEEING HOW HIGH THE COST WOULD HAVE BEEN...THE WHOLE THING HAS MADE US FEEL PRETTY LUCKY, REALLY.
IT MIGHT HAPPEN SOMEDAY, BUT RIGHT NOW WE'RE FOCUSED ON GETTING THE OTHER GHOSTS BACK TO WHERE THEY WANT TO BE, AND THIS T.V. PROJECT OF LEO'S...

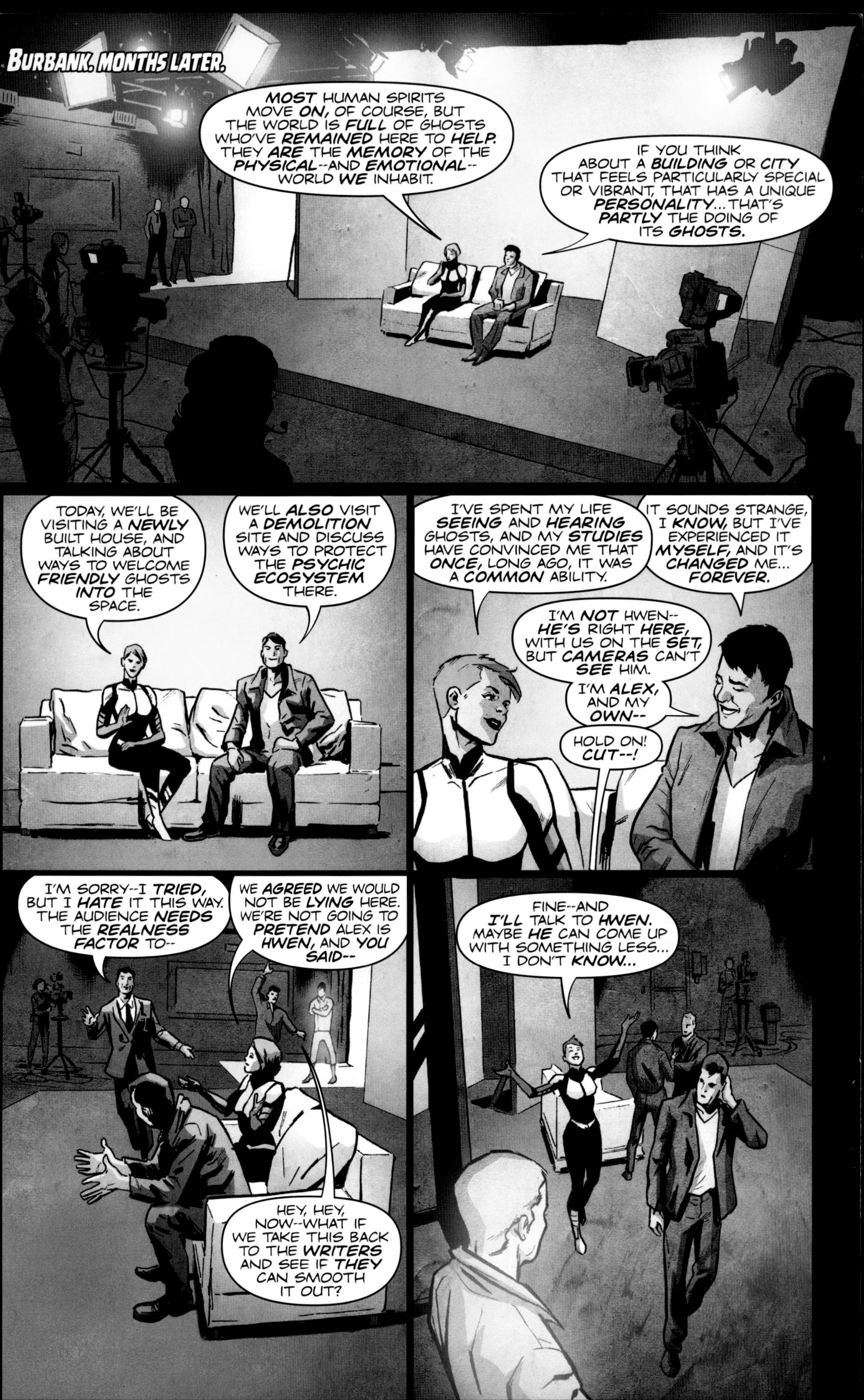
BURBANK. MONTHS LATER.
MOST HUMAN SPIRITS MOVE ON, OF COURSE, BUT THE WORLD IS FULL OF GHOSTS WHO'VE REMAINED HERE TO HELP. THEY ARE THE MEMORY OF THE PHYSICAL--AND EMOTIONAL--WORLD WE INHABIT.
IF YOU THINK ABOUT A BUILDING OR CITY THAT FEELS PARTICULARLY SPECIAL OR VIBRANT, THAT HAS A UNIQUE PERSONALITY... THAT'S PARTLY THE DOING OF ITS GHOSTS.
TODAY, WE'LL BE VISITING A NEWLY BUILT HOUSE, AND TALKING ABOUT WAYS TO WELCOME FRIENDLY GHOSTS INTO THE SPACE.
WE'LL ALSO VISIT A DEMOLITION SITE AND DISCUSS WAYS TO PROTECT THE PSYCHIC ECOSYSTEM THERE.
I'VE SPENT MY LIFE SEEING AND HEARING GHOSTS, AND MY STUDIES HAVE CONVINCED ME THAT ONCE, LONG AGO, IT WAS A COMMON ABILITY.
IT SOUNDS STRANGE, I KNOW, BUT I'VE EXPERIENCED IT MYSELF, AND IT'S CHANGED ME... FOREVER.
I'M NOT HWEN--HE'S RIGHT HERE, WITH US ON THE SET, BUT CAMERAS CAN'T SEE HIM.
I'M ALEX, AND MY OWN--
HOLD ON! CUT--!
I'M SORRY--I TRIED, BUT I HATE IT THIS WAY. THE AUDIENCE NEEDS THE REALNESS FACTOR TO--
WE AGREED WE WOULD NOT BE LYING HERE. WE'RE NOT GOING TO PRETEND ALEX IS HWEN, AND YOU SAID--
HEY, HEY, NOW--WHAT IF WE TAKE THIS BACK TO THE WRITERS AND SEE IF THEY CAN SMOOTH IT OUT?
FINE--AND I'LL TALK TO HWEN. MAYBE HE CAN COME UP WITH SOMETHING LESS... I DON'T KNOW...

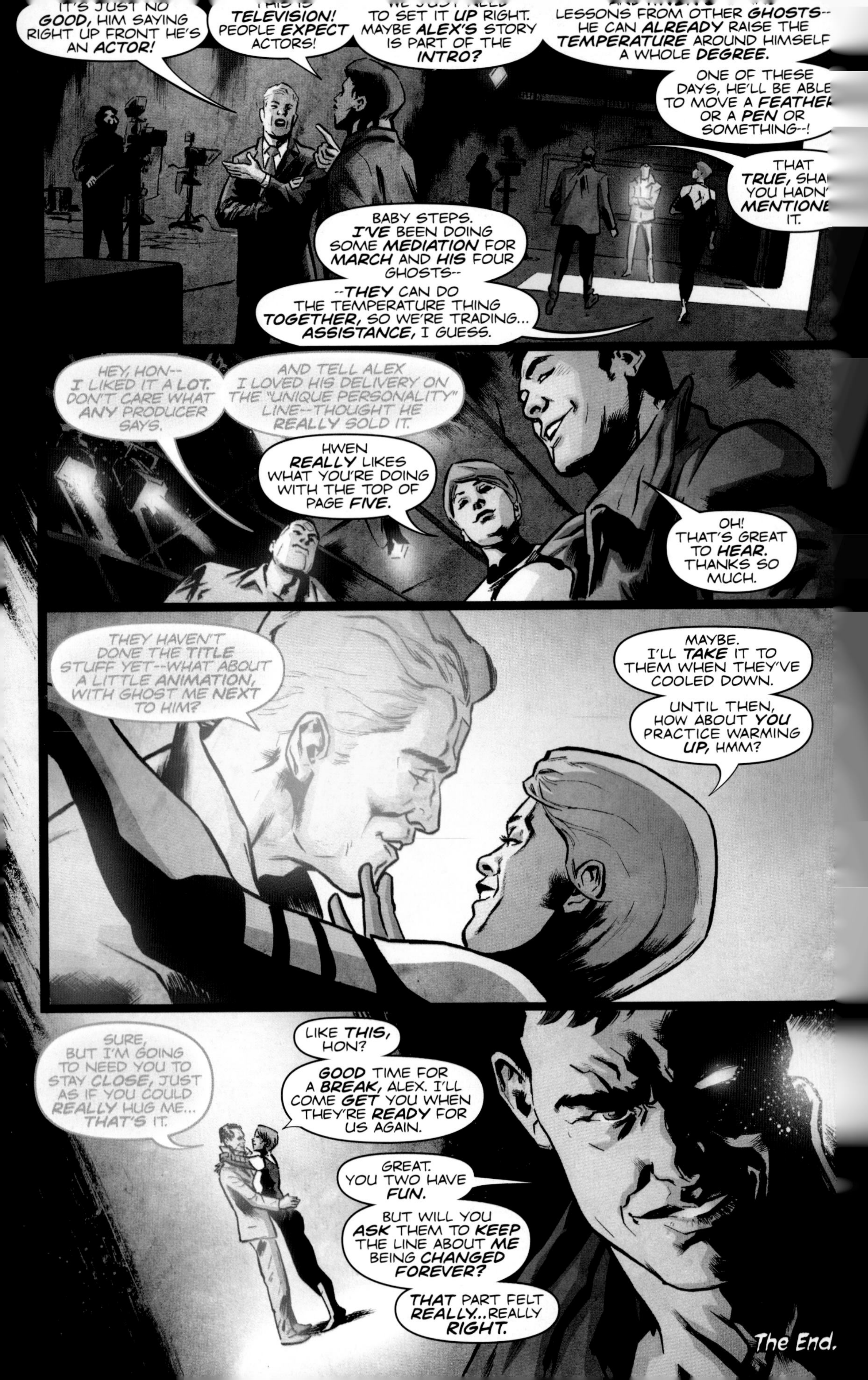
IT'S JUST NO GOOD, HIM SAYING RIGHT UP FRONT HE'S AN ACTOR!
TELEVISION! PEOPLE EXPECT ACTORS!
TO SET IT UP RIGHT. MAYBE ALEX'S STORY IS PART OF THE INTRO?
LESSONS FROM OTHER GHOSTS-- HE CAN ALREADY RAISE THE TEMPERATURE AROUND HIMSELF A WHOLE DEGREE.
ONE OF THESE DAYS, HE'LL BE ABLE TO MOVE A FEATHE OR A PEN OR SOMETHING--!
THAT TRUE, SHA YOU HADN' MENTIONE IT.
BABY STEPS. I'VE BEEN DOING SOME MEDIATION FOR MARCH AND HIS FOUR GHOSTS--
--THEY CAN DO THE TEMPERATURE THING TOGETHER, SO WE'RE TRADING... ASSISTANCE, I GUESS.
HEY, HON-- I LIKED IT A LOT. DON'T CARE WHAT ANY PRODUCER SAYS.
AND TELL ALEX I LOVED HIS DELIVERY ON THE "UNIQUE PERSONALITY" LINE--THOUGHT HE REALLY SOLD IT.
HWEN REALLY LIKES WHAT YOU'RE DOING WITH THE TOP OF PAGE FIVE.
OH! THAT'S GREAT TO HEAR. THANKS SO MUCH.
THEY HAVEN'T DONE THE TITLE STUFF YET--WHAT ABOUT A LITTLE ANIMATION, WITH GHOST ME NEXT TO HIM?
MAYBE. I'LL TAKE IT TO THEM WHEN THEY'VE COOLED DOWN.
UNTIL THEN, HOW ABOUT YOU PRACTICE WARMING UP, HMM?
SURE, BUT I'M GOING TO NEED YOU TO STAY CLOSE, JUST AS IF YOU COULD REALLY HUG ME... THAT'S IT.
LIKE THIS, HON?
GOOD TIME FOR A BREAK, ALEX. I'LL COME GET YOU WHEN THEY'RE READY FOR US AGAIN.
GREAT. YOU TWO HAVE FUN.
BUT WILL YOU ASK THEM TO KEEP THE LINE ABOUT ME BEING CHANGED FOREVER?
THAT PART FELT REALLY...REALLY RIGHT.
The End.

GALLERY

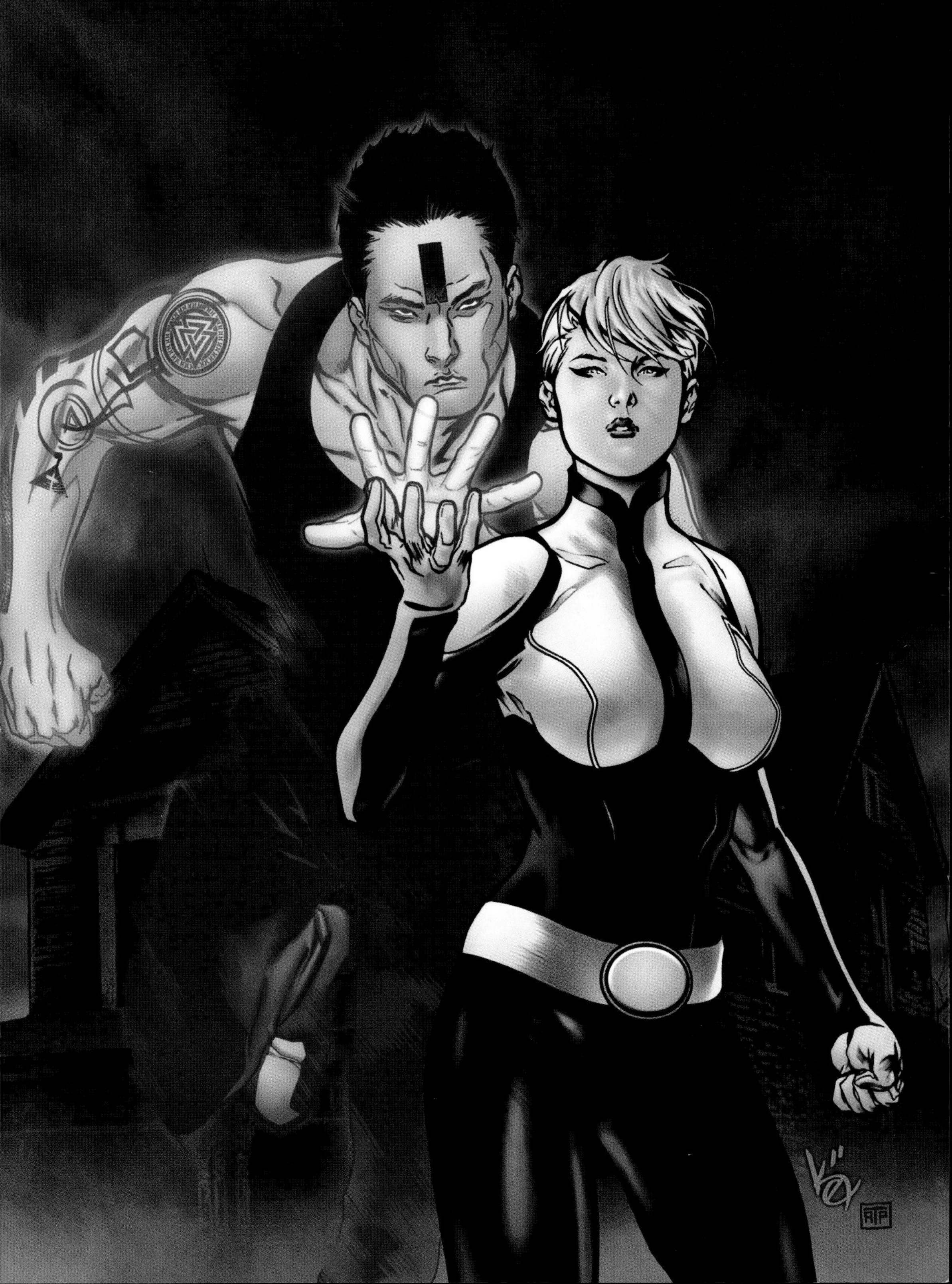

THE DEATH-DEFYING DOCTOR MIRAGE: SECOND LIVES #1 VARIANT COVER
Art by KHARI EVANS with
ALLEN PASSALAQUA

THE DEATH-DEFYING DOCTOR MIRAGE: SECOND LIVES #2 VARIANT COVER
Art by EMI LENOX

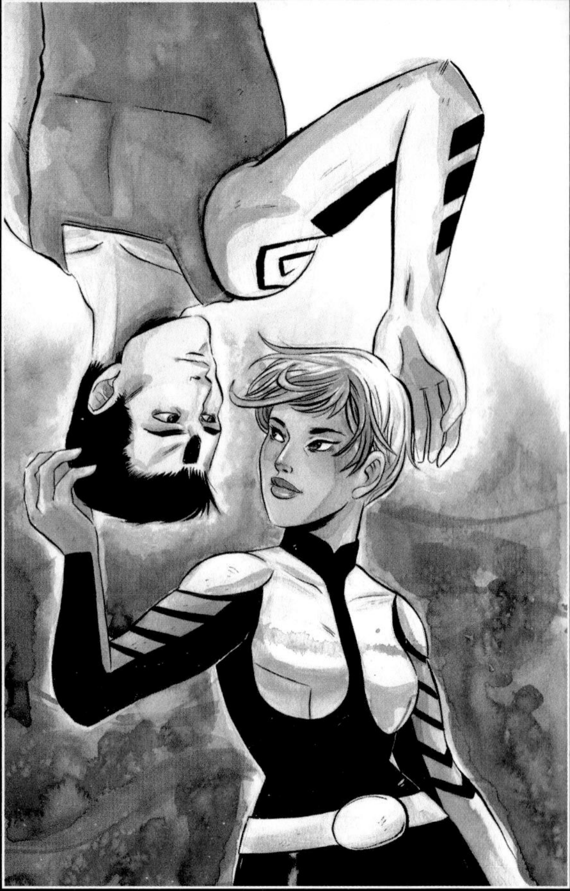

THE DEATH-DEFYING DOCTOR MIRAGE: SECOND LIVES #3 COVER B
Art by KEVIN WADA

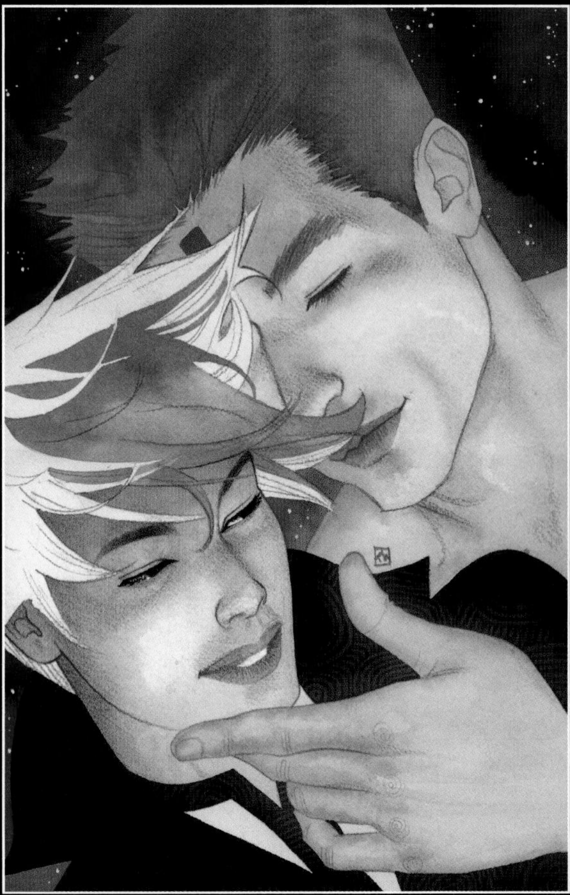

THE DEATH-DEFYING DOCTOR MIRAGE: SECOND LIVES #4 COVER C
Art by JULIAN TOTINO TEDESCO

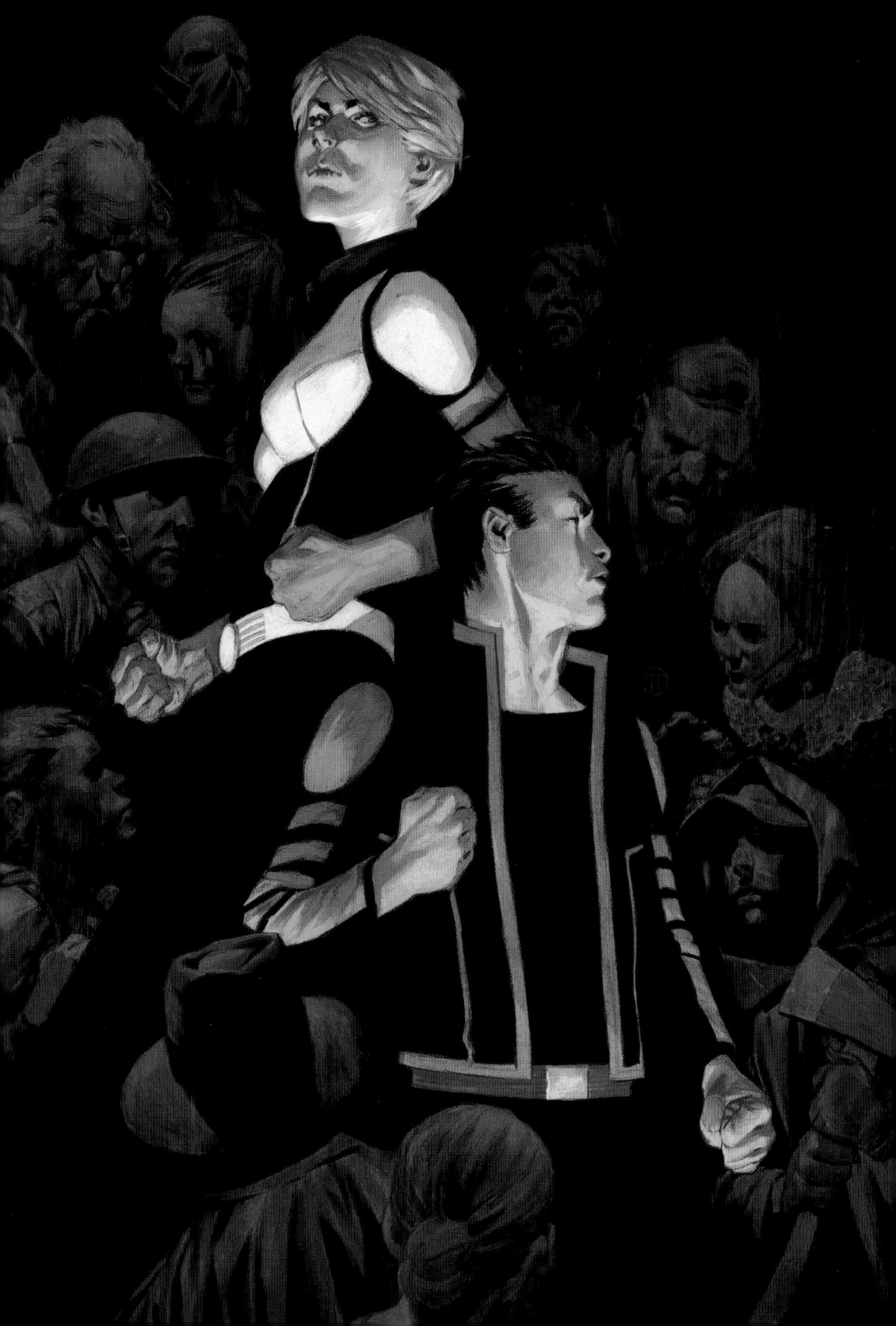

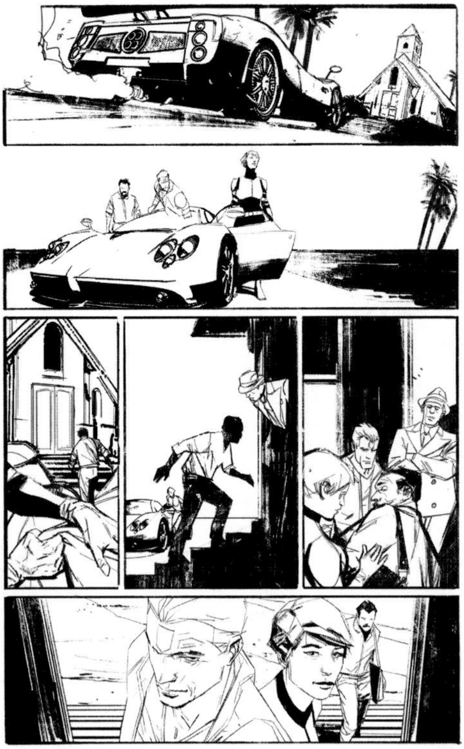

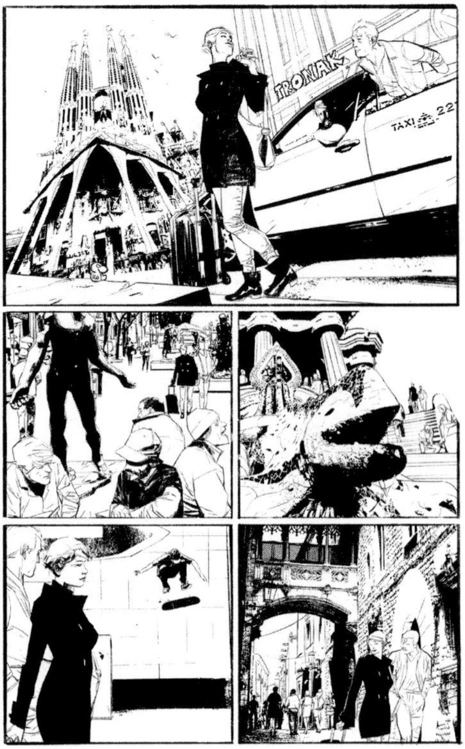
TRONAK
TAXI

THE DEATH-DEFYING DOCTOR MIRAGE: SECOND LIVES #1,
pages 4 and 12 (top)
Art by ROBERTO DE LA TORRE

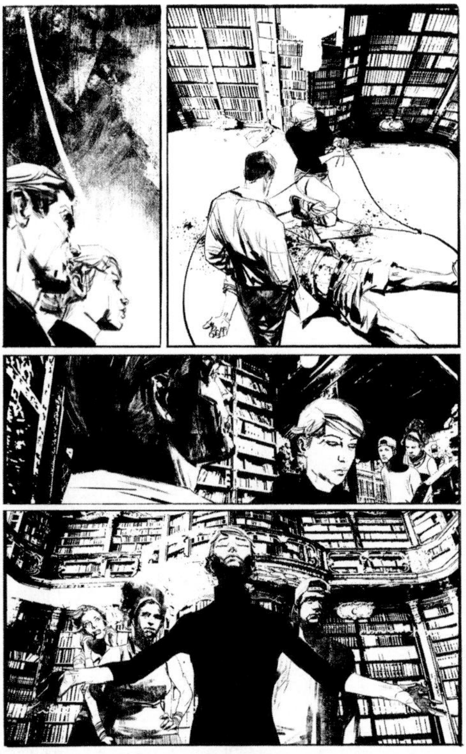

THE DEATH-DEFYING DOCTOR MIRAGE: SECOND LIVES #2,
pages 1 (right) and 2 (facing)
Art by ROBERTO DE LA TORRE

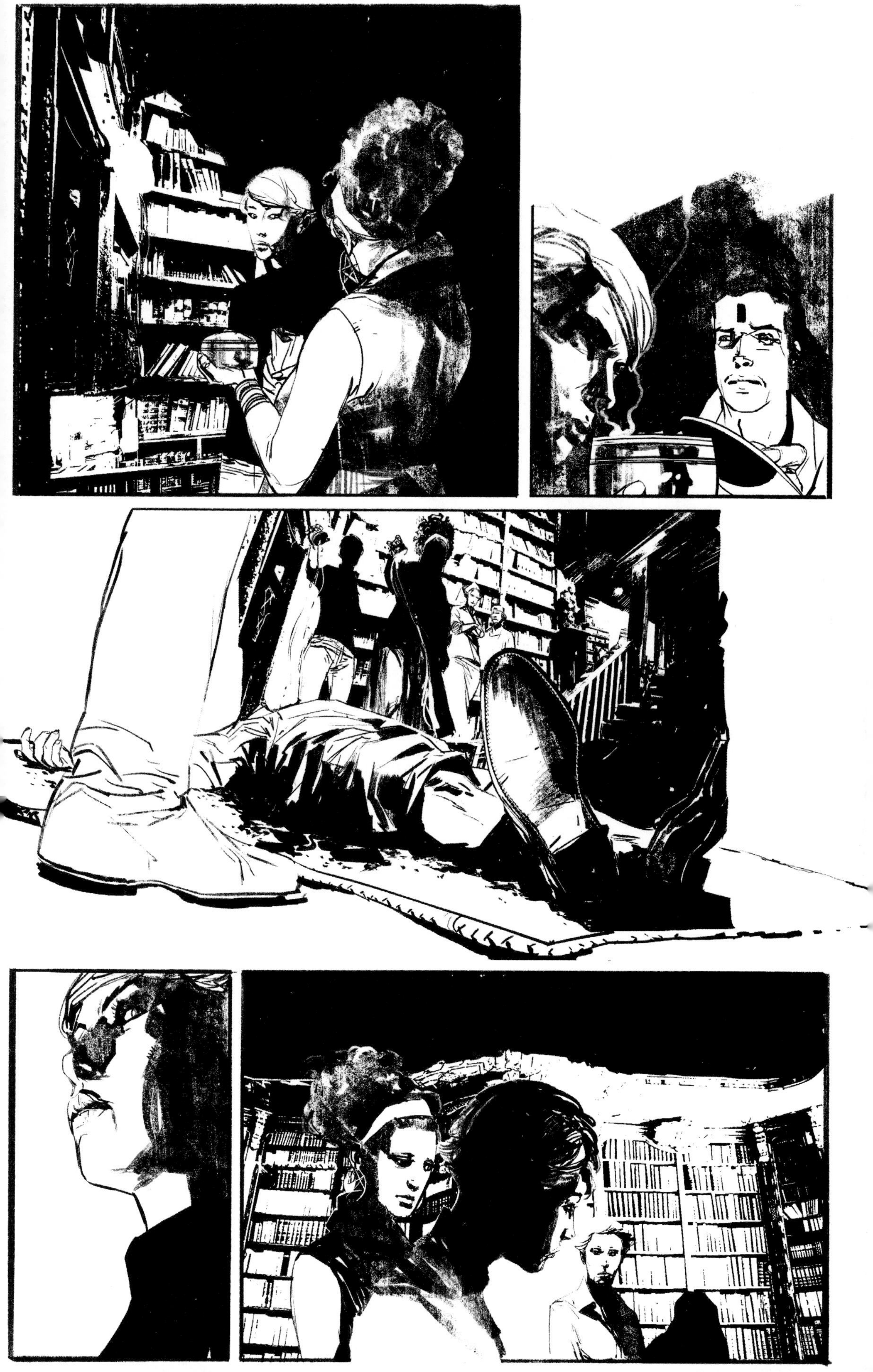

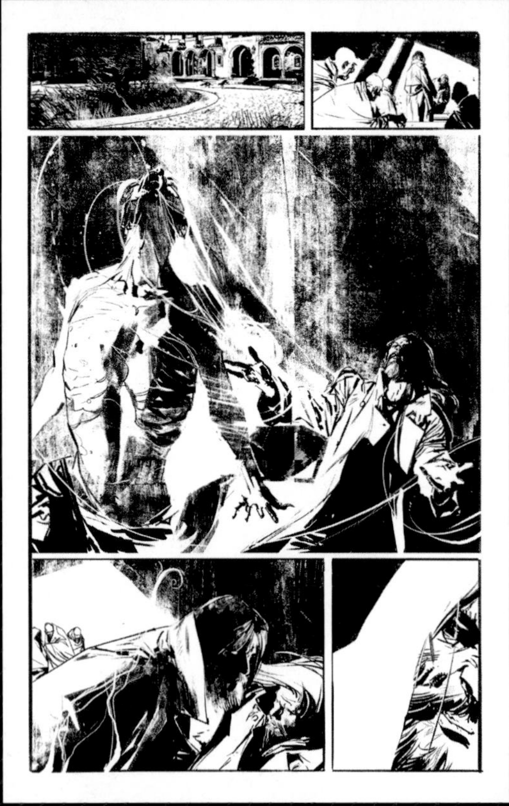

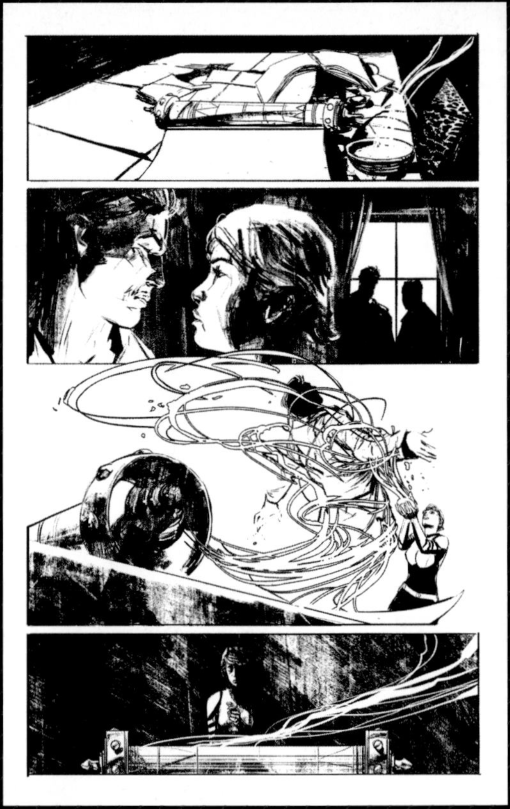

THE DEATH-DEFYING DOCTOR MIRAGE: SECOND LIVES #3,
pages 6 and 22 (top)
Art by ROBERTO DE LA TORRE

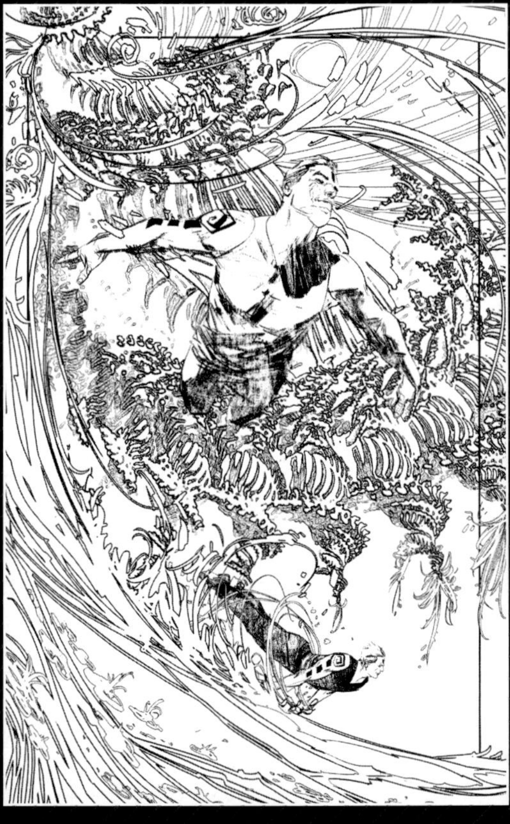

THE DEATH-DEFYING DOCTOR MIRAGE: SECOND LIVES #4,
pages 2 (right) and 3 (facing)
Art by ROBERTO DE LA TORRE

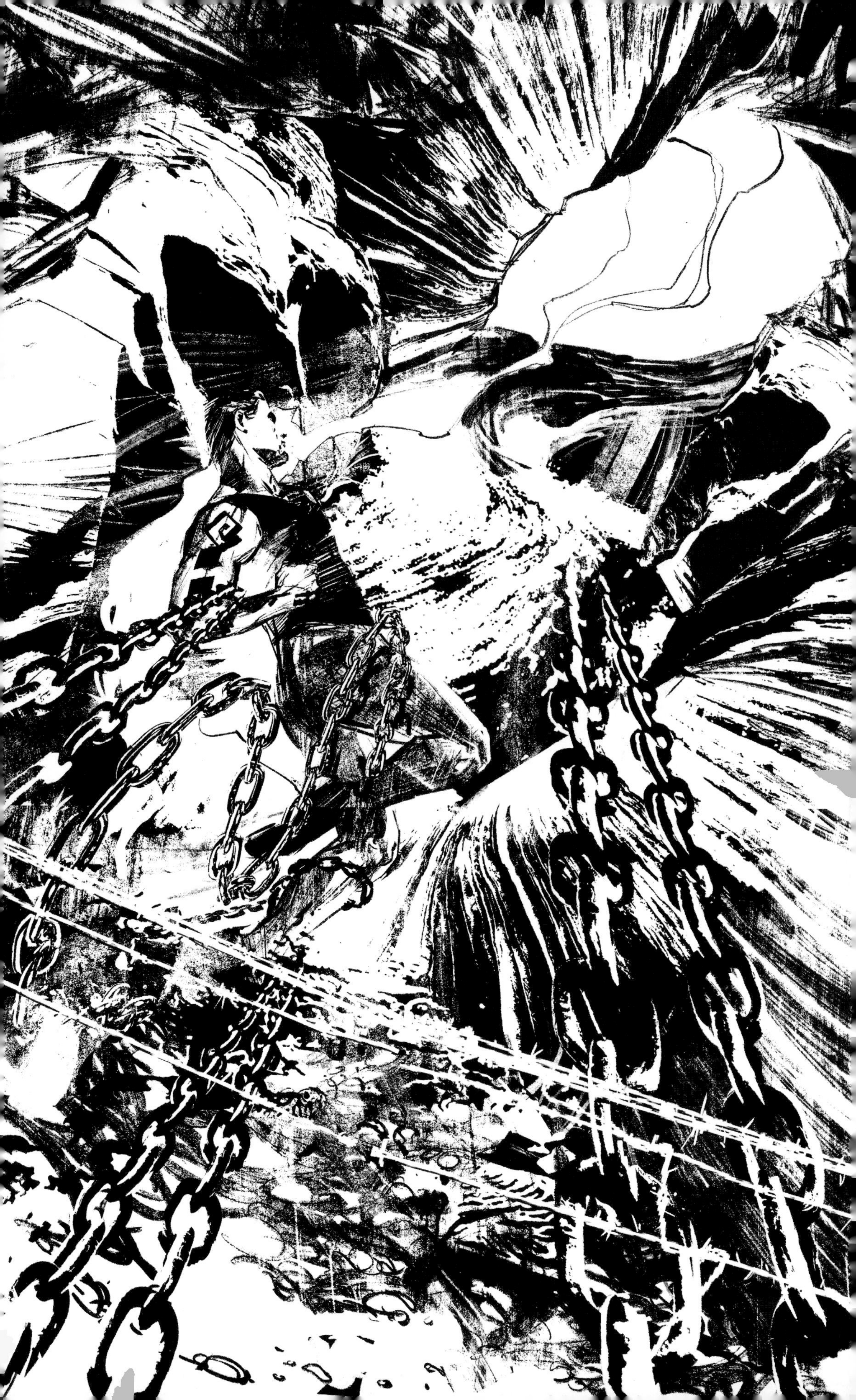

EXPLORE THE VALIANT UNIVERSE

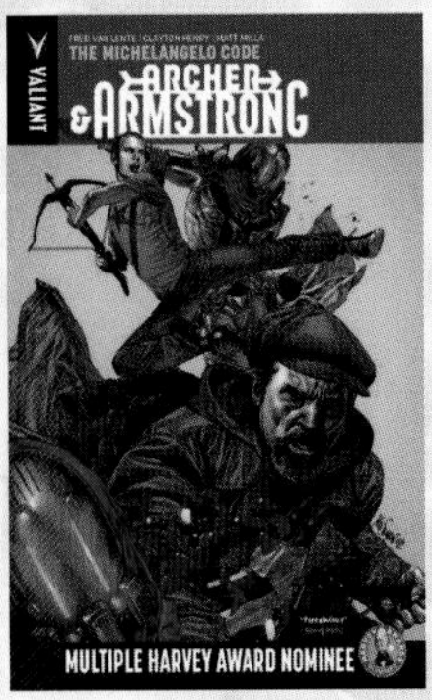
THE MICHELANGELO CODE
VALIANT
ARCHER & ARMSTRONG
MULTIPLE HARVEY AWARD NOMINEE

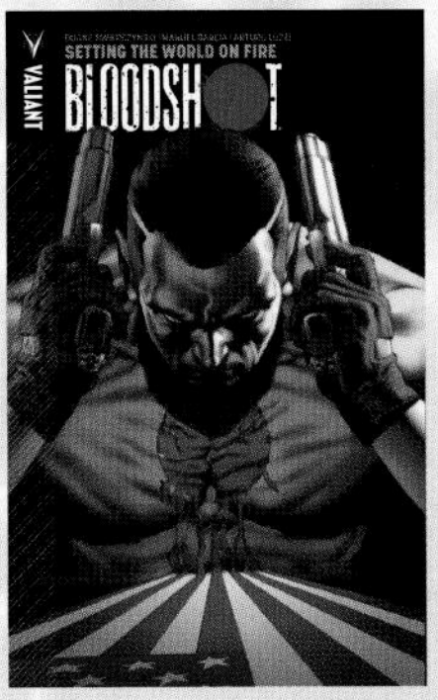
SETTING THE WORLD ON FIRE
VALIANT
BLOODSHOT

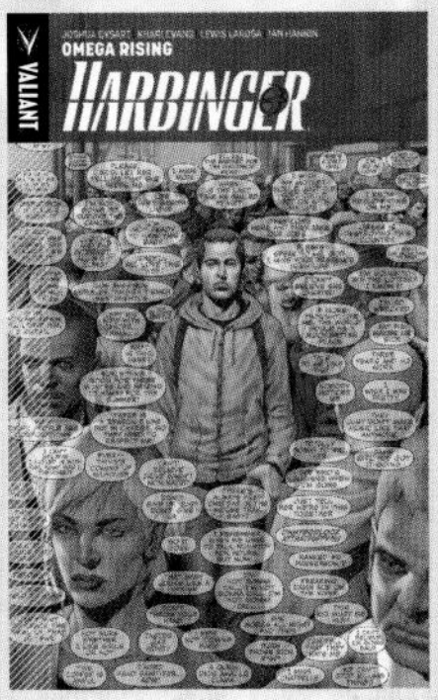
OMEGA RISING
VALIANT
HARBINGER

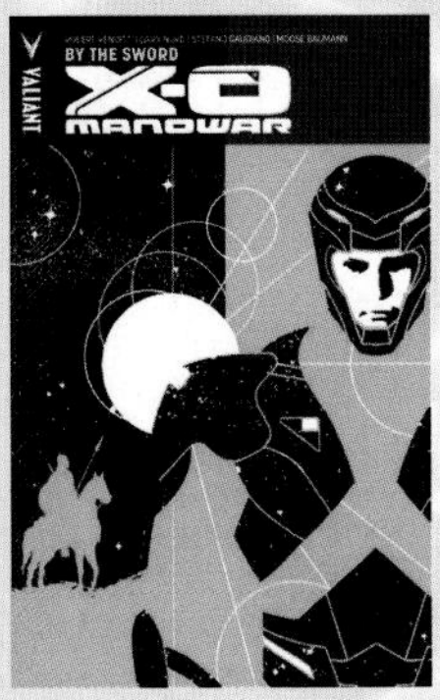
BY THE SWORD
VALIANT
X-O MANOWAR

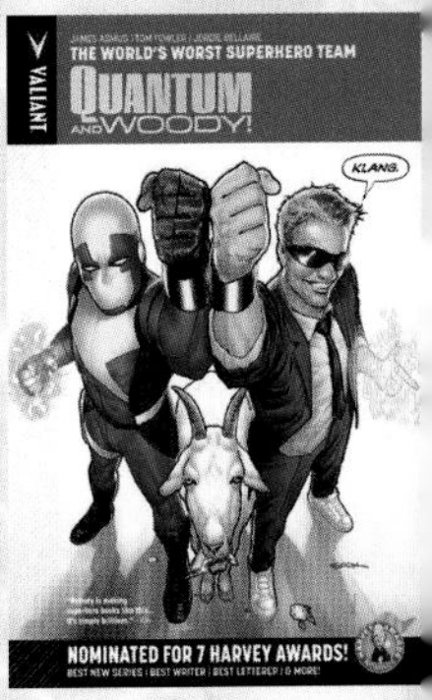
THE WORLD'S WORST SUPERHERO TEAM
VALIANT
QUANTUM AND WOODY!
KLANG
NOMINATED FOR 7 HARVEY AWARDS!

ARCHER & ARMSTRONG

Volume 1: The Michelangelo Code
ISBN: 9780979640988

Volume 2: Wrath of the Eternal Warrior
ISBN: 9781939346049

Volume 3: Far Faraway
ISBN: 9781939346148

Volume 4: Sect Civil War
ISBN: 9781939346254

Volume 5: Mission: Improbable
ISBN: 9781939346353

Volume 6: American Wasteland
ISBN: 9781939346421

Volume 7: The One Percent and Other Tales
ISBN: 9781939346537

ARMOR HUNTERS

Armor Hunters
ISBN: 9781939346452

Armor Hunters: Bloodshot
ISBN: 9781939346469

Armor Hunters: Harbinger
ISBN: 9781939346506

Unity Vol. 3: Armor Hunters
ISBN: 9781939346445

X-O Manowar Vol. 7: Armor Hunters
ISBN: 9781939346476

BLOODSHOT

Volume 1: Setting the World on Fire
ISBN: 9780979640964

Volume 2: The Rise and the Fall
ISBN: 9781939346032

Volume 3: Harbinger Wars
ISBN: 9781939346124

Volume 4: H.A.R.D. Corps
ISBN: 9781939346193

Volume 5: Get Some!
ISBN: 9781939346315

Volume 6: The Glitch and Other Tales
ISBN: 9781939346711

BLOODSHOT REBORN

Volume 1: Colorado
ISBN: 9781939346674

Volume 2: The Hunt
ISBN: 9781939346827

Volume 3: The Analog Man
ISBN: 9781682151334

BOOK OF DEATH

Book of Death
ISBN: 9781939346971

Book of Death: The Fall of the Valiant Universe
ISBN: 9781939346988

DEAD DROP

ISBN: 9781939346858

THE DEATH-DEFYING DOCTOR MIRAGE

Volume 1
ISBN: 9781939346490

Volume 2: Second Lives
ISBN: 9781682151297

THE DELINQUENTS

ISBN: 9781939346513

DIVINITY

ISBN: 9781939346766

ETERNAL WARRIOR

Volume 1: Sword of the Wild
ISBN: 9781939346209

Volume 2: Eternal Emperor
ISBN: 9781939346292

Volume 3: Days of Steel
ISBN: 9781939346742

WRATH OF THE ETERNAL WARRIOR

Volume 1: Risen
ISBN: 9781682151235

HARBINGER

Volume 1: Omega Rising
ISBN: 9780979640957

Volume 2: Renegades
ISBN: 9781939346025

Volume 3: Harbinger Wars
ISBN: 9781939346117

Volume 4: Perfect Day
ISBN: 9781939346155

Volume 5: Death of a Renegade
ISBN: 9781939346339

Volume 6: Omegas
ISBN: 9781939346384

HARBINGER WARS

Harbinger Wars
ISBN: 9781939346094

Bloodshot Vol. 3: Harbinger Wars
ISBN: 9781939346124

Harbinger Vol. 3: Harbinger Wars
ISBN: 9781939346117

EXPLORE THE VALIANT UNIVERSE

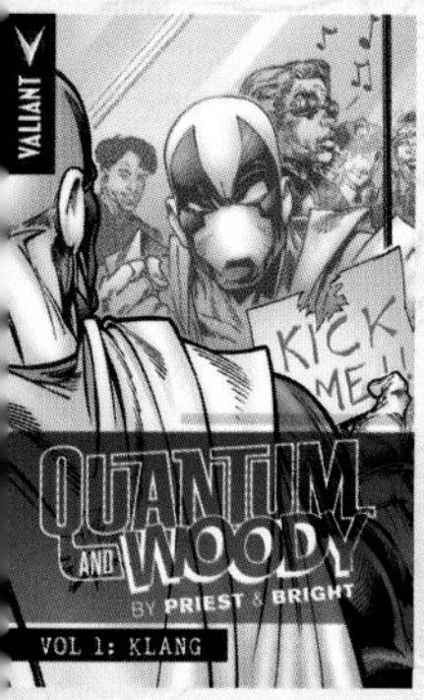

VALIANT
QUANTUM AND WOODY
BY PRIEST & BRIGHT
VOL 1: KLANG

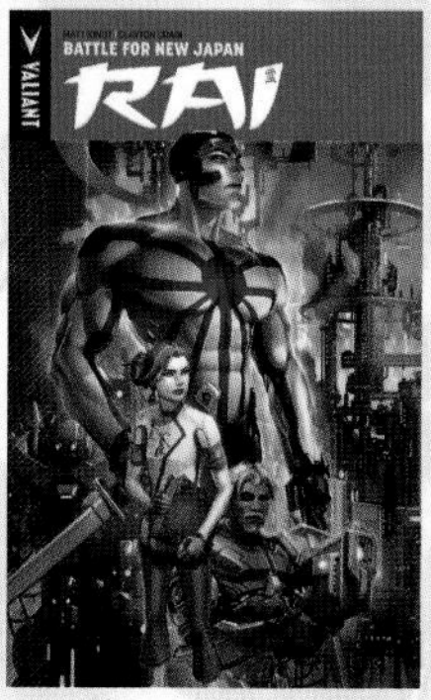

VALIANT
BATTLE FOR NEW JAPAN
RAI

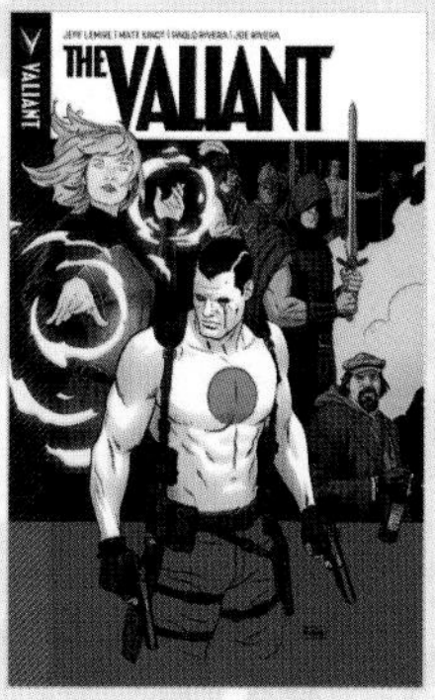

VALIANT
THE VALIANT

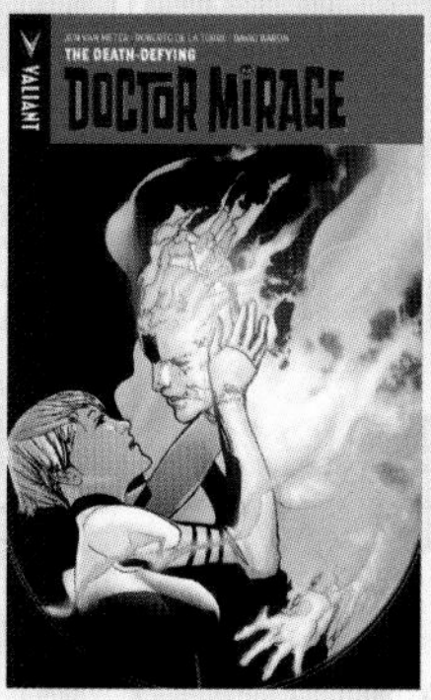

VALIANT
THE DEATH-DEFYING
DOCTOR MIRAGE

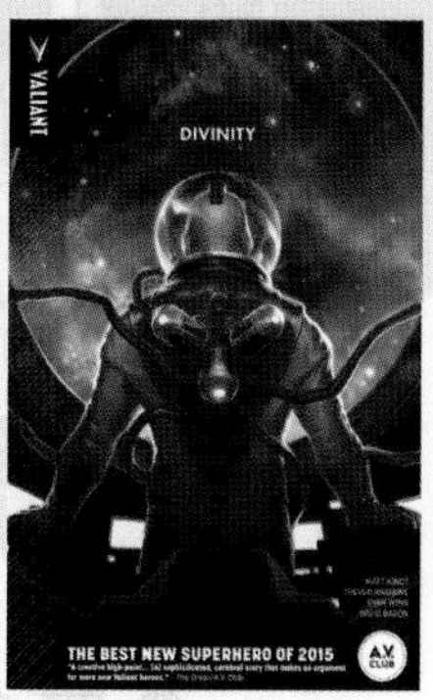

VALIANT
DIVINITY
THE BEST NEW SUPERHERO OF 2015

IMPERIUM

Volume 1: Collecting Monsters
ISBN: 9781939346759

Volume 2: Broken Angels
ISBN: 9781939346896

Volume 3: The Vine Imperative
ISBN: 9781682151112

NINJAK

Volume 1: Weaponeer
ISBN: 9781939346667

Volume 2: The Shadow Wars
ISBN: 9781939346940

Volume 3: Operation: Deadside
ISBN: 9781682151259

QUANTUM AND WOODY

Volume 1: The World's Worst Superhero Team
ISBN: 9781939346186

Volume 2: In Security
ISBN: 9781939346230

Volume 3: Crooked Pasts, Present Tense
ISBN: 9781939346391

Volume 4: Quantum and Woody Must Die!
ISBN: 9781939346629

QUANTUM AND WOODY BY PRIEST & BRIGHT

Volume 1: Klang
ISBN: 9781939346780

Volume 2: Switch
ISBN: 9781939346803

Volume 3: And So...
ISBN: 9781939346865

Volume 4: Q2 - The Return
ISBN: 9781682151099

RAI

Volume 1: Welcome to New Japan
ISBN: 9781939346414

Volume 2: Battle for New Japan
ISBN: 9781939346612

Volume 3: The Orphan
ISBN: 9781939346841

SHADOWMAN

Volume 1: Birth Rites
ISBN: 9781939346001

Volume 2: Darque Reckoning
ISBN: 9781939346056

Volume 3: Deadside Blues
ISBN: 9781939346162

Volume 4: Fear, Blood, And Shadows
ISBN: 9781939346278

Volume 5: End Times
ISBN: 9781939346377

IVAR, TIMEWALKER

Volume 1: Making History
ISBN: 9781939346636

Volume 2: Breaking History
ISBN: 9781939346834

Volume 3: Ending History
ISBN: 9781939346995

UNITY

Volume 1: To Kill a King
ISBN: 9781939346261

Volume 2: Trapped by Webnet
ISBN: 9781939346346

Volume 3: Armor Hunters
ISBN: 9781939346445

Volume 4: The United
ISBN: 9781939346544

Volume 5: Homefront
ISBN: 9781939346797

Volume 6: The War-Monger
ISBN: 9781939346902

Volume 7: Revenge of the Armor Hunters
ISBN: 9781682151136

THE VALIANT

ISBN: 9781939346605

VALIANT ZEROES AND ORIGINS

ISBN: 9781939346582

X-O MANOWAR

Volume 1: By the Sword
ISBN: 9780979640940

Volume 2: Enter Ninjak
ISBN: 9780979640995

Volume 3: Planet Death
ISBN: 9781939346087

Volume 4: Homecoming
ISBN: 9781939346179

Volume 5: At War With Unity
ISBN: 9781939346247

Volume 6: Prelude to Armor Hunters
ISBN: 9781939346407

Volume 7: Armor Hunters
ISBN: 9781939346476

Volume 8: Enter: Armorines
ISBN: 9781939346551

Volume 9: Dead Hand
ISBN: 9781939346650

Volume 10: Exodus
ISBN: 9781939346933

Volume 11: The Kill List
ISBN: 9781682151273

VALIANT
JOSHUA DYSART | BARRY KITSON | CLAYTON HENRY
KHARI EVANS | RAFA SANDOVAL
HARBINGER
DELUXE EDITION 2

VALIANT
ROBERT VENDITTI | MATT KINDT | JOSHUA DYSART | JOE HARRIS | ROBERT GILL
DOUG BRAITHWAITE | DIEGO BERNARD | TREVOR HAIRSINE | STEPHEN SEGOVIA
ARMOR HUNTERS
DELUXE EDITION

VALIANT
JIM SHOOTER | DAVID LAPHAM
CHILDREN OF THE EIGHTH DAY
HARBINGER
VALIANT MASTERS
L8-AGIN

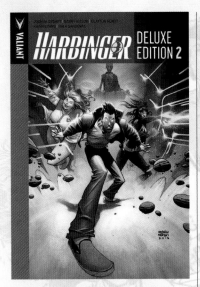

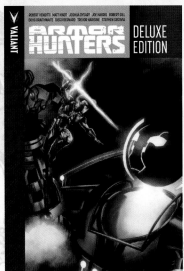

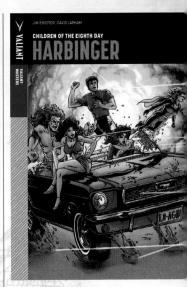

Omnibuses

Archer & Armstrong: The Complete Classic Omnibus
ISBN: 9781939346872
Collecting ARCHER & ARMSTRONG (1992) #0-26, ETERNAL WARRIOR (1992) #25 along with ARCHER & ARMSTRONG: THE FORMATION OF THE SECT.

Quantum and Woody: The Complete Classic Omnibus
ISBN: 9781939346360
Collecting QUANTUM AND WOODY (1997) #0, 1-21 and #32, THE GOAT: H.A.E.D.U.S. #1, and X-O MANOWAR (1996) #16

X-O Manowar Classic Omnibus Vol. 1
ISBN: 9781939346308
Collecting X-O MANOWAR (1992) #0-30, ARMORINES #0, X-O DATABASE #1, as well as material from SECRETS OF THE VALIANT UNIVERSE #1

Deluxe Editions

Archer & Armstrong Deluxe Edition Book 1
ISBN: 9781939346223
Collecting ARCHER & ARMSTRONG #0-13

Archer & Armstrong Deluxe Edition Book 2
ISBN: 9781939346957
Collecting ARCHER & ARMSTRONG #14-25, ARCHER & ARMSTRONG: ARCHER #0 and BLOODSHOT AND H.A.R.D. CORPS #20-21.

Armor Hunters Deluxe Edition
ISBN: 9781939346728
Collecting Armor Hunters #1-4, Armor Hunters: Aftermath #1, Armor Hunters: Bloodshot #1-3, Armor Hunters: Harbinger #1-3, Unity #8-11, and X-O MANOWAR #23-29

Bloodshot Deluxe Edition Book 1
ISBN: 9781939346216
Collecting BLOODSHOT #1-13

Bloodshot Deluxe Edition Book 2
ISBN: 9781939346810
Collecting BLOODSHOT AND H.A.R.D. CORPS #14-23, BLOODSHOT #24-25, BLOODSHOT #0, BLOODSHOT AND H.A.R.D. CORPS: H.A.R.D. CORPS #0, along with ARCHER & ARMSTRONG #18-19

Book of Death Deluxe Edition
ISBN: 9781682151150
Collecting BOOK OF DEATH #1-4, BOOK OF DEATH: THE FALL OF BLOODSHOT #1, BOOK OF DEATH: THE FALL OF NINJAK #1, BOOK OF DEATH: THE FALL OF HARBINGER #1, and BOOK OF DEATH: THE FALL OF X-O MANOWAR #1.

Divinity Deluxe Edition
ISBN: 97819393460993
Collecting DIVNITY #1-4

Harbinger Deluxe Edition Book 1
ISBN: 9781939346131
Collecting HARBINGER #0-14

Harbinger Deluxe Edition Book 2
ISBN: 9781939346773
Collecting HARBINGER #15-25, HARBINGER: OMEGAS #1-3, and HARBINGER: BLEEDING MONK #0

Harbinger Wars Deluxe Edition
ISBN: 9781939346322
Collecting HARBINGER WARS #1-4, HARBINGER #11-14, and BLOODSHOT #10-13

Ivar, Timewalker Deluxe Edition Book 1
ISBN: 9781682151198
Collecting IVAR, TIMEWALKER #1-12

Quantum and Woody Deluxe Edition Book 1
ISBN: 9781939346681
Collecting QUANTUM AND WOODY #1-12 and QUANTUM AND WOODY: THE GOAT #0

Q2: The Return of Quantum and Woody Deluxe Edition
ISBN: 9781939346568
Collecting Q2: THE RETURN OF QUANTUM AND WOODY #1-5

Rai Deluxe Edition Book 1
ISBN: 9781682151174
Collecting RAI #1-12, along with material from RAI #1 PLUS EDITION and RAI #5 PLUS EDITION

Shadowman Deluxe Edition Book 1
ISBN: 9781939346438
Collecting SHADOWMAN #0-10

Shadowman Deluxe Edition Book 2
ISBN: 9781682151075
Collecting SHADOWMAN #11-16, SHADOWMAN #13X, SHADOWMAN: END TIMES #1-3 and PUNK MAMBO #0

Unity Deluxe Edition Book 1
ISBN: 9781939346575
Collecting UNITY #0-14

The Valiant Deluxe Edition
ISBN: 97819393460986
Collecting THE VALIANT #1-4

X-O Manowar Deluxe Edition Book 1
ISBN: 9781939346100
Collecting X-O MANOWAR #1-14

X-O Manowar Deluxe Edition Book 2
ISBN: 9781939346520
Collecting X-O MANOWAR #15-22, and UNITY #1-4

X-O Manowar Deluxe Edition Book 3
ISBN: 9781682151310
Collecting X-O MANOWAR #23-29 and ARMOR HUNTERS #1-4.

Valiant Masters

Bloodshot Vol. 1 - Blood of the Machine
ISBN: 9780979640933

H.A.R.D. Corps Vol. 1 - Search and Destroy
ISBN: 9781939346285

Harbinger Vol. 1 - Children of the Eighth Day
ISBN: 9781939346483

Ninjak Vol. 1 - Black Water
ISBN: 9780979640971

Rai Vol. 1 - From Honor to Strength
ISBN: 9781939346070

Shadowman Vol. 1 - Spirits Within
ISBN: 9781939346018

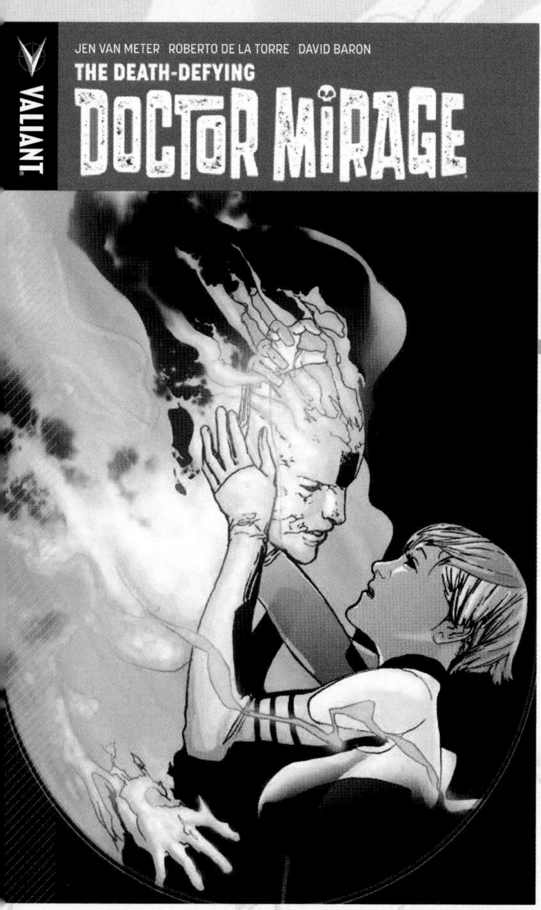
VALIANT
JEN VAN METER ROBERTO DE LA TORRE DAVID BARON
THE DEATH-DEFYING
DOCTOR MIRAGE
The Death-Defying Dr. Mirage

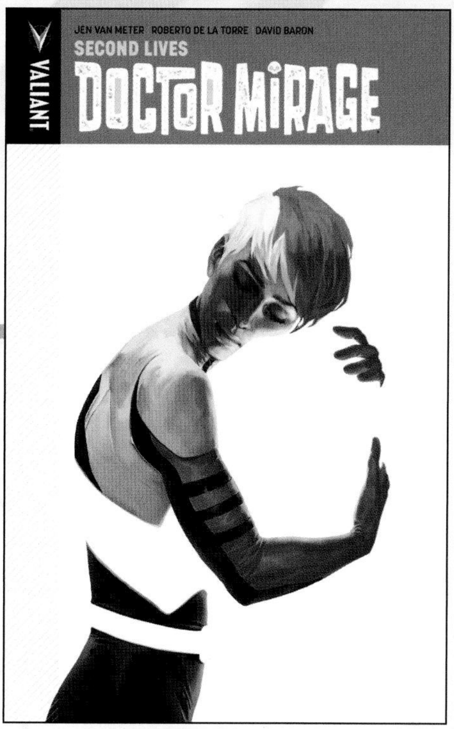
VALIANT
JEN VAN METER ROBERTO DE LA TORRE DAVID BARON
SECOND LIVES
DOCTOR MIRAGE
The Death-Defying Dr. Mirage
Vol. 2: Second Lives

"★★★★...Equal parts clever and emotional as it sets up an impressive new hero..."
-Comic Book Resources

"Everything you could want in a paranormal story...with mystery and intrigue around every corner."
-Bloody Disgusting

READ DR. MIRAGE'S EARLIEST APPEARANCES

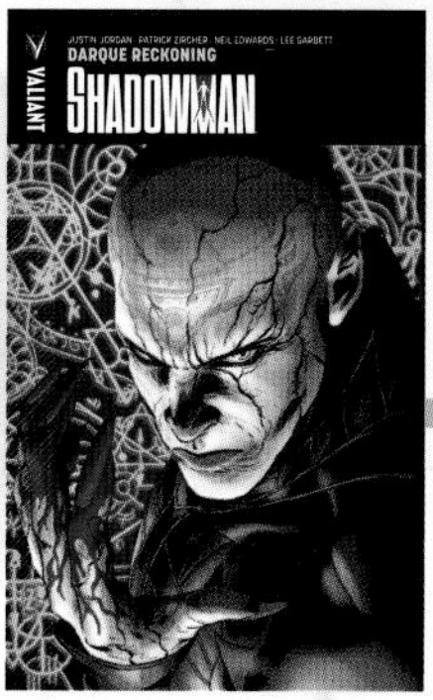
VALIANT
DARQUE RECKONING
SHADOWMAN
Shadowman Vol. 2:
Darque Reckoning
(OPTIONAL)

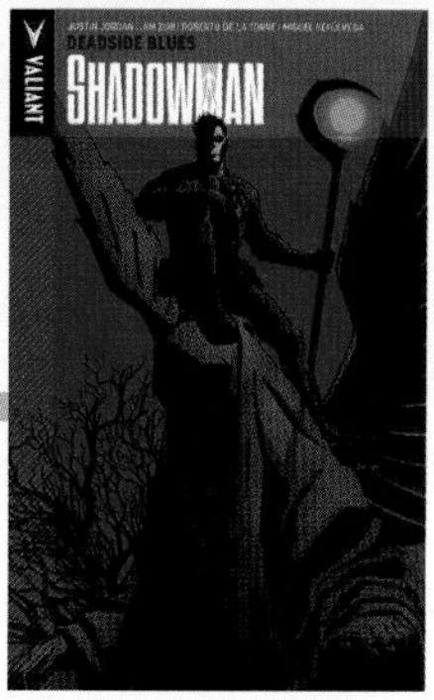
VALIANT
DEADSIDE BLUES
SHADOWMAN
Shadowman Vol. 3:
Deadside Blues
(OPTIONAL)

Go beyond and back with Valiant's spirited occult adventurer for a breathtaking, heartbreaking journey into realms of the unknown!

From Eisner Award-nominated writer
JEN VAN METER
(HOPELESS SAVAGES, CAPTAIN MARVEL)

and

Visionary artist
ROBERTO DE LA TORRE
(DAREDEVIL)

VALIANT®

Faith®

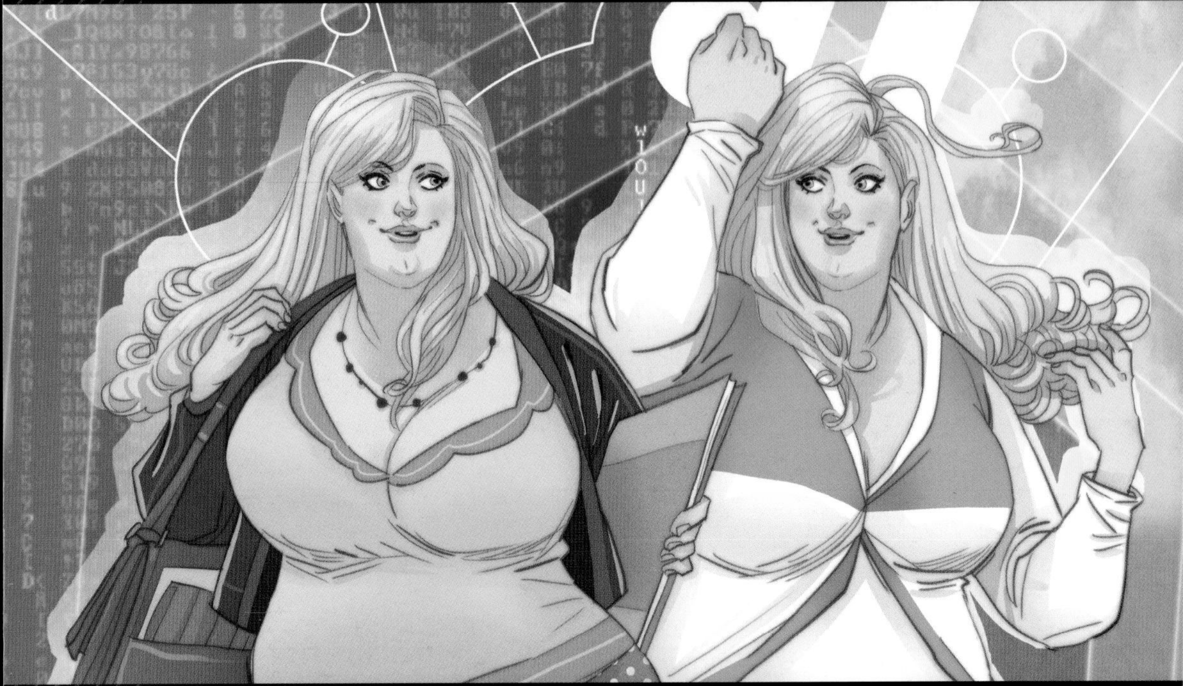

VALIANT'S MOST DEMANDED HERO STEPS OUT OF HARBINGER... AND INTO AN ALL-NEW ADVENTURE!

Orphaned at a young age, Faith Herbert - a psionically gifted "psiot" discovered by the Harbinger Foundation - has always aspired to greatness. But now this once-ordinary teenager is taking control of her destiny and becoming the hard-hitting hero she's always known she can be - complete with a mild-mannered secret identity, unsuspecting colleagues, and a day job as a reporter that routinely throws her into harm's way! Well, at least she thought it would... When she's not typing up listicles about cat videos, Faith makes a secret transformation to patrol the night as the City of Angels' own leading superhero - the skysoaring Zephyr!

Rising star Jody Houser (*Orphan Black*) and explosive artists Francis Portela (*Green Lantern*) and Marguerite Sauvage (*DC Comics Bombshells*) pilot a new chapter for the high-flying hero that *People Magazine* calls "a superhero we can all admire."

Collecting FAITH (LIMITED SERIES) #1-4.

TRADE PAPERBACK
ISBN: 978-1-68215-121-1

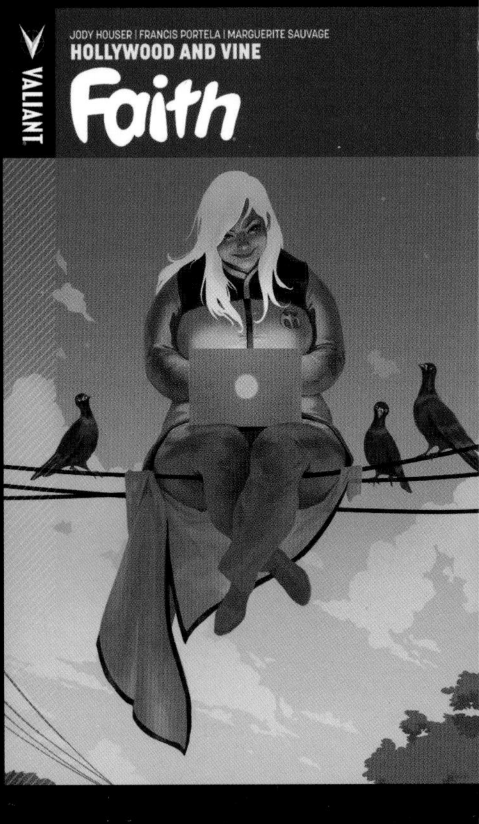
VALIANT
JODY HOUSER | FRANCIS PORTELA | MARGUERITE SAUVAGE
HOLLYWOOD AND VINE
Faith